JOSÉ ROBERTO A. IGREJA

INGLÊS FLUENTE EM 30 LIÇÕES!

VOCABULÁRIO, GRAMÁTICA APLICADA, DIÁLOGOS E EXERCÍCIOS PRÁTICOS PARA VOCÊ REATIVAR A FLUÊNCIA DE UMA FORMA PROGRESSIVA E DINÂMICA

Veja como acessar o áudio p. 359

8ª reimpressão

DISAL EDITORA

© 2012 José Roberto A. Igreja

Preparação de texto: Juliane Kaori / Verba Editorial

Capa e projeto gráfico: Paula Astiz

Editoração eletrônica: Paula Astiz Design

Assistente editorial: Aline Naomi Sassaki

Ilustrações: Rafael Dourado

Áudio
Produtora: jm produção de áudio
Locutores: Christopher Johnston, Robert Young e Sarah Johnson

Dados Internacionais de Catalogação na Publicação (CIP)
(Câmara Brasileira do Livro, SP, Brasil)

Igreja, José Roberto A.

    Igreja, José Roberto A. Inglês fluente em 30 lições! / José
Roberto A. Igreja. — Barueri, SP : DISAL, 2012.

    ISBN 978-85-7844-102-9

    1. Inglês - Estudo e ensino I. Título.

12-02341   CDD-420.7

Índices para catálogo sistemático:
1. Inglês : Estudo e ensino 420.7

DISAL EDITORA

Todos os direitos reservados em nome de:
Bantim, Canato e Guazzelli Editora Ltda.

Alameda Mamoré 911 – cj. 107
Alphaville – BARUERI – SP
CEP: 06454-040
Tel. / Fax: (11) 4195-2811
Visite nosso site: www.disaleditora.com.br
Televendas: (11) 3226-3111

Fax gratuito: 0800 7707 105/106
E-mail para pedidos: comercialdisal@disal.com.br

SUMÁRIO

APRESENTAÇÃO

Bem-vindo a **Inglês fluente em 30 lições!**. O conteúdo deste livro foi cuidadosamente planejado para oferecer a você uma forma dinâmica e interativa de praticar o idioma inglês.

O livro abrange as quatro habilidades de aprendizado de um idioma (leitura, compreensão auditiva, escrita e expressão oral) e proporciona a oportunidade de aprender, revisar e consolidar diversos tópicos e conceitos importantes da língua inglesa de uma maneira progressiva e prática. Desta forma você vai poder se preparar para situações realistas de comunicação no idioma, tornando-se melhor capacitado à compreensão auditiva, bem como mais confiante ao se expressar oralmente em diversas situações.

Veja abaixo as seções presentes em cada uma das 30 lições do livro:

DIALOGUES (DIÁLOGOS)

Cada lição traz um diálogo que reflete alguma situação do dia a dia. Dessa forma **Inglês fluente em 30 lições!** reúne 30 diálogos realistas abrangendo os principais tópicos da conversação cotidiana. A grande gama de assuntos tratados nos diálogos garante a presença de vocabulário e expressões coloquiais relativas a variados temas. O áudio que acompanha o livro e que traz a gravação dos diálogos feita por falantes nativos proporciona a oportunidade de você praticar e melhorar gradualmente a compreensão auditiva do idioma inglês a respeito de diversos assuntos. Você poderá também conferir a tradução dos diálogos que foi propositalmente inserida no fim do livro, para que você procure em um primeiro momento compreender os diálogos em inglês, sem o auxílio e a interferência do português.

FOCUS ON VOCABULARY, PHRASES AND EXPRESSIONS
(ENFOQUE NO VOCABULÁRIO, LOCUÇÕES E EXPRESSÕES)

Esta seção explora palavras e expressões usuais importantes na comunicação diária e que aparecem destacadas em negrito no diálogo.

É apresentado sempre que possível um ou mais sinônimos da palavra ou expressão em destaque, bem como uma explicação para a mesma quando necessário. Você poderá também conferir a equivalência em português das palavras e expressões abordadas nesta seção.

DIALOGUE – COMPREHENSION QUESTIONS
(DIÁLOGO – PERGUNTAS DE COMPREENSÃO)

São apresentadas nesta seção questões para verificar a compreensão do diálogo. Após a audição do diálogo, você poderá também ouvir essas perguntas no áudio e tentar respondê-las em voz alta, conferindo depois as respostas no fim do livro: uma maneira lúdica de melhorar tanto a compreensão auditiva quanto a expressão oral.

APPLIED GRAMMAR
(GRAMÁTICA APLICADA)

Esta seção apresenta conceitos fundamentais da gramática do idioma inglês de uma forma objetiva e prática. Como o próprio nome da seção sugere (Gramática aplicada), a intenção é proporcionar a aplicação imediata desses conceitos estruturais na comunicação do dia a dia. Desta forma, variados exemplos realistas e usuais da conversação cotidiana são apresentados para cada conceito gramatical abordado. Você terá também a oportunidade de praticar e consolidar o aprendizado desses conceitos com a seção de exercícios (*Practice set*) que aborda as estruturas gramaticais em destaque de cada lição.

Todos os principais conceitos gramaticais necessários para a comunicação no idioma inglês são apresentados de forma progressiva ao longo das 30 lições.

USUAL VOCABULARY
(VOCABULÁRIO USUAL)

A seção *Usual vocabulary* traz palavras e expressões agrupadas em torno de um tema específico e relevante para a comunicação cotidiana. Você poderá conferir vários exemplos de uso em frases contextualizadas que retratam de forma realista e natural a utilização do vocabulário, assim como é feita pelos falantes nativos, em contextos usuais de conversação.

Ao longo das 30 lições você terá a oportunidade de aprender, relembrar e reativar mais de 1200 palavras e expressões muito importantes para a comunicação, relativas a variados assuntos, tais como: a vida em família, relacionamentos, diversão e entretenimento, saúde e bem-estar, viagens, o uso de computadores, a vida escolar, o clima, trabalho e carreira etc. Você também poderá praticar o vocabulário apresentado em cada lição ao fazer os exercícios propostos na seção *Practice set*.

Um dos destaques da seção *Usual vocabulary* é que ela também apresenta uma seleção das principais expressões idiomáticas e *phrasal verbs,* que podem ser resumidamente definidos como combinações de verbos e preposições que produzem significados distintos. Ao todo são apresentadas 30 expressões idiomáticas e 30 *phrasal verbs*, em grupos intercalados a partir da lição 25. Essas seções incluem também exemplos de uso em frases contextualizadas e o conteúdo das mesmas poderá também ser praticado nas seções *Practice set* correspondentes a essas lições.

PRACTICE SET
(CONJUNTO DE EXERCÍCIOS)

Esta é uma seção de grande importância já que oferece várias formas de você colocar em prática todo o conteúdo apresentado nas seções anteriores de uma maneira lúdica e interativa. A seção *Pratice set* é dividida em cinco partes, que podem variar um pouco dependendo da lição. As principais atividades propostas são explicadas a seguir:

I. Listen to the questions and circle the right answer.

Uma atividade de compreensão auditiva interessante que reúne dez perguntas gravadas em áudio. Para cada uma dessas perguntas, são apresentadas no livro três opções de resposta a sua escolha. Uma excelente maneira de praticar a compreensão auditiva, revisando e consolidando ao mesmo tempo os aspectos gramaticais e o vocabulário em destaque de cada lição.

II. Dictation: listen to the sentences and write them.

Esta é mais uma atividade que visa desenvolver a habilidade da compreensão auditiva. Aqui você deverá escrever as cinco frases ou perguntas que vai ouvir no áudio. São apresentadas frases ou perguntas realistas da comunicação cotidiana que refletem os tópicos de gramática e vocabulário presentes em cada lição, o que torna este exercício bastante interessante. Além do desenvolvimento gradual da compreensão auditiva, este exercício também proporciona a prática da escrita, que é muito importante.

III. Circle the right answer.

Um exercício de múltipla escolha com três opções de respostas. Esta atividade apresenta cinco perguntas que serão lidas e que, desta forma, proporcionam mais uma oportunidade de contato e visualização das estruturas gramaticais e do vocabulário abordados em cada lição.

IV. Write questions/ phrases for the following answers.

Ao invés de responder perguntas, este exercício propõe justamente o contrário, ou seja, a formulação de perguntas a partir das respostas apresentadas. Uma ótima oportunidade de treinar o uso dos verbos auxiliares (ex. *Do, Does, Did, Will, Would*), dos verbos modais (ex. *Can, May, Could, Might, Must, Should*) e também das *questions words* (*What, Who, Whose, Where, When, Why, How* etc.).

V. Circle the word or expression that is different from the group.

Este exercício trabalha o vocabulário e as expressões abordadas em cada lição. Você deverá identificar a palavra ou expressão que não pertence ao grupo de palavras e/ ou expressões apresentado: uma maneira prática de revisar e consolidar o vocabulário.

A partir da lição 13, esse exercício é substituído por outro com o nome "Fill in the blanks with an appropriate word/ expression from the box". Essa atividade apresenta frases ou perguntas contextualizadas em que há alguma lacuna a ser preenchida. Você deverá completá-las a partir das opções de vocabulário e expressões apresentadas no início do exercício. Desta forma você estará relembrando o vocabulário abordado na lição de forma prática e interativa.

Inglês fluente em 30 lições! traz as respostas a todos os exercícios propostos, o que o torna um excelente material para o autoestudo. Outras seções importantes incorporadas ao livro e que incrementam o conteúdo:

USOS DO VERBO GET

O verbo *get* é conhecido como um dos verbos mais versáteis e recorrentes da língua inglesa, podendo ser usado em diversos contextos com significados muito diferentes. Esta seção apresenta os 12 significados mais importantes e usuais desse verbo-chave na comunicação do dia a dia.

LISTA DE VERBOS PRINCIPAIS E SEUS SIGNIFICADOS

Você poderá conferir nesta lista o significado dos 180 verbos principais regulares e irregulares mais importantes para a conversação cotidiana. Essa lista apresenta os tempos presente, passado e particípio passado e inclui todos os verbos que aparecem ao longo dos 30 diálogos do livro.

Seja ao escrever, ler, compreender o que é falado ou ao se expressar, tenho certeza que o conteúdo de todas as seções de **Inglês fluente em 30 lições!** vai ajudar você a se sentir mais confiante e apto à comunicação em inglês.

Enjoy!

José Roberto A. Igreja

LESSON 1

DIALOGUE 1
What do you do for a living?

Brian: Nice to meet you Jane!
Jane: Nice to meet you too.
Brian: So, **what do you do for a living**?
Jane: Me? I'm a **vet**.
Brian: Really? You probably love animals.
Jane: I do. I have two dogs and three birds. How about you? Do you have any **pets**?
Brian: No, I don't. I don't have time to **take care of** them.
Jane: I see. Wow, it's almost **noon**, I'm sorry, I'm late for work, I have to go. See you around!
Brian: Sure, Jane. Take care!

▶ Veja a tradução desse diálogo na p. 289.

FOCUS ON VOCABULARY, PHRASES AND EXPRESSIONS 1

What do you do for a living? = What do you do?; What's your occupation? (O que você faz?; Qual é a sua ocupação?)
Vet = veterinarian (veterinário; veterinária)
Pet = domesticated animal (animal de estimação)
Take care of = look after (cuidar de)
Noon = midday (meio-dia)

1. What's Jane's occupation?
2. Does Brian have any pets?
3. How many pets does Jane have?
4. Why doesn't Brian have any pets?
5. Why does Jane have to go?

APPLIED GRAMMAR 1
verbo auxiliar *do* (presente) e verbo *to be* (presente)

VERBO AUXILIAR *DO* (TEMPO PRESENTE)

Os verbos auxiliares indicam em que tempo (presente, passado, futuro ou condicional) uma pergunta está sendo feita. No caso do **tempo presente** usamos o verbo auxiliar *do* para fazer perguntas com os sujeitos *I* (eu); *you* (você); *we* (nós) e *they* (eles, elas). Veja os exemplos:

Do you speak Spanish? (Você fala espanhol?)
Do they travel on business very often?
(Eles viajam a negócios com muita frequência?)
Do you play tennis? (Você joga tênis?)

Obs.: Nos exemplos acima, **do** é o verbo auxiliar e **speak**, **travel** e **play** são os verbos principais. Veja na p. 281 uma lista com os verbos principais mais utilizados na conversação cotidiana.

Para as respostas curtas usamos *"Yes, I do"*, no caso da resposta afirmativa, ou *"No, I don't"*, quando a resposta for negativa. Veja os exemplos:

Do you speak Spanish? **Yes, I do. / No, I don't.**
Do they travel on business very often? **Yes, they do. / No, they don't.**
Do you play tennis? **Yes, I do. / No, I don't.**

16

Para as respostas completas repetimos o verbo principal na resposta afirmativa e usamos a forma negativa **don't** (contração de **do** + **not**) antes do verbo principal na resposta negativa. Veja os exemplos:

Do you speak Spanish? **Yes, I speak Spanish.** / **No, I don't speak Spanish.**
Do they travel on business very often? **Yes, they travel on business very often.** / **No, they don't travel on business very often.**
Do you play tennis? **Yes, I play tennis.** / **No, I don't play tennis.**

Agora veja mais alguns exemplos de perguntas e respostas no tempo presente com o verbo auxiliar do e as *WH-questions*: **What** (O que/ Qual) – **Where** (Onde) – **When** (Quando) – **Why** (Por que) – **Who** (Quem) – **How** (Como):

What do you do? (O que você faz?) – **I'm a teacher.** (Sou professor.)
▶ Veja *Occupations* (ocupações) p. 30
Where do you live? (Onde você mora?) – **I live in Rio de Janeiro.** (Moro no Rio de Janeiro.)
When do you have English classes? (Quando você tem aulas de inglês?) – **I have English classes on Tuesdays and Thursdays.** (Tenho aulas de inglês às terças e quintas-feiras.)
Why do you get up early every day? (Por que você levanta cedo todos os dias?) – **I get up early every day because I need to take my daughter to school.** (Levanto cedo todos os dias porque preciso levar minha filha à escola.)
Who do you live with? (Com quem você mora?) – **I live with my wife and children.** (Moro com minha esposa e filhos.)
How do you spell your name? (Como se soletra seu nome?) – It's FREDERICK: F – R – E – D – E – R – I – C – K

ᴵ|ᴵ|ᴵ 3 THE ALPHABET: HOW TO PRONOUNCE
O ALFABETO: COMO PRONUNCIAR

Saber pronunciar as letras do alfabeto em inglês pode ser bastante útil em uma viagem internacional de negócios ou turismo. É muito comum, por exemplo, ao fazer o *check-in* no aeroporto ou hotel, ouvir a pergunta **How do you spell... ?** (Como se soletra... ?) para confirmação de nomes, sobrenomes e outras informações. Portanto, não deixe de treinar ouvindo a pronúncia das letras do alfabeto no áudio e aproveite para praticar soletrando as letras de seu nome e sobrenome.

A B C D E F G H I J K L M N
O P Q R S T U V W X Y Z

VERBO TO BE (TEMPO PRESENTE)

Veja no quadro abaixo a conjugação do verbo *to be* (ser, estar) no tempo presente, nas formas afirmativa, negativa e interrogativa.

Affirmative	Negative	Interrogative
I am (= I'm)*	I'm not	Am I?
You are (= You're)	You aren't **	Are you?
He is (= He's)	He isn't ***	Is he?
She is (= She's)	She isn't	Is she?
It is (= It's)	It isn't	Is it?
We are (= We're)	We aren't	Are we?
You are (= You're)	You aren't	Are you?
They are (= They're)	They aren't	Are they?

* formas contraídas

** aren't = contração de are + not

*** isn't = contração de is + not

Observe que, para transformar uma frase afirmativa com o verbo *to be* em interrogativa, basta inverter a posição do sujeito e a do verbo. Veja o exemplo:

Paul is a lawyer. (Paul é advogado)
Is Paul a lawyer? (Paul é advogado?)

Agora veja alguns exemplos de uso do verbo *to be* no tempo presente, nas formas afirmativa, negativa e interrogativa:

How are you today? (Como você está hoje?) – **I'm fine, thanks!** (Estou bem, obrigado!)

Sam and Joe are both college students. (Sam e Joe são ambos estudantes universitários.)

Are you married? (Você é casado/a?) – **No, I'm single.** (Não, sou solteiro/a.)

Kate isn't at home now. She's at school. (Kate não está em casa agora. Ela está na escola.)

Who's that girl? (Quem é aquela garota?)

Is Jeff your friend? (Jeff é seu amigo?)

What's your occupation? (Qual a sua ocupação?)

It's really cold today! (Está mesmo frio hoje!)

How old are you? (Quantos anos você tem?)

Nick is nineteen years old. (Nick tem dezenove anos de idade.)

Jeniffer isn't late for the meeting. (Jeniffer não está atrasada para a reunião.)

Whose is that cell phone? (De quem é aquele telefone celular?)

Are they ready to go? (Eles estão prontos para ir?)

Where are you from? (De onde você é?) – **I'm from Canada. / I'm Canadian.** (Sou do Canadá. / Sou canadense.)

➤ Veja *Countries and nationalities* (países e nacionalidades) p. 20

USUAL VOCABULARY 1

DAYS OF THE WEEK

Monday (segunda-feira)
Tuesday (terça-feira)
Wednesday (quarta-feira)
Thursday (quinta-feira)
Friday (sexta-feira)
Saturday (sábado)
Sunday (domingo)

MONTHS OF THE YEAR

January (janeiro)
February (fevereiro)
March (março)
April (abril)
May (maio)
June (junho)
July (julho)
August (agosto)
September (setembro)
October (outubro)
November (novembro)
December (dezembro)

POLITE EXPRESSIONS

Thank you./ Thanks. (Obrigado.)
You're welcome. (Não há de quê.)

GREETINGS 1

Good morning (Bom dia)
Good afternoon (Boa tarde)
Good evening (Boa noite)
Good night* (Boa noite)
Hello (Olá/ Oi)
Hi (Oi)
How are you? (Como você está?)
I'm fine, thank you, and you? (Estou bem, obrigado, e você?)
* Usado ao se retirar ou antes de ir dormir.

COUNTRIES AND NATIONALITIES

Brazil (Brasil)/ **Brazilian** (brasileiro/a)
Germany (Alemanha)/ **German** (alemão/ alemã)
Australia (Austrália)/**Australian** (australiano/a)
Canada (Canadá)/ **Canadian** (canadense)
China (China)/ **Chinese** (chinês/ chinesa)
Cuba (Cuba) / **Cuban** (cubano/a)

Egypt (Egito) / **Egyptian** (egípcio/a)
Scotland (Escócia)/ **Scottish, Scot** (escocês/ escocesa)
Spain (Espanha)/ **Spanish** (espanhol/a)
United States (Estados Unidos)/ **American** (americano/a)
France (França)/ **French** (francês/ francesa)
Greece (Grécia) / **Greek** (grego/a)
Holland, The Netherlands/ (Holanda)/ **Dutch** (holandês/ holandesa)
England (Inglaterra)/ **English** (inglês/ inglesa)
Ireland (Irlanda)/ **Irish** (irlandês/ irlandesa)
Italy (Itália)/ **Italian** (italiano/a)
Japan (Japão)/ **Japanese** (japonês/ japonesa)
Mexico (México)/ **Mexican** (mexicano/a)
New Zealand (Nova Zelândia)/ **New Zealander** (neozelandês/ neozelandesa)
Portugal (Portugal)/ **Portuguese** (português/ portuguesa)
Sweden (Suécia)/ **Swedish** (sueco/a)
Switzerland (Suíça)/ **Swiss** (suíço/a)

PRACTICE SET 1

🎵 4 I. Listen to the questions and circle the right answer.

1. a) Yes, I did.
   b) No, I don't.
   c) No, he doesn't.

2. a) Yes, she is.
   b) Yes, he does.
   c) Yes, he is.

3. a) On Mondays and Wednesdays.
   b) Yes, I study Spanish.
   c) No, I don't speak Spanish

4. a) Yes, that's a man.
   b) Yes, I do.
   c) That's Harry.

5. a) No, I don't.
   b) I'm twenty-six years old.
   c) No, I don't speak Portuguese.

6. a) I have a phone number.
   b) It's 504-6571.
   c) Yes, it is.

7. a) Me? I'm from Los Angeles.
   b) Yes, I do.
   c) Me? I'm a webdesigner.

8. a) Yes, that's Pamella.
   b) She's twenty-three years old.
   c) Yes, Pamella is my friend.

9. a) He's Australian.
   b) He's okay.
   c) Yes, he is.

10. a) Yes, I am.
    b) Yes, I do.
    c) It's Mike: M - I - K - E

ılıılıı 5 II. Dictation: listen to the sentences and write them.

1. _____

2. _____

3. _____

4. _____

5. _____

III. Rewrite the sentences with contractions.
Ex.: What is your occupation? What's your occupation?

1. Kate is a teacher. _____

2. What is your phone number? _____

3. It is hot today. _____

4. Sam is not American, he is from Canada. _____

5. I am thirty-two years old. _____

IV. Write questions/ phrases for the following answers.

1. _____?
   I'm an engineer.

2. _____?
   I'm fine, thanks!

3. _____?
   Victor is twenty-six years old.

4. _____?
   No, I don't smoke.

5. _____
   You're welcome.

V. Circle the word or expression that is different from the group.

1. Wednesday – Monday – Friday – April – Tuesday – Sunday
2. February – December – July – October – March – Thursday
3. Why – Where – Saturday – Who – What – When
4. Italy – Australian – French – Canadian – American – Spanish
5. Good afternoon – Where are you from? – Good morning – Good evening – Good night

🔊 6 **DIALOGUE 2**

Why don't we go camping for a change?

Rita: Why don't we do something different next weekend?
Joe: **Sure**, **honey**, what do you have in mind?
Rita: I don't know, **perhaps** we could **go camping for a change**.
Joe: Sounds exciting! Hey, I had an idea. Why don't you call your friend Karen and check if she and Arnold would like to **come along with** us? Don't you think it would be a lot more **fun**?
Rita: **Definitely**. We could go in just one car and share the expenses. Listen, I think we'll need to buy a new **tent**.
Joe: I agree, ours is very old and I think it's too small. I can't remember the last time we used it!
Rita: I can't either! Great, I'll give Karen a call. I hope they can join us. Wow, I'm **looking forward to** our weekend!
Joe: Me too, honey!

▶ Veja a tradução desse diálogo na p. 289.

FOCUS ON VOCABULARY, PHRASES AND EXPRESSIONS 2

Sure = of course (claro, com certeza)
Honey = 1. sweet substance made by bees; 2. (inf.) dear (1. mel; 2. querido/a)

25

Perhaps = maybe (talvez)
Go camping = go somewhere and stay in a tent (acampar)
For a change = as something different (para variar)
Come along with = come together with (vir junto)
Fun = enjoyable; amusing (divertido)
Definitely = absolutely (sem dúvida, com certeza)
Tent = a shelter made of cloth (barraca)
Look forward to = feel happy and excited about something that is going to happen (aguardar ansiosamente)

ᵢₗᵢₗ 7 DIALOGUE 2 – COMPREHENSION QUESTIONS

1. What does Rita want to do next weekend?
2. Does Joe like the idea of going camping?
3. Who do they plan to invite to go camping with them?
4. Why do they need to buy a new tent?

APPLIED GRAMMAR 2
perguntas no tempo presente com o verbo auxiliar *don't* e plural dos substantivos

Usamos o verbo auxiliar **don't** (contração de **do** + **not**) para fazer perguntas negativas no tempo presente com os sujeitos *I* (eu); *you* (você); *we* (nós) e *they* (eles, elas). Veja os exemplos abaixo:

Don't you need to work today? (Você não precisa trabalhar hoje?) – **Yes, I do. / No, I don't.**
Don't they speak English? (Eles não falam inglês?) – **Yes, they do. / No, they don't.**
Don't you like her? (Você não gosta dela?) – **Yes, I do. / No, I don't.**

Agora veja mais alguns exemplos de perguntas e respostas no tempo presente com o verbo auxiliar *don't* e as *question words What*

(O que) e *Why* (Por que):

Why don't we go to the club tomorrow?
(Por que não vamos ao clube amanhã?)
Why don't you invite your friend to go with us?
(Por que você não convida seu amigo para ir conosco?)
What part of the sentence don't you understand?
(Qual parte da sentença você não entende?)
Why don't you sit down and relax for a few minutes?
(Por que você não senta e relaxa por alguns minutos?)

PLURAL DOS SUBSTANTIVOS

O plural da maioria dos substantivos em inglês é formado com o acréscimo da letra "s". Veja alguns exemplos:

friend (amigo/a) – **friends** (amigos/as)
house (casa) – **houses** (casas)
car (carro) – **cars** (carros)
window (janela) – **windows** (janelas)
book (livro) – **books** (livros)

Para os substantivos que terminam em "y" e são precedidos de vogal, acrescenta-se "s". Veja os exemplos:

boy (garoto) – **boys** (garotos)
key (chave) – **keys** (chaves)
day (dia) – **days** (dias)
toy (brinquedo) – **toys** (brinquedos)
guy (cara, sujeito) – **guys** (caras, sujeitos)

Para os substantivos que terminam em "y" e são precedidos de consoante, substitui-se o "y" por "ies". Veja os exemplos:

story (estória) – **stories** (estórias)
party (festa) – **parties** (festas)

city (cidade) – **cities** (cidades)
family (família) – **families** (famílias)
country (país) – **countries** (países)

Para os substantivos que terminam em "ch", "s", "ss", "sh", "x" e a maioria dos substantivos que terminam em "o", acrescenta-se "es". Veja os exemplos:

church (igreja) – **churches** (igrejas)
watch (relógio) – **watches** (relógios)
bus (ônibus) – **buses** (ônibus)
glass (copo) – **glasses** (copos)
kiss (beijo) – **kisses** (beijos)
brush (escova) – **brushes** (escovas)
box (caixa) – **boxes** (caixas)
potato (batata) – **potatoes** (batatas)
tomato (tomate) – **tomatoes** (tomates)

Para os substantivos que terminam em "f"ou "fe", troca-se o "f" ou "fe" por "ves". Veja os exemplos:

knife (faca) – **knives** (facas)
wife (esposa) – **wives** (esposas)
shelf (prateleira) – **shelves** (prateleiras)
life (vida) – **lives** (vidas)

O plural de alguns substantivos é irregular; veja alguns exemplos:

man (homem) – **men** (homens)
woman (mulher) – **women** (mulheres)
child (criança) – **children** (crianças)
tooth (dente) – **teeth** (dentes)

USUAL VOCABULARY 2

NUMBERS 1

one (1)	**eleven** (11)
two (2)	**twelve** (12)
three (3)	**thirteen** (13)
four (4)	**fourteen** (14)
five (5)	**fifteen** (15)
six (6)	**sixteen** (16)
seven (7)	**seventeen** (17)
eight (8)	**eighteen** (18)
nine (9)	**nineteen** (19)
ten (10)	**twenty** (20)

Ex.: **What's your telephone number?** (Qual é o número de seu telefone?)
It's 759-4216. (É 759-4216.)

MARITAL STATUS

married (casado/a)
single (solteiro/a)
engaged (noivo/a)
divorced (divorciado/a)
separated (separado/a)
widowed (viúvo/a)

GREETINGS 2

How are you doing? (Como está?/ Como vai?)
How's it going? (Como estão indo as coisas?)
What's up? (E aí?)
Long time no see! (Há quanto tempo a gente não se vê!)
Bye! (Tchau!)
See you later! (Te vejo mais tarde!/ Até mais tarde)
See you tomorrow! (Até amanhã!)
See you around! (Te vejo por aí!)
Take care! (Cuide-se!)

OCCUPATIONS

teacher (professor/a)
professor (professor/a universitário/a)
lawyer (advogado/a)
doctor (médico/a)
taxi driver (motorista de táxi)
architect (arquiteto/a)
housewife (dona de casa)
accountant (contador/a)
waiter (garçom)
waitress (garçonete)
dentist (dentista)
businessman (empresário)
manager (gerente)
secretary (secretária)
clerk (balconista)
barber (barbeiro)
hairdresser (cabeleireiro/a)
singer (cantor/a)
cook (cozinheiro/a)
chef (chefe de cozinha)
real estate agent (corretor de imóveis)
engineer (engenheiro/a)
writer (escritor/a)
consultant (consultor/a)
flight attendant (comissário/a de bordo)
nurse (enfermeira/o)
cleaner (faxineiro/a)
maid (empregada doméstica)
baby sitter (babá)
psychologist (psicólogo/a)
veterinarian/vet (veterinário/a)
tour guide (guia turístico)
travel agent (agente de viagens)
actor (ator)
actress (atriz)

PRACTICE SET 2

🎵 8 I. Listen to the questions and circle the right answer.

1. a) I live in Chicago.
    b) I live in an apartment.
    c) I live with my wife and children.

2. a) Yes, I speak Italian fluently.
    b) No, I don't.
    c) No, I live in France.

3. a) Yes, it is.
    b) No, it isn't.
    c) Very good, thanks!

4. a) I have to study.
    b) No, I don't.
    c) Yes, I like to go to the club on Sunday.

5. a) That's a woman.
    b) That's Mary.
    c) That's John.

6. a) Yes, she's my friend.
    b) It's Elizabeth.
    c) Yes, it is.

7. a) She's a teacher.
    b) No, she's married.
    c) She's from Brazil.

8. a) He's nineteen years old.
    b) She's sixteen years old.
    c) Yes, he is old.

9. a) Yes, I am.
   b) It's 539-6742.
   c) Yes, that's my telephone number.

10. a) Yes, I go to the club on Saturdays.
    b) Yes, I have to work every day.
    c) Yes, I go to the club every Sunday.

🔊 9 II. Dictation: listen to the sentences and write them.

1. _____

2. _____

3. _____

4. _____

5. _____

III. Write the plural of the following words:

1. computer _____
2. box _____
3. family _____
4. wife _____
5. child _____

IV. Write questions/ phrases for the following answers.

1. _____?
   No, I don't have a car.

2. _____?

Yes, I'm married.

3. _____?

Linda is thirty-five years old.

4. _____?

No, Rita's single.

5. _____

Nice to meet you too.

V. Circle the word or expression that is different from the group.

1. tables – houses – boxes – girls – cities – child
2. married – single – divorced – separated – webdesigner – engaged
3. how are you? – what's up? – how's it going? – uncle
4. teacher – husband – engineer – doctor – lawyer – taxi driver
5. Italian – Germany – Japan – France – Spain – England

LESSON 3

🔊 10 **DIALOGUE 3**
What does your dad do?

Mel: What does your **dad** do?
Josh: My dad? He's a lawyer.
Mel: Oh, really? Does he work in an office **downtown**?
Josh: He does, he **catches** the subway to work every day.
Mel: I see, and you have only one sister, right?
Josh: That's right, Helen, she's younger than I am.
Mel: How old is she?
Josh: She just **turned** fifteen.
Mel: Does she have a boyfriend?
Josh: Well, not that I know of!

▶ Veja a tradução desse diálogo na p. 290.

FOCUS ON VOCABULARY, PHRASES AND EXPRESSIONS 3

Dad = father (pai, papai)
Downtown = the center of a city, especially the business area (centro da cidade)
Catch/ caught/ caught = get on a bus, train, subway etc. (pegar ônibus, trem, metrô etc.)
Turn/ turned/ turned = become a particular age (fazer anos)

DIALOGUE 3 – COMPREHENSION QUESTIONS

1. What does Josh's father do?
2. How does Josh's father go to work?
3. How many sisters does Josh have?
4. What's Josh's sister's name?
5. How old is Josh's sister?

APPLIED GRAMMAR 3
tempo presente com o verbo auxiliar does, pronome pessoal e pronome objeto

Usamos o verbo auxiliar *does* para fazer perguntas no tempo presente com os sujeitos *he* (ele); *she* (ela) e *it** (ele, ela). Veja os exemplos:

* Pronome usado para referir-se a objetos e animais.

Does she smoke? (Ela fuma?) – **Yes, she does. / No, she doesn't*.**
Does he speak French? (Ele fala francês?) – **Yes, he does. / No, he doesn't.**
Does it drink milk? (Ele bebe leite?) – **Yes, it does. / No, it doesn't.**
Does Mary have a car? (Mary tem carro?) – **Yes, she does. / No, she doesn't.**
Does Ralph understand Spanish? (Ralph entende espanhol?) – **Yes, he does. / No he doesn't.**

* **doesn't** = contração de **does + not**

Para a resposta completa afirmativa repetimos o verbo principal usado na pergunta acrescido de "s". No caso da resposta completa negativa usamos *"doesn't"* (contração de *does* + *not*) antes do verbo principal. Veja os exemplos:

Does she smoke ? – **Yes, she smokes. / No, she doesn't smoke.**
Does he speak French? – **Yes, he speaks French. / No, he doesn't speak French.**

Does it drink milk? – **Yes, it drinks milk. / No, it doesn't drink milk.**

O verbo "have" (ter) é substituído por "has" na resposta afirmativa completa. Veja o exemplo:

Does Mary have a car? – **Yes, she has a car. / No, she doesn't have a car.**

Para os verbos que terminam em "o", "ch", "sh" e "ss", acrescenta-se "es" na resposta afirmativa completa. Veja os exemplos:

Does Nick go to the club on Sundays? – **Yes, he goes to the club on Sundays. / No, he doesn't go to the club on Sundays.**
Does Liz teach every day? – **Yes, she teaches every day. / No, she doesn't teach every day.**
Does Amanda brush her teeth after meals? – **Yes, she brushes her teeth after meals. / No, she doesn't brush her teeth after meals.**

Agora veja mais alguns exemplos de perguntas e respostas no tempo presente com o verbo auxiliar *does* e as *question words* **What** (O que/ Qual) – **Where** (Onde) – **When** (Quando) – **Why** (Por que) – **Who** (Quem) – **How** (Como):

What does she do for a living? (O que ela faz?) – **She's a dentist** (Ela é dentista.)
Where does Joe live? (Onde Joe mora?) – **He lives in an apartment downtown.** (Ele mora em um apartamento na cidade.)
When does Jane come here? (Quando Jane vem aqui?) – **She comes here on Wednesdays and Fridays.** (Ela vem aqui nas quartas e sextas.)
Why does he get up so early? (Por que ele levanta tão cedo?) – **He gets up early because he has to go to work.** (Ele levanta cedo porque tem que ir ao trabalho.)
Who does Bob live with? (Com quem Bob mora?) – **Bob lives with his wife and kids.** (Bob mora com a esposa e filhos.)

How does Maggy come to work? (Como Maggy vem ao trabalho?) –
Maggy comes to work by subway. (Maggy vem ao trabalho de metrô.)

Usamos o verbo auxiliar **doesn't** (contração de **does** + **not**) para fazer perguntas negativas no tempo presente com os sujeitos *he* (ele); *she* (ela) e *it* (ele, ela). Veja os exemplos:

Doesn't she work on Saturdays? (Ela não trabalha aos sábados?)
Doesn't Terry go to the gym every day?
(Terry não vai à academia todos os dias?)
Doesn't Linda have a job? (Linda não tem emprego?)

PRONOME PESSOAL E PRONOME OBJETO

Observe na tabela abaixo os pronomes pessoais e os pronomes objetos:

Pronome pessoal	Pronome objeto
I	me
you	you
he	him
she	her
it	it
we	us
you	you
they	them

Agora veja alguns exemplos de uso em frases contextualizadas:

Do you understand me? (Você me entende?)
Susan doesn't need us. (Susan não precisa de nós.)
Does Harry like her? (Harry gosta dela?)
Where's Jeff? I need to talk to him.
(Onde está Jeff? Preciso falar com ele.)
I don't understand them. (Eu não os entendo.)
Do you see her every day? (Você a vê todos os dias?)

USUAL VOCABULARY 3

FAMILY CONNECTIONS

father/ dad (pai)
mother/ mom (mãe)
parents (pais)
relatives (parentes)
husband (marido)
wife (esposa)
son (filho)
daughter (filha)
children/ kids (filhos)
brother (irmão)
sister (irmã)
grandfather (avô)
grandmother (avó)
grandparents (avôs)
grandson (neto)
granddaughter (neta)
grandchildren (netos)
brother-in-law (cunhado)
sister-in-law (cunhada)
uncle (tio)
aunt (tia)
cousin (primo/a)
nephew (sobrinho)
niece (sobrinha)
father-in-law (sogro)
mother-in-law (sogra)
son-in-law (genro)
daughter-in-law (nora)

DEMONSTRATIVE PRONOUNS

this (isto, este, esta)
these (estes, estas)
that (aquilo, aquele, aquela)

those (aqueles, aquelas)

MEANS OF TRANSPORTATION

subway (metrô)
bus (ônibus)
train (trem)
car (carro)
plane (avião)
ship (navio)

Ex.: **How do you come to work?** (Como você vem ao trabalho?) – **I come to work by subway.** (Eu venho ao trabalho de metrô.)

PRACTICE SET 3

🔊 12 I.   Listen to the questions and circle the right answer.

1. a) No, she doesn't.
    b) Yes, Sophie works here.
    c) No, Sophie doesn't speak Spanish.

2. a) That's my nephew.
    b) That's my brother-in-law.
    c) That's my sister-in-law.

3. a) I don't have a car.
    b) By bus.
    c) I don't work on Saturdays.

4. a) That's Mary.
    b) That's right.
    c) That's Bill.

5. a) No, my husband doesn't speak Spanish.
    b) Yes, he speaks German.
    c) Yes, he does.

6. a) He's nineteen years old.
    b) She's sixteen years old.
    c) Yes, Nick is my brother.

7. a) He works in a bank.
    b) Yes, he does.
    c) He's Spanish.

8. a) Yes, I do. I have a son and a daughter.
    b) Yes, I like children.
    c) No, they aren't good kids.

9. a) Susan? She's from Miami.
    b) Susan? She's a dentist.
    c) Susan? She's thirty-four years old.

10. a) Yes, he does.
    b) Yes, he works every day.
    c) He comes to work by car.

🎵 13 II. Dictation: listen to the sentences and write them.

1. _____

2. _____

3. _____

4. _____

5. _____

III. Replace the underlined word(s) by a pronoun.
Ex.: Does Jeff like <u>Rita</u>? > Does Jeff like her?

1. I don't understand <u>Sam</u>. > I don't understand _____ .
2. Susan likes <u>Peter and I</u>. > Susan likes _____ .
3. I see <u>Liz and Sandra</u> every day. > I see _____ every day.
4. Do you like <u>Mary</u>? > Do you like _____ ?
5. We don't know <u>that man</u>. > We don't know _____ .

IV. Write questions/ phrases for the following answers.

1. _____?
   No, Rita doesn't smoke.

2. _____?
   Nick is from Australia.

3. _____?
   My daughter is five years old.

4. _____?
   My brother works in a bank.

5. _____?
   Barry comes to work by subway.

V. Circle the word or expression that is different from the group.

1. sister – father – boy – daughter – aunt – cousin
2. bus – subway – train – ship – plane – husband
3. that – these – this – they – those
4. she – me – they – I – you – he
5. August – Tuesday – Friday – Wednesday – Monday – Saturday

🔊 14 DIALOGUE 4
You have a great memory!

Tyler: Is that your dad's car parked out front?
Neil: No, that's my uncle's car. My dad had a problem with his car so he **borrowed** his brother's car.
Tyler: Ah, I thought maybe your dad had bought another car or something. **By the way**, I saw your sister at school this morning.
Neil: Did you?
Tyler: Yeah, she was talking to Kate during the **break**.
Neil: Oh, yeah Kate is one of her best friends. They **get along** really well. Remember those **guys** we met at the park yesterday?
Tyler: Sure.
Neil: I was trying to remember their names.
Tyler: Josh and Oliver?
Neil: That's right! You have a great memory!
Tyler: But what about them? Why were you trying to remember their names?
Neil: Well, I think they'll be playing on our basketball team. I saw the **coach** talking to them in the **gym** this morning. That's why!

▶ Veja a tradução desse diálogo na p. 290.

FOCUS ON VOCABULARY, PHRASES AND EXPRESSIONS 4

Borrow/ borrowed/ borrowed = receive and use something from someone and promise to give it back (pegar emprestado)
By the way = expression used to introduce a new subject (a propósito)
Break = pause, interval (intervalo)
Get along = have a good relationship (dar-se bem)
Guy = a man (cara, sujeito)
Coach = someone who trains a team (técnico)
Gym = 1. a large room for doing physical exercises 2. a place where people go to do physical exercises (1. ginásio esportivo 2. academia de ginástica)

ılıļı 15 DIALOGUE 4 – COMPREHENSION QUESTIONS

1. Did Neil's father buy a new car?
2. Why did Neil's father borrow his brother's car?
3. Who did Tyler see at school this morning?
4. Who's Kate?
5. Why was Neil trying to remember the names of the guys he and Tyler met at the park?

APPLIED GRAMMAR 4
pronomes possessivos e o caso possessivo ('s)

Observe na tabela abaixo o pronome possessivo e o pronome possessivo adjetivo:

Pronome possessivo adjetivo	Pronome possessivo
my	mine
your	yours
his	his
her	hers

its	**its**
our	**ours**
your	**yours**
their	**theirs**

my/ mine (meu, meus, minha, minhas)
your/ yours (seu, seus, sua, suas)
his (dele)
her/ hers (dela)
its (dele, dela)
our (nosso, nossos, nossa, nossas)
your/ yours (seus, suas, de vocês)
their/ theirs (deles, delas)

Agora veja alguns exemplos de uso em frases contextualizadas:

Where's my cell phone? (Onde está o meu celular?)
This is not Mike's book. It's mine. (Este livro não é do Mike. É meu.)

Is Thomas your friend? (O Thomas é seu amigo?)
My car is parked here. Where is yours?
(Meu carro está estacionado aqui. Onde está o seu?)

Do you know his family? (Você conhece a família dele?)
This is John's iPod. I'm sure it's his.
(Este iPod é do John. Tenho certeza que é dele.)

Her father is a singer. (O pai dela é cantor.)
This handbag is hers. (Esta bolsa é dela.)

Our new house is big. (Nossa casa nova é grande.)
That's not Peter's dog. It's ours.
(Aquele cachorro não é do Peter. É nosso.)

Where are their friends? (Onde estão os amigos deles?)
Those CDs are theirs. (Aqueles CDs são deles.)

O CASO POSSESSIVO ('S)

O caso possessivo ('s) é usado para mostrar que algo pertence a alguém. Veja os exemplos:

Nick's apartment is small. (O apartamento do Nick é pequeno.)
Whose dog is that? That's Mary's dog.
(De quem é aquele cachorro? Aquele cachorro é da Mary.)
Is this cell phone yours? No, it's Bob's.
(Este celular é seu? Não é do Bob.)
Where are Bill's friends? (Onde estão os amigos de Bill?)
My brother's car is red. (O carro do meu irmão é vermelho.)
Nina's boyfriend is nineteen years old.
(O namorado de Nina tem dezenove anos.)
Jeff's sister is a nurse. (A irmã de Jeff é enfermeira.)

USUAL VOCABULARY 4

NUMBERS 2

twenty-one (21)
twenty-two (22)
twenty-three (23)
twenty-four (24)
twenty-five (25)
twenty-six (26)
twenty-seven (27)
twenty-eight (28)
twenty-nine (29)
thirty (30)
forty (40)
fifty (50)
sixty (60)
seventy (70)
eighty (80)

ninety (90)
one hundred (100)
two hundred (200)
three hundred (300)
one thousand (1000)
two thousand (2000)
three thousand (3000)
ten thousand (10.000)

Ex.: **101 – one hundred and one**
212 – two hundred and twelve
568 – five hundred and sixty-eight
1793 – one thousand, seven hundred and ninety-three
7256 – seven thousand, two hundred and fifty-six

SPORTS

soccer (futebol)
basketball (basquetebol)
volleyball (voleibol)
handball (handebol)
swimming (natação)
baseball (beisebol)
cycling (ciclismo)
golf (golfe)
hockey (hóquei)
jogging/ running (corrida)
athletics (atletismo)
skiing (esqui)
skating (patinação)
ice skating (patinação no gelo)
boxing (boxe)
mountain climbing (alpinismo)
bowling (boliche)
skateboarding (skatismo)
football (futebol americano)
tennis (tênis)

table tennis (tênis de mesa)
surfing (surfe)

PRACTICE SET 4

🎵 16 I.   Listen to the questions and circle the right answer.

1.   a) No, she doesn't.
     b) Yes, he does.
     c) Yes, he works every day.

2.   a) Yes, they are.
     b) That's my brother.
     c) Those are Jeff's friends.

3.   a) Yes, I do.
     b) Yes, I come here every day.
     c) No, I don't have time.

4.   a) Yes, she's my sister.
     b) It's Sandra.
     c) Yes, it is.

5.   a) She plays volleyball with her friends.
     b) Yes, she likes to play volleyball.
     c) Yes, she does.

6.   a) Yes, I have a brother.
     b) He's twenty-six years old.
     c) Yes, my brother's friend is a teacher.

7.   a) She works in a hospital.
     b.) Yes, she's from France.
     c) Yes, she has a son and two daughters.

8.   a) She's at school.

b) She's my sister.
c) She's Nick's sister.

9. a) Her father is fifty-five years old.
b) Her father is my friend.
c) Her father is a doctor.

10. a) Yes, I like sports.
b) Volleyball.
c) Yes, I am.

🔊 17 II. Dictation: listen to the sentences and write them.

1. _____

2. _____

3. _____

4. _____

5. _____

III. Write the following numbers.

a) 83 _____

b) 407 _____

c) 6.354 _____

d) 9.971 _____

e) 729 _____

IV. Write questions/ phrases for the following answers.

1. _____?
   Yes, that umbrella is mine.

2. _____?
   That cell phone is mine.

3. _____
   That's Daniel's sister.

4. _____?
   Yes, I do. I play soccer on Saturdays.

5. _____?
   Samantha works in a hospital.

V. Circle the word or expression that is different from the group.

1. our – my – their – his – she – your
2. swimming – window – volleyball – soccer – jogging – basketball
3. September – January – November – July – February – Monday
4. teacher – dentist – lawyer – nephew – secretary – taxi driver
5. Mexico – Canadian – New Zealand – Brazil – France – Portugal

LESSON 5

DIALOGUE 5
You missed out on a great party!

Sarah: So, how was the party last night?
Dustin: Great, I **had** a lot of **fun.**
Sarah: Did Josh **show up** with his new girlfriend?
Dustin: He did, but he arrived really late. We all thought he wasn't coming anymore. By the way, your friend Dana was also there.
Sarah: Was she? **What a pity** I couldn't come!
Dustin: Yeah, you **missed out on** a great party, but don't worry, we are planning to organize another party soon.
Sarah: Sounds good! Do **keep me posted**.
Dustin: Sure! I hope you can **make it** next time.

▶ Veja a tradução desse diálogo na p. 291.

FOCUS ON VOCABULARY, PHRASES AND EXPRESSIONS 5

Have fun = have a good time; enjoy oneself (divertir-se)
Show up = arrive or appear (chegar, aparecer)
What a pity = an expression meaning "that's too bad" (que pena)
Miss out on = lose an opportunity to do something (perder a oportunidade de fazer algo)
Keep me posted = keep me informed (mantenha-me informado)
Make it = go to an event (ir a um evento)

DIALOGUE 5 – COMPREHENSION QUESTIONS

1. Did Dustin enjoy the party last night?
2. Did Josh go to the party?
3. Who's Dana?
4. Does Sarah enjoy going to parties?

APPLIED GRAMMAR 5
verbo auxiliar *did* (passado) e verbo *to be* (passado)

VERBO AUXILIAR *DID* (TEMPO PASSADO)

O verbo auxiliar **did** é usado para fazer perguntas no tempo passado com todos os sujeitos. Veja os exemplos:

Did you like the movie? (Você gostou do filme?)
Did they come here last night? (Eles vieram aqui ontem à noite?)
Did Barry go to the club yesterday? (Barry foi ao clube ontem?)

Para as respostas curtas usamos *"Yes, I did"*, no caso da resposta afirmativa, ou *"No, I didn't"* quando a resposta for negativa. Veja os exemplos:

Did you like the movie? **Yes, I did. / No, I didn't.**
Did they come here last night? **Yes, they did. / No, they didn't.**
Did Barry go to the club yesterday? **Yes, he did. / No, he didn't.**

Para as respostas completas usamos o verbo principal no tempo passado (veja a coluna do passado na lista de verbos na p. 281) na resposta afirmativa, e usamos a forma negativa **didn't** (contração de **did** + **not**) antes do verbo principal na resposta negativa. Veja os exemplos:

Did you like the movie? **Yes, I liked the movie. / No, I didn't like the movie.**

Did they come here last night? **Yes, they came here last night. / No, they didn't come here last night.**
Did Barry go to the club yesterday? **Yes, he went to the club yesterday. / No, he didn't go to the club yesterday.**

Agora veja mais alguns exemplos de perguntas e respostas no tempo passado com o verbo auxiliar *did* e as *question words* **What** (O que/ Qual) – **Where** (Onde) – **When** (Quando) – **Why** (Por que) – **Who** (Quem) – **How** (Como) – **How much** (Quanto/a):

What did you do yesterday? (O que você fez ontem?)
Where did Dennis go last night? (Aonde o Dennis foi ontem à noite?) – **He went to the movies.** (Ele foi ao cinema.)
When did she arrive from the United States? (Quando ela chegou dos Estados Unidos?) – **She arrived from the United States on Thursday night.** (Ela chegou dos Estados Unidos na quinta à noite.)
Why did she close the window? (Por que ela fechou a janela?) – **She closed the window because it's cold.** (Ela fechou a janela porque está frio.)
Who did Liz dance with? (Com quem a Liz dançou?) – **Liz danced with Eric.** (A Liz dançou com o Eric.)
How did you do that? (Como você fez isso?)
How much did the tickets cost? (Quanto custaram os ingressos?) – **They cost twenty-five dollars.** (Custaram vinte e cinco dólares.)

VERBO *TO BE* (TEMPO PASSADO)

Veja no quadro abaixo a conjugação do verbo *to be* (ser, estar) no tempo passado, nas formas afirmativa, negativa e interrogativa.

Affirmative	Negative	Interrogative
I was	I wasn't *	Was I?
You were	You weren't **	Were you?
He was	He wasn't	Was he?
She was	She wasn't	Was she?
It was	It wasn't	Was it?

We were	**We weren't**	**Were we?**
You were	**You weren't**	**Were you?**
They were	**They weren't**	**Were they?**

* wasn't = contração de was + not

** weren't = contração de were + not

Observe que, para transformar uma frase afirmativa com o verbo *to be* em interrogativa, basta inverter a posição do sujeito e a do verbo. Veja o exemplo:

Samuel was the best student in his class.
(Samuel foi o melhor aluno da sala.)
Was Samuel the best student in his class?
(Samuel foi o melhor aluno da sala?)

Agora veja alguns exemplos de uso do verbo **to be** no tempo passado, nas formas afirmativa, negativa e interrogativa.

I was very busy yesterday. (Estive muito ocupado ontem.)
Were you at home last night? (Você estava em casa ontem à noite?)
Kate and Nick were here last Tuesday.
(Kate e Nick estiveram aqui na terça passada.)
Where was Mike yesterday? (Onde o Mike esteve ontem?)
Gary and Michael weren't at the meeting last Monday.
(Gary e Michael não estiveram na reunião na segunda passada.)
Who was that girl with you? (Quem era aquela garota com você?)
Was Melissa busy yesterday? (Melissa estava ocupada ontem?)
Was that new cell phone expensive?
(Aquele novo telefone celular foi caro?)
It was very cold yesterday! (Fez muito frio ontem!)
How old were you when you moved to Brazil? (Quantos anos você tinha quando se mudou para o Brasil?) – **I was five years old when I moved to Brazil.** (Eu tinha cinco anos quando me mudei para o Brasil.)
Richard wasn't late for the meeting.
(Richard não estava atrasado para a reunião.)

That computer wasn't expensive. It was cheap.
(Aquele computador não foi caro. Foi barato.)

USUAL VOCABULARY 5

TIME EXPRESSIONS

today (hoje)
tonight (hoje à noite)
every day (todos os dias)
every week (todas as semanas)
every month (todos os meses)
every year (todos os anos)
tomorrow (amanhã)
tomorrow night (amanhã à noite)
yesterday (ontem)
last night (ontem à noite)
last week (semana passada)
last month (mês passado)
last year (ano passado)
last Monday (segunda-feira passada)
last Sunday (domingo passado) etc.

Ex.: **What day is today?** (Que dia é hoje?) – **Today is Wednesday.**
(Hoje é quarta.)
What did David do last night? (O que David fez ontem à noite?)
He played cards with his friends. (Ele jogou cartas com os amigos.)

CLOTHES AND SHOES

shirt (camisa)
t-shirt (camiseta)
pants (calças)
dress (vestido)
skirt (saia)
blouse (blusa de mulher)

coat (casaco)
jacket (jaqueta)
socks (meias)
sweatshirt (moletom)
suit (terno)
underpants (cueca)
boxers (cueca samba-canção)
panties (calcinha)
bra (sutiã)
scarf (cachecol)
hat (chapéu)
tie (gravata)
trunks (calção)
bathing suit (maiô)
shoes (sapatos)
boots (botas)
slippers (chinelos)
cleats (chuteira)
sneakers (tênis)
sandals (sandálias)

Ex.: **Your new red dress is beautiful.**
(Seu novo vestido vermelho é bonito.)
This green shirt is mine. (Esta camisa verde é minha.)

COLORS

blue (azul)
red (vermelho)
yellow (amarelo)
green (verde)
orange (laranja)
pink (rosa)
brown (marron)
grey (cinza)
black (preto)
white (branco)

Ex.: **What color is it?** (De que cor é?)
Whose are those black pants? (De quem é aquela calça preta?)
Those black pants are Phillip's. (Aquela calça preta é do Phillip.)

PRACTICE SET 5

20 I. Listen to the questions and circle the right answer.

1. a) Yes, we did.
   b) Yes, we do.
   c) Yes, we are.

2. a) Yes, he is.
   b) No, he wasn't.
   c) No, he isn't.

3. a) Yes, it does.
   b) No, it isn't.
   c) It cost two hundred dollars.

4. a) He needs to go to the bank.
   b) Yes, he does.
   c) He is Jane's brother.

5. a) Yes, it is.
   b) No, it wasn't.
   c) No, it isn't.

6. a) Yes, he did.
   b) He went to the club.
   c) Yes, he does.

7. a) Yes, they did.
   b) Yes, they do.
   c) No, they don't.

8. a) Yes, he likes to travel.
   b) No, he doesn't.
   c) He went to Miami.

9. a) Yes, it is.
   b) No, it isn't.
   c) Today is Monday.

10. a) Yes, he did.
    b) He played soccer last Friday.
    c) No, he didn't.

⏸ 21 II. Dictation: listen to the sentences and write them.

1. _____

2. _____

3. _____

4. _____

5. _____

III. Complete the following questions.

1. _____ you here yesterday? Yes, I was.

2. _____ are those socks? They're mine.

3. _____ color is it? It's blue.

4. _____ Phillip smoke? No, he doesn't.

5. _____ Susan come here last week? Yes, she did.

IV. Write questions/ phrases for the following answers.

1. _____?
   Yes, David was here last night.

2. _____?
   No, that green shirt isn't mine.

3. _____?
   That's my friend Bill.

4. _____?
   I went to the club on Friday.

5. _____?
   Her name's Samantha.

V. Circle the word or expression that is different from the group.

1. they – we – I – she – his – you
2. baseball – hat – tennis – golf – skiing – cycling
3. pants – shoes – newspaper – shirt – jacket – socks
4. blue – white – red – sneakers – yellow – black
5. last week – today – last year – tomorrow – last night – bowling

> ## LESSON 6

Hi darling. How was your day?

Great!

DIALOGUE 6
It's great to be back home!

James: It's great to be back home!
Liz: Hi, **darling**. How was your day?
James: Great! What are you doing in the kitchen, **honey**?
Liz: I'm making a **strawberry** cake, your favorite!
James: Wow, my **mouth** is already starting to **water**. Where are Pamella and Jake?
Liz: Pamella is taking a shower. She's going out with her boyfriend tonight. Jake is probably listening to music in his bedroom.
James: Good, I'll go upstairs to say hello to him. Actually there's something I want to talk to him about.
Liz: Now I'm curious, what is it?
James: Oh, **no big deal**! I **got** tickets for the hockey game on Friday night.
Liz: Jake's gonna love it!
James: I know!

▶ Veja a tradução desse diálogo na p. 291.

FOCUS ON VOCABULARY, PHRASES AND EXPRESSIONS 6

Darling = sweetheart, dear, honey (querida/o)
Honey = 1. sweet substance made by bees; 2. (inf.) dear (1. mel; 2. querido/a)

Strawberry = red pulpy fruit (morango)
Mouth = the part of your face below your nose that you use to eat and speak (boca)
Water/ watered/ watered = if your mouth waters, saliva begins to form in your mouth (dar água na boca)
No big deal = something that is not very important (nada muito importante)
Got: veja Usos do verbo *get* **p. 275**

ıı|ı|ı· 23 **DIALOGUE 6 – COMPREHENSION QUESTIONS**

1. How was James's day?
2. What's Liz doing in the kitchen?
3. Where are Pamella and Jake?
4. Who's Pamella going out with tonight?
5. What does James want to talk to Jake about?

APPLIED GRAMMAR 6
o gerúndio e o tempo verbal *present progressive*

GERÚNDIO

A formação do gerúndio em inglês é muito simples. Enquanto em português temos as terminações -ando/ -endo/ -indo (ex.: trabalhando, vendendo, sorrindo) em inglês usa-se a terminação -*ing*. Vejas os exemplos abaixo:

Work (trabalhar) – **working** (trabalhando)
Read (ler) – **reading** (lendo)
Go (ir) – **going** (indo)

Obs.: Quando o verbo principal termina em "e", omite-se o "e" e acrescenta-se "ing". Veja os exemplos:

Make (fazer) – **making** (fazendo)
Write (escrever) – **writing** (escrevendo)
Give (dar) – **giving** (dando)

PRESENT PROGRESSIVE

O tempo verbal **present progressive**, também conhecido como **present continuous**, descreve uma ação que está acontecendo no momento. É formado através da combinação do verbo *to be* no presente (conjugado) e do verbo principal no gerúndio, ou seja, acrescido da terminação "*ing*". Veja abaixo alguns exemplos de uso nas formas afirmativa, negativa e interrogativa:

Tony is studying for a test. (Tony está estudando para uma prova.)

Rita isn't working now. She's at home watching a movie. (Rita não está trabalhando agora. Ela está em casa assistindo a um filme.)

What's Bianca doing? (O que a Bianca está fazendo?) – **She's making a cake for Jim's birthday party.** (Ela está fazendo um bolo para a festa de aniversário do Jim.)

Joe is taking a shower. (Joe está tomando uma ducha.)
Are you enjoying the show? (Você está gostando do show?)

O *present progressive* também pode ser usado para expressar o futuro quando nos referimos a ações previamente planejadas. Veja os exemplos abaixo:

I'm meeting Carol at the mall later.
(Vou encontrar Carol no shopping mais tarde.)
Are you working tomorrow? (Você vai trabalhar amanhã?)
David is playing tennis with Tony at 7 pm today.
(David vai jogar tênis com Tony hoje às 19 horas.)
What are you doing this weekend? (O que você vai fazer neste final de semana?) – **I'm traveling to the beach.** (Vou viajar para a praia.)

USUAL VOCABULARY 6

TELLING THE TIME: WHAT TIME IS IT? (*QUE HORAS SÃO?*)

It's seven o'clock in the morning./ It's seven a.m. (São sete horas da manhã.)
It's seven o'clock in the evening./ It's seven p.m. (São sete horas da noite.)
It's five past seven. (São sete e cinco.)
It's a quarter past seven. (São sete e quinze.)
It's twenty past seven. (São sete e vinte.)
It's half past seven. (São sete e meia.)
It's a quarter to eight. (São sete e quarenta e cinco. / São quinze para as oito.)
It's ten to eight. (São sete e cinquenta. / São dez para as oito.)
It's noon./ It's midday. (É meio-dia.)
It's midnight. (É meia-noite.)

watch (relógio de pulso)
clock (relógio de parede ou de mesa)
my watch is fast (meu relógio está adiantado)
my watch is slow (meu relógio está atrasado)
eight o'clock sharp (oito horas em ponto)

PRACTICE SET 6

🔊 24 I. Listen to the questions and circle the right answer.

1. a) He's reading a book.
    b) Yes, he is.
    c) Yes, he does.

2. a) Yes, he is.
    b) No, he doesn't.
    c) No, he isn't.

3. a) Yes, she does.
   b) No, it isn't.
   c) No, she isn't. It's a holiday, remember?

4. a) It's beautiful.
   b) It cost forty-five dollars.
   c) Yes, it was.

5. a) Yes, it was.
   b) No, it wasn't.
   c) No, I wasn't.

6. a) It's noon.
   b) No, it isn't.
   c) Yes, it's good.

7. a) Yes, he did.
   b) He went to the movies with his friends.
   c) No, David is from New Zealand.

8. a) They cost eighty dollars.
   b) Yes, they are new sneakers.
   c) No, they weren't.

9. a) Yes, he works on Saturdays.
   b) No, it isn't.
   c) I think it's Friday.

10. a) They arrived last Tuesday.
    b) They travel every month.
    c) They have a big car.

25 II. Dictation: listen to the sentences and write them.

1. _____

2. _____

3. _____

4. _____

5. _____

III. Circle the right answer.

1. Is that yellow dress yours?
   a) No, it doesn't.
   b) Yes, it is.
   c) Yes, it does.

2. What time is it?
   a) It's midnight.
   b) It's hot.
   c) Yes, it is.

3. Where does Fred go every day?
   a) Yes, he does.
   b) He goes to school.
   c) No, he doesn't have a sister.

4. What's Bill doing?
   a) He's sleeping.
   b) He's Mary's friend.
   c) He plays basketball.

5. Does Phillip have a job?
   a) Yes, he is.
   b) Yes, he works in a bank.
   c) Yes, she does.

IV. Write questions/ phrases for the following answers.

1. _____?
   I'm going to the movies tonight.

2. _____?
   Yes, those black shoes are mine.

3. _____?
   That shirt costs fifty dollars.

4. _____?
   We went to the beach last weekend.

5. _____?
   It's ten past nine.

V. Circle the word or expression that is different from the group.

1. accountant – secretary – manager – daughter – singer – waiter
2. pink – white – yellow – brown – grey – that
3. New Zealand – Italy – New York – Germany – Argentina – U.S.A.
4. son-in-law – student – grandfather – cousin – son – brother
5. July – Tuesday – February – December – May – November

26 **DIALOGUE 7**
A surprise birthday party

Bill: I saw a **guy** who **looked** just **like** you yesterday!
Harry: Where was that?
Bill: At the Bayshore **mall**, around 4:00 pm
Harry: That was probably me, I was there in the afternoon. I was shopping for **sneakers**. How about you? What were you doing at the mall yesterday?
Bill: I went there to **get** Barbara a gift. Today's her birthday. By the way, I tried to reach you yesterday, I called you twice but I didn't leave a message.
Harry: I remember I was taking a shower when the phone rang yesterday, so that must have been you, sorry! What did you want to talk to me about?
Bill: We're planning a surprise party for Barbara tonight, so I was wondering if you'd care to **drop by** our place and join us.
Harry: **Cool!** Barbara's gonna love this!
Bill: I really hope so. I've **taken care of** all the arrangements so I hope it all **works out** fine.
Harry: It will, don't worry. What time should I **show up** then?
Bill: Around six would be fine. Barbara will be arriving a little later.
Harry: Great, I'll be there before six. And Bill?
Bill: Yeah?
Harry: Thanks a lot for inviting me!

▶ Veja a tradução desse diálogo na p. 291.

FOCUS ON VOCABULARY, PHRASES AND EXPRESSIONS 7

Guy = a man (cara, sujeito)
Look like = resemble (parecer-se com)
Mall = shopping center (shopping)
Sneakers = sports shoes (tênis)
Get: veja Usos do verbo *get* p. 275
Drop by = visit informally (dar um pulo na casa de)
Cool = excellent, very good (legal)
Take care of = look after (cuidar de)
Work out = develop in a particular way (dar certo)
Show up = arrive or appear (chegar, aparecer)

ᶦᵗᶦᶦ 27 DIALOGUE 7 – COMPREHENSION QUESTIONS

1. What was Harry doing at the mall yesterday?
2. Why did Bill go to the mall yesterday?
3. Why is Bill planning a surprise party for Barbara tonight?
4. What did Bill want to talk to Harry about?

APPLIED GRAMMAR 7
tempo verbal *past progressive* e o verbo haver:
there + to be

PAST PROGRESSIVE

O tempo verbal ***past progressive***, ou ***past continuous***, descreve uma ação que estava acontecendo quando outra a interrompeu. É formado pela combinação do verbo *to be* no passado (conjugado) e do verbo principal no gerúndio, ou seja, acrescido da terminação *-ing*. Veja os exemplos contextualizados abaixo, nas formas afirmativa, negativa e interrogativa:**Fred was having lunch when Linda called.** (Fred estava almoçando quando Linda ligou.)

What were you doing when I called you this morning? (O que você estava fazendo quando eu te liguei de manhã?) – **I was shaving when you called me.** (Estava fazendo a barba quando você ligou.)

It was raining a lot when we left the office last night. (Estava chovendo muito quando saímos do escritório ontem à noite.)

Were you having dinner when Lucy arrived? (Vocês estavam jantando quando Lucy chegou?) – **No, we were watching TV when she arrived.** (Não, estávamos assistindo TV quando ela chegou.)

O VERBO HAVER: *THERE + TO BE*

O verbo "haver" em inglês é formado a partir da combinação da palavra there com o verbo to be conjugado. Veja abaixo as combinações possíveis:

there is = há (singular)
there are = há (plural)
there was = houve, havia (singular)
there were = houve, havia (plural)
there will be = haverá
there is going to be = vai haver (singular)
there are going to be = vai haver (plural)
there would be = haveria
there can be = pode haver
there may be = pode haver; talvez haja
there could be = poderia haver
there should be = deveria haver
there must be = deve haver
there has been = tem havido (singular)
there have been = tem havido (plural)
there had been = tinha havido

Obs.: A forma negativa do verbo "haver" em inglês é feita pela forma negativa do verbo *to be* e dos verbos auxiliares e modais.
Ex.: **there isn't** = não há

there aren't = não há (plural)

there wasn't – não houve; não havia – etc.

USUAL VOCABULARY 7

THE HOUSE

bedroom (dormitório)
bathroom (banheiro)
living-room (sala de estar)
dining-room (sala de jantar)
kitchen (cozinha)
laundry (lavanderia)
attic (sótão)
basement (porão, subsolo)
garage (garagem)
garden (jardim)
pool (piscina)
fence (cerca)
gate (portão)
yard (quintal)
backyard (quintal nos fundos da casa)

MEALS

breakfast (café da manhã)
lunch (almoço)
dinner (jantar)
 supper (ceia)
snack (lanche)

BREAKFAST

coffee (café)
milk (leite)
tea (chá)

water (água)
sugar (açúcar)
sweetner (adoçante)
juice (suco)
bread (pão)
rolls (pãezinhos)
toast (torrada)
bagel (pequeno pão em forma de anel)
butter (manteiga)
jam (geleia)
cream cheese (requeijão)
peanut butter (pasta de amendoim)
cereal (cereal)
scrambled eggs (ovos mexidos)
ham (presunto)
cheese (queijo)
cottage cheese (queijo fresco)
cake (bolo)
cracker (biscoito de água e sal)
cookie (biscoito doce/ bolacha)
muffin (bolinho, geralmente com frutas)

Ex.: **What do you usually have for breakfast?** (O que você geralmente come no café da manhã?) – **I usually have orange juice, coffee and toast.** (Eu geralmente tomo suco de laranja, café e como torrada.)

PRACTICE SET 7

28 I. Listen to the questions and circle the right answer.

1. a) No, I wasn't.
    b) Yes, I was.
    c) I was taking a shower.

2. a) Yes, he is.
   b) No, he doesn't.
   c) No, he isn't.

3. a) Yes, our house is big.
   b) We have just one bathroom.
   c) We have three bedrooms.

4. a) It cost one hundred and fifty-four dollars.
   b) Yes, that is a new dress.
   c) It is black.

5. a) Yes, I was.
   b) No, it wasn't.
   c) No, I wasn't.

6. a) I had orange juice, bacon and eggs and coffee.
   b) yes, I have breakfast at home every day.
   c) No, I don't like to drink milk.

7. a) He went to the supermarket with his wife.
   b) He was watching TV when you called him.
   c) Yes, James has breakfast at home every morning.

8. a) Yes, she drank coffee yesterday.
   b) No, she doesn't like milk.
   c) She drank orange juice in the morning.

9. a) It was midnight.
   b) Yes, it was.
   c) Bill has lunch at noon every day.

10. a) Yes, we have a nice apartment.
    b) Yes, it does.
    c) There's just one bedroom.

◀ıı||ı 29 II. Dictation: listen to the sentences and write them.

1. _____

2. _____

3. _____

4. _____

5. _____

III. Circle the right answer.

1. Is there a bank near here?
    a) No, it doesn't.
    b) Yes, there is.
    c) Yes, it does.

2. What does Sandra usually have for breakfast?
    a) She has breakfast at 9 am.
    b) No, she's not hungry now.
    c) She has orange juice and cereal.

3. Were there many students at school last night?
    a) I was there with my friends.
    b) Yes, there were.
    c) No, he didn't.

4. What time do you have lunch?
    a) At noon.
    b) Yes, I do.
    c) I like hamburgers.

5. What does Carol do?
   a) She's sleeping now.
   b) She has two brothers and a sister.
   c) She's a doctor.

IV. Write questions/ phrases for the following answers.

1. _____?
   There are two bedrooms.

2. _____?
   I usually have a chocolate milk shake and a muffin for breakfast.

3. _____?
   Yes, there's a drugstore on the next block.

4. _____?
   No, there isn't any milk in the refrigerator.

5. _____?
   No, the kitchen is small.

V. Circle the word or expression that is different from the group.

1. shoes – dress – jacket – t-shirt – pants – neighbor
2. tennis – basketball – soccer – volleyball – television – golf
3. kitchen – breakfast – bathroom – living room – bedroom –
   backyard
4. fireman – nurse – friend – lawyer – taxi driver – writer
5. bread – milk – cake – juice – kitchen – muffin

LESSON 8

🔊 30 **DIALOGUE 8**
Why don't we throw a party?

Harry: I heard Jane won't be coming with us to the beach anymore next week.
Sam: Yeah, I think she'll be very busy **taking care of** her nephew. I'm sure we'll miss her, but what can we do?
Harry: Well, maybe we can **stop by** to see her when we come back.
Sam: Sounds good! Let's do that.
Harry: Sure. Listen, we'll be going to university next year, so I was thinking, why don't we **throw a party** to celebrate?
Sam: That's a very good idea, Harry! Maybe we could have it in December? What do you think?
Harry: Great! It will be a good opportunity to see all our colleagues from school again before we **move away**. I'll talk to Steve, he's very good at organizing events.
Sam: Yeah, I'm sure he'll be **excited** about it. Let me know if you two **come up with** any interesting ideas.
Harry: Sure Sam! I will.

▶ Veja a tradução desse diálogo na p. 292.

FOCUS ON VOCABULARY, PHRASES AND EXPRESSIONS 8

Take care of = look after (cuidar de)
Stop by = visit someone for a short time (fazer uma visita breve a alguém)

Sounds good = great; good idea (ótimo; boa ideia)
Throw a party = arrange a party; have a party (dar uma festa)
Move away = move to another place (mudar-se para outro lugar)
Excited = very happy and enthusiastic (animado; entusiasmado)
Come up with = think of a plan, idea etc. (ter uma ideia, um plano etc.)

ᴵᴵᴵᴵ 31 DIALOGUE 8 – COMPREHENSION QUESTIONS

1. Why can't Jane go to the beach with Harry and Sam?
2. What do Harry and Sam plan to do when they come back from the beach?
3. Does Sam like Harry's idea of throwing a party?
4. When do they plan to throw the party?
5. Who's very good at organizing events?

APPLIED GRAMMAR 8

verbo auxiliar *will* (futuro) e futuro imediato com verbo *to be* + *going to*

VERBO AUXILIAR *WILL* (FUTURO)

Usamos o verbo auxiliar **will** para expressar o futuro. Veja os exemplos abaixo:

I will travel to Miami next Tuesday.
(Viajarei para Miami na próxima terça-feira.)
We will see Sandra at school tomorrow.
(Veremos Sandra na escola amanhã.)
Harry will talk to Alan tonight.
(Harry conversará com Alan hoje à noite.)

Obs.: As formas contraídas **I'll** (= I will); **you'll** (= you will); **he'll** (= he will); **she'll** (= she will); **we'll** (= we will); **they'll** (= they will) são bastante usuais na conversação.

Para fazer uma pergunta no tempo futuro basta iniciar com o verbo auxiliar *will*, veja os exemplos:

Will we have time to visit them next Saturday?
(Teremos tempo para visitá-los no próximo sábado?)
Will Barry come here next week?
(O Barry virá aqui na próxima semana?)
Will you need these books tomorrow?
(Você precisará destes livros amanhã?)

Para as respostas curtas usamos *"Yes, I will"*, no caso da resposta afirmativa, ou *"No, I won't"* quando a resposta for negativa. Veja os exemplos:

Will you need these books tomorrow? **Yes, I will. / No, I won't.**
Will Barry come here next week? **Yes, he will. / No, he won't.**

A forma negativa de **will** é **won't**, contração de **will** + **not**. Veja os exemplos abaixo:

They won't travel with us to San Francisco.
(Eles não viajarão conosco para São Francisco.)
I won't have time to finish the report today.
(Não terei tempo para terminar o relatório hoje.)
We won't see them tomorrow.
(Não os veremos amanhã.)

Veja agora alguns exemplos do uso do *will* com *WH-questions*:

When will Ana travel to Europe?
(Quando a Ana viajará para a Europa?)
What will you do tomorrow? (O que você fará amanhã?)
Where will they stay? (Onde eles ficarão?)

Uma outra forma de expressar o futuro é através da combinação do verbo *to be* + *going to* (futuro imediato). Veja os exemplos abaixo:

We are going to travel to the beach next weekend.
(Vamos viajar para a praia no próximo fim de semana.)
What time are you going to meet Jeniffer tonight?
(A que horas você vai encontrar a Jeniffer hoje à noite?)
What is Jack going to do tomorrow?
(O que o Jack vai fazer amanhã?)

Obs.: Veja também o uso do *present progressive* para expressar futuro na seção Applied grammar 6 na p. 62.

USUAL VOCABULARY 8

THE WEATHER

hot/ warm (quente)
cold (frio)
sunny (ensolarado)
rainy (chuvoso)
cloudy (nublado)
windy (ventando)
snowy (nevando)
mild (ameno)

Ex.: **What's the weather like today?**
(Como está o tempo hoje?)
It's warm and sunny.
(Está quente e ensolarado.)
What's the weather forecast for the weekend?
(Qual é a previsão do tempo para o fim de semana?)
It's going to be hot all weekend, but it's going to rain on Saturday afternoon.
(Vai fazer calor o fim de semana inteiro, mas vai chover no sábado à tarde.)

SEASONS OF THE YEAR

summer (verão)
winter (inverno)
fall/ autumn (outono)
spring (primavera)

Ex.: **What's your favorite season?**
(Qual sua estação do ano preferida?)
I prefer the summer.
(Prefiro o verão.)

LUNCH AND DINNER

pasta (massas)
spaghetti with meatballs (espaguete com almôndegas)
lasagna (lasanha)
hamburger (hambúrguer)
cheeseburger (hambúrguer com queijo)
French fries (batata frita)
rice and beans (arroz com feijão)
eggs (ovos)
lettuce and tomato salad (salada de alface e tomate)
chicken soup (canja de galinha)
vegetable soup (sopa de legumes)
meat (carne)
roast beef (carne assada)
roast chicken (frango assado)
pork (carne de porco)
steak (bife)
sausage (linguiça)
turkey (peru)
fish (peixe)
tuna (atum)
cod/ codfish (bacalhau)
shrimp (camarão)
salmon (salmão)
potato (batata)

olive (azeitona)
onion (cebola)
garlic (alho)
carrot (cenoura)
cucumber (pepino)
eggplant (berinjela)
hearts of palm (palmito)
cabbage (repolho)

Ex.: **What kind of food do you prefer?**
(Que tipo de comida você prefere?)
I like vegetables and fish.
(Gosto de legumes e peixe.)

Ex.: **At the restaurant**
(No restaurante)
Waiter: Are you ready to order sir?
(Garçom: O senhor está pronto para fazer o pedido?)
Yes, I'll have the grilled steak and the potato salad, please.
(Sim, eu vou querer o bife grelhado e a salada de batata, por favor.)

PRACTICE SET 8

▥▥ 32 I.   Listen to the questions and circle the right answer.

1. a) Yes, I am.
    b) I'll probably go to the club and play tennis.
    c) Yes, I saw her yesterday.

2. a) I think so.
    b) Yes, she does.
    c) Yes, she will.

3. a) I prefer the spring.
    b) It's time to go home now.
    c) It's cold and rainy.

4. a) At twelve o'clock.
   b) I have pasta and sometimes just a hamburger.
   c) Yes, I love sandwiches.

5. a) Yes, I will.
   b) No, I don't.
   c) Yes, I do.

6. a) Yes, she did.
   b) No, not really.
   c) She lives with her husband.

7. a) I'll see them tomorrow night.
   b) Yes, they will.
   c) I see her every day.

8. a) She gets up at six o'clock every morning.
   b) Yes, she will.
   c) Around 10 pm.

9. a) I go to that restaurant every Saturday.
   b) I like hamburgers and other kinds of sandwiches.
   c) Yes, I do.

10. a) I went to the mall to see a movie.
    b) Yes, I did.
    c) I like to go to the movies.

᪑᪑᪑ 33 II. Dictation: listen to the sentences and write them.

1. _____

2. _____

3. _____

4. _____

5. _____

III. Circle the right answer.

1. Does Patricia smoke?
   a) Yes, she will.
   b) No, she won't.
   c) No, she doesn't

2. What's the weather forecast for today?
   a) Yes, it will.
   b) It's going to be a hot day.
   c) I prefer cold weather.

3. Does your husband like to eat meat?
   a) No, he doesn't. He's a vegetarian.
   b) Yes, I do.
   c) No, he didn't.

4. Are you ready to order?
   a) Yes, I do.
   b) No, I don't.
   c) Yes, I am.

5. Did you talk to Barry yesterday?
   a) No, I didn't.
   b) Yes, he does.
   c) No, I don't.

IV. Write questions/ phrases for the following answers.

1. _____?
   I prefer the winter.

2. _____?
   I like chicken, fish and vegetables.

3. _____?
   Yes, I'll see him tomorrow.

4. _____?
   It's cold and cloudy.

5. _____?
   No, Sheila doesn't have a brother. She has two sisters.

V. Circle the word or expression that is different from the group.

1. chicken – French fries – tuna – spring – carrot – lasagna
2. uncle – cousin – weather – aunt – father – nephew
3. warm – cloudy – windy – pretty – cold – sunny
4. she – his – my – our – their – your
5. Brazilian – Russian – German – England – Japanese – Spanish

🎵 34 **DIALOGUE 9**
Would you like to see a movie?

Mike: So, what would you do if you were **in his shoes**?
Ray: To be honest with you I **don't have a clue**.
Mike: I know what you mean. I feel the same myself. One thing I'm sure, I'd never like to experience a situation like that.
Ray: Yeah, it's **awful**.
Mike: I'm going to the kitchen, would you like some water or coffee?
Ray: No, thanks, I'm ok. Hey, I was thinking, you're not doing anything tonight, are you?
Mike: No, not really, why?
Ray: Would you like to see a movie?
Mike: Good idea. Do you know **what's on** at the Arcade mall?
Ray: It seems there's a new action movie actually, we can **check out** their website.
Mike: Great, maybe we could also go **grab a bite to eat** at the new **hamburger joint** they have there.
Ray: Fine by me!

▶ Veja a tradução desse diálogo na p. 293.

FOCUS ON VOCABULARY, PHRASES AND EXPRESSIONS 9

In someone's shoes = experience someone's life (estar no lugar de outra pessoa; "na pele de outra pessoa")

Not have a clue = have no knowledge or information about something (não ter conhecimento ou informação sobre algo; "não ter a mínima ideia")
Awful = terrible (terrível; muito ruim)
What's on = what movie is on (que filme está passando)
Check out = take a look at (olhar para alguém ou algo)
Grab a bite to eat = eat some food or a small meal (comer algo)
Hamburger joint = a snack bar that serves hamburgers (lanchonete que serve hambúrguer)

ꜱ｜ꞁ｜ꞁꜱ 35 DIALOGUE 9 – COMPREHENSION QUESTIONS

1. What kind of situation are Mike and Ray talking about? A good one or a bad one?
2. Do they know what they would do in that situation?
3. Does Ray want to drink anything?
4. What does Ray invite Mike to do?
5. What else do they plan to do?

APPLIED GRAMMAR 9
verbo auxiliar *would* (condicional)

O verbo auxiliar **would** expressa o tempo condicional e corresponde em português às terminações "ia", "iam", "íamos" dos verbos, como é o caso de "gostar<u>ia</u>"; "prefer<u>iriam</u>" e "comprar<u>íamos</u>". A forma contraída de *would* é bastante usual: I'd; you'd; he'd; she'd; we'd; they'd. Veja alguns exemplos:

I would prefer to travel next weekend.
= I'd prefer to travel next weekend.
(Prefiriria viajar no próximo final de semana.)

We would buy that house if we had money.
= We'd buy that house if we had money.
(Compraríamos aquela casa se tivéssemos dinheiro.)
They'd like to travel to Europe this year.
(Eles gostariam de viajar para a Europa este ano.)

Para fazer uma pergunta no tempo condicional basta iniciar com o verbo auxiliar **would**, veja os exemplos:

Would you like some coffee? (Você gostaria de um café?)
Would they prefer to stay home tonight?
(Eles prefeririam ficar em casa hoje à noite?)
Would you like to go with us? (Você gostaria de ir conosco?)

Para as respostas curtas usamos *"Yes, I would"*, no caso da resposta afirmativa, ou *"No, I wouldn't"* quando a resposta for negativa. Veja os exemplos:

Would you like some coffee? **Yes, I would. / No, I wouldn't.**
Would they prefer to stay home tonight? **Yes, they would. / No, they wouldn't.**

A forma negativa de *would* é *wouldn't*, contração de *would + not*. Veja os exemplos abaixo:

I wouldn't like to live in that city.
(Não gostaria de viver naquela cidade.)
We wouldn't have time to visit that museum.
(Não teríamos tempo de visitar aquele museu.)
They wouldn't get up so early.
(Eles não levantariam tão cedo.)

Veja agora alguns exemplos do uso do *will* com *WH-questions*:

Where would you prefer to go today?
(Aonde você preferiria ir hoje?)

What would they like to do tonight?
(O que eles gostariam de fazer hoje à noite?)
When would you prefer to travel to the U.S.?
(Quando você preferiria viajar para os Estados Unidos?)
Why wouldn't you like to see them tomorrow?
(Por que você não gostaria de vê-los amanhã?)

USUAL VOCABULARY 9

KINDS OF MOVIES

action movies (filmes de ação)
comedies (comédias)
love stories (filmes românticos)
thrillers (suspenses)
war movies (filmes de guerra)
western (*western*)
sci-fi* (ficção científica)
whodunits (filmes policiais)
sitcoms** (séries)
* Abreviação de science-fiction = ficção científica.
** Abreviação de situation comedies = seriado cômico.

Ex.: **What kind of movies do you prefer/ like?**
(Que tipo de filme você prefere/ gosta?)
I prefer comedies. (Prefiro comédias.)
I like thrillers. (Gosto de suspenses.)

Ex.: **How often do you go to the movies?**
(Com que frequência você vai ao cinema?)
I go to the movies about once a month.
(Vou ao cinema aproximadamente uma vez por mês.)

FRUIT

apple (maçã)
banana (banana)
orange (laranja)
pear (pera)
grapes (uvas)
lemon (limão)
strawberry (morango)
papaya (papaia)
passion fruit (maracujá)
melon (melão)
watermelon (melancia)
peach (pêssego)
cherry (cereja)
coconut (coco)
pineapple (abacaxi)
tangerine (mexerica)
grapefruit (toranja)
mango (manga)
avocado (abacate)
plum (ameixa)
guava (goiaba)

PRACTICE SET 9

▐▏▌▐ 36   I.   Listen to the questions and circle the right answer.

1.   a) Yes, I would.
     b) He'll go to the club.
     c) I'd prefer to stay home.

2.   a) No, thanks, I'm ok.
     b) No, I don't.
     c) Yes, I will.

3. a) I prefer pasta.
   b) I love action movies.
   c) I go to the movies every weekend.

4. a) She'd like to visit her brother.
   b) She went to the movies.
   c) She has a house on the beach.

5. a) I prefer geography.
   b) Yes, I did.
   c) I didn't have time.

6. a) No, she doesn't. She prefers comedies.
   b) Yes, she will.
   c) No, she won't.

7. a) I eat an apple every day.
   b) Passion fruit juice, please.
   c) No, I didn't.

8. a) No, I wouldn't.
   b) Yes, he does.
   c) No, I prefer sitcoms.

9. a) I went to a restaurant with friends.
   b) I prefer to eat vegetables.
   c) No, I wouldn't.

10. a) Yes, I do.
    b) About once a week.
    c) I prefer action movies.

🔊 37 II. Dictation: listen to the sentences and write them.

1. _____

2. _____

3. _____

4. _____

5. _____

III. Circle the right answer.

1. Do you like comedies?
   a) Yes, I would.
   b) Oh, yeah, I love comedies.
   c) No, he doesn't.

2. When would you like to visit them?
   a) I don't know, maybe next Saturday.
   b) Yes, I would.
   c) I talked to them yesterday.

3. What would you like to drink?
   a) Strawberry juice, please.
   b) No, I prefer orange juice.
   c) Yes, I would.

4. How often do you see them?
   a) Yes, I do.
   b) I see them every week.
   c) No, I wouldn't.

5. Does your wife like sitcoms?
   a) Yes, she does.
   b) She has two brothers.
   c) Yes, I do.

IV. Write questions/ phrases for the following answers.

1. _____?
   Rachel visits her sister about once a month.

2. _____?
   Yes, I'd love to go to the beach next weekend.

3. _____?
   No, Monica doesn't speak Japanese.

4. _____?
   She'd prefer to stay home tonight.

5. _____?
   No, I don't like war movies.

V. Circle the word or expression that is different from the group.

1. pineapple – cherry – grapes – bacon – pear – strawberry
2. thrillers – sci-fi – geography – westerns – love stories – comedies
3. she – they – his – we – you – it
4. dentist – baby sitter – waitress – lawyer – woman – teacher
5. magazine – sunny – cloudy – cold – warm – windy

38
DIALOGUE 10
Have you been on a diet?

Ben: Hi, Rod, **long time no see**. How's it going?

Rod: Pretty good. Hey, you look **thinner** than the last time I saw you. Have you been on a diet?

Ben: Me? Oh, no! I've been **working out** at the gym three times a week now, that's why, you're right, I did use to be **fatter**.

Rod: Wow, you probably feel a lot **healthier** now, don't you?

Ben: I do, it's great to be **in shape**. So, I heard you moved into a bigger apartment, right? How's the new place?

Rod: Very good. My family is really happy about this new apartment, more spacious and comfortable than the last one. We have a bigger living room and one extra bedroom now, and that makes all the difference.

Ben: Great, you do sound happy. How about the **neighborhood**, is it quieter?

Rod: It is and the good thing is we have great **neighbors**.

Ben: Wow, sounds like you made the right move. You're also living closer to the company now, aren't you?

Rod: I am. I can **get** to work faster now. My **commute** to work used to take about half an hour, but now it only takes me about fifteen minutes.

Ben: Good for you!

▶ Veja a tradução desse diálogo na p. 293.

FOCUS ON VOCABULARY, PHRASES AND EXPRESSIONS 10

Long time no see = I haven't seen you for a long time (há quanto tempo a gente não se vê)
Pretty good = very good; very well (muito bem)
Thin = slender; slim (magro)
Thinner: veja Applied grammar 11 na p. 106
Work out = do physical exercise (fazer exercício físico; "malhar")
Fat = heavy; obese (gordo)
Fatter: veja Applied grammar 11 na p. 106
Healthy = enjoying good health; fit (saudável)
Healthier: veja Applied grammar 11 na p. 106
In shape = in good physical condition; fit (em boa forma física; em forma)
Neighborhood = a particular area of a city (bairro)
Neighbor = someone who lives near you (vizinho)
Get: veja Usos do verbo *get* na p. 275
Commute = the trip to and from work every day (o trajeto de casa para o trabalho e vice-versa)

39 DIALOGUE 10 – COMPREHENSION QUESTIONS

1. Why does Rod look thinner now?
2. Does Rod feel healthier now?
3. How's Rod's new apartment?
4. Does Rod have any problems with his neighbors?
5. How long does it take Rod to get to work now?

APPLIED GRAMMAR 10
adjectives

Os adjetivos em inglês são invariáveis, ou seja, usamos a mesma palavra para masculino, feminino, singular e plural. Veja nos exemplos abaixo que o adjetivo *new* (novo, nova, novos, novas) permanece o mesmo, enquanto em português há variação:

Um carro novo = A **new** car
Uma casa nova = A **new** house
Carros novos = **New** cars
Casas novas = **New** houses

É importante também lembrar que a posição dos adjetivos é sempre antes dos substantivos, ou seja, o contrário do português. Veja o exemplo abaixo:

My sister is a *tall* girl. (Minha irmã é uma menina alta.)
Obs.: Observe que, no exemplo acima, o adjetivo **tall** vem antes do substantivo **girl.**

Veja alguns outros exemplos:

We watched a *good* movie last night.
(Assistimos a um bom filme ontem à noite.)
Who's that *fat* man over there? (Quem é aquele homem gordo ali?)
Nelson has a *red* bicycle. (Nelson tem uma bicicleta vermelha.)
Our friend Lucy lives in a *big* apartment.
(Nossa amiga Lucy mora em um apartamento grande.)

ADJECTIVES – COMPARISON OF EQUALITY

Veja abaixo a comparação de igualdade:

Equality: **as** + **adjective** + **as**
Ex.: *as tall as* (tão alto quanto); *as big as* (tão grande quanto); *as expensive as* (tão caro quanto); *as beautiful as* (tão bonito quanto)

Agora veja alguns exemplos em frases contextualizadas:

Peter is as young as Paul. (O Peter é tão jovem quanto o Paul.)
The blue house is as expensive as the yellow one.
(A casa azul é tão cara quanta a amarela.)
Susan is as tall as Rachel. (A Susan é tão alta quanto a Rachel.)

The movie we saw yesterday is as interesting as the movie we saw today. (O filme que vimos ontem é tão interessante quanto o filme que vimos hoje.)

USUAL VOCABULARY 10

THE BODY

hand (mão)
fingers (dedos das mãos)
arm (braço)
wrist (pulso)
head (cabeça)
shoulder (ombro)
chest (peito)
stomach/ belly (barriga)
waist (cintura)
back (costas)
elbow (cotovelo)
thigh (coxa)
leg (perna)
knee (joelho)
foot/ feet (pé/ pés)
toes (dedos do pé)
ankle (tornozelo)
heel (calcanhar)
lungs (pulmões)
kidneys (rins)
liver (fígado)
heart (coração)

THE FACE

eyes (olhos)
ears (orelhas)

mouth (boca)
tooth/ teeth (dente/ dentes)
nose (nariz)
head (cabeça)
forehead (testa)
hair (cabelo)
neck (pescoço)
chin (queixo)
jaw (maxilar)
throat (garganta)
gum (gengiva)
lips (lábios)
tongue (língua)
cheek (bochecha)
eyebrow (sobrancelha)
eyelashes (cílios)
eyelid (pálpebra)

Ex.: **How often do you brush your teeth?**
(Com que frequência você escova os dentes?)
I brush my teeth three times a day.
(Escovo os dentes três vezes por dia.)
Do you brush your teeth after every meal?
(Você escova os dentes após todas as refeições?)

ACHES

headache (dor de cabeça)
toothache (dor de dente)
stomachache (dor de barriga)
earache (dor de ouvido)
backache (dor nas costas)

Ex.: **Are you feeling all right?** (Você está sentindo-se bem?)
No, I have a headache, I need to take an aspirin.
(Não, estou com dor de cabeça, preciso tomar uma aspirina.)

Ex.: **What's the matter with Sandra?**
(Qual é o problema com a Sandra?)
She has a cold. (Ela está com resfriado.)

PRACTICE SET 10

🎵 40 I. Listen to the questions and circle the right answer.

1. a) Yes, she was.
    b) No, she isn't.
    c) Yes, she does.

2. a) No, he didn't.
    b) Yes, he will.
    c) Yes, he does.

3. a) She loves vegetables.
    b) She has a stomachache.
    c) Yes, she did.

4. a) Yes, it is.
    b) Yes, I like the blue tie.
    c) No, it won't.

5. a) I need to brush my teeth.
    b) Three times a day.
    c) I didn't have time to brush my teeth yesterday.

6. a) I went there last night.
    b) Yes, I like to go out on Saturdays.
    c) I'd prefer to play tennis.

7. a) Yes, he is.
    b) Yes, he does.
    c) Yes, he was.

8. a) No, she wouldn't.
   b) I don't know. I have no idea.
   c) Yes, she would.

9. a) About four times a week.
   b) Yes, I do.
   c) I prefer to shave in the morning.

10. a) No, she wouldn't.
    b) No, she doesn't.
    c) No, she has a headache.

ıＩıＩı 41 II. Dictation: listen to the sentences and write them.

1. _____

2. _____

3. _____

4. _____

5. _____

III. Circle the right answer.

1. Are you all right?
   a) Yes, I was.
   b) Sure, I'm fine.
   c) Yes, I will.

2. How do you plan to go there?
   a) I'll probably go by car.
   b) Yes, I would.
   c) I'm going there with some friends.

3. Would you like to see a movie now?
   a) Yes, the movie was very interesting.
   b) No, I don't like action movies.
   c) No, I don't have time for that now.

4. What's the matter with Bob?
   a) Bob works in a bank.
   b) I think he has a cold.
   c) No, he wasn't.

5. Would Tony like to go with us?
   a) Yes, he would.
   b) Tony went there yesterday.
   c) No, he won't.

IV. Write questions/ phrases for the following answers.

1. _____?
Sabrina brushes her teeth three times a day.

2. _____?
No, he isn't. He has a cold.

3. _____?
I'd prefer to play soccer with my friends today.

4. _____?
She went to visit her sisters.

5. _____?

No, Sarah doesn't smoke.

V. Circle the word or expression that is different from the group.

1. foot – backache – hand – arm – leg – chest
2. water – milk – bread – juice – coffee – tea
3. mouth – nose – tongue – foot – eyes – ears
4. stomachache – earache – toothache – shoulder – headache – backache
5. steak – tuna – chicken – fish – beer – turkey

🎵 42 **DIALOGUE 11**
How's school?

Jeff: Hi Brian, how was the movie last night?
Brian: It **sucked**!
Jeff: Really?
Brian: Oh yeah, I guess I could say that was the worst movie I've ever seen in my entire life.
Jeff: Wow, I'm surprised! That movie **got** a **rave review**. Some great actors work in it, right?
Brian: That's right, but the **plot** is **awful**, anyway, I don't **wanna** talk about it, it's a waste of time.
Jeff: Ok. So, how's school?
Brian: So far so good. I guess I could say I'm doing well, the only thing is I'm having a hard time with physics, that's the **toughest** subject for me.
Jeff: Oh yeah? And what is the easiest subject for you?
Brian: Geography, that's actually my favorite subject.
Jeff: The most difficult subject for me has always been math, but I guess I'm **getting to grips with** it now.
Brian: Good for you! Well, we can't really complain, you know, we study at a great school and we do have some of the best teachers working there.
Jeff: That's right!

➤ Veja a tradução desse diálogo na p. 294.

FOCUS ON VOCABULARY, PHRASES AND EXPRESSIONS 11

Suck = to be very bad (ser horrível)
Got: veja Usos do verbo *get* na p. 275
Rave review = a very enthusiastic review (uma crítica muito elogiosa e favorável)
Plot = the story of a film, book, etc. (enredo)
Awful = terrible (terrível; muito ruim)
Wanna = want to (querer)
So far so good = up to this point all is ok (até aqui tudo bem)
Tough = hard; difficult (difícil)
Toughest: veja Applied grammar 12 na p. 114
Get to grips with = understand and deal with a situation; face something (entender e lidar com uma situação; encarar algo)

꜔꜔꜔ꜜ 43 **DIALOGUE 11 – COMPREHENSION QUESTIONS**

1. Did Brian like the movie he saw last night?
2. Why is Jeff surprised that Brian didn't like the movie?
3. What's the most difficult subject at school for Brian?
4. What's Brian's favorite subject at school?
5. Are Jeff and Brian happy about the school where they study?

APPLIED GRAMMAR 11
adjectives – comparison of superiority

A comparação de superioridade dos adjetivos curtos é feita de forma diferente dos adjetivos longos. Veja abaixo a comparação de superioridade para os adjetivos curtos:

Superiority: short adjective+**er** + **than**
Ex.: *older than* (mais velho do que); *taller than* (mais alto do que); *cheaper than* (mais barato do que); *hotter than* (mais quente do

que); *bigger than* (maior do que); *happier than* (mais feliz do que); *easier than* (mais fácil do que); *prettier than* (mais bonita do que)

Obs.: Quando um adjetivo terminar em consoante, vogal, consoante (CVC) – por exemplo, *big, hot* – dobra-se a última letra do adjetivo antes de acrescentar -*er*, na comparação de superioridade. No caso dos adjetivos que terminam em "y" (por exemplo, happy, easy, pretty, busy, heavy etc.) é preciso substituir o "y" por "i" antes de acrescentar -*er*, na comparação de superioridade.

Veja alguns exemplos em frases contextualizadas:

John is taller than Brian.
(John é mais alto do que Brian.)
Today is hotter than yesterday.
(Hoje está mais quente do que ontem.)
I think Mary is prettier than Jane.
(Eu acho que a Mary é mais bonita do que a Jane.)
Is Jeff younger than Harry?
(O Jeff é mais jovem do que o Harry?)

Agora veja a comparação de superioridade para os adjetivos longos:

Superiority: more + long adjective + **than**
Ex.: *more expensive than* (mais caro do que); *more interesting than* (mais interessante do que); *more difficult than* (mais difícil do que)

Exemplos em frases contextualizadas:

Japanese is more difficult than English.
(Japonês é mais difícil do que inglês.)
The movie I saw yesterday was more interesting than this one.
(O filme que eu vi ontem foi mais interessante do que este.)
This apartment is more comfortable than the other one.
(Este apartamento é mais confortável do que o outro.)

USUAL VOCABULARY 11

HOUSEHOLD CHORES

clean the house (limpar a casa)
do/ wash the dishes (lavar os pratos)
vacuum (passar aspirador de pó)
iron the clothes (passar as roupas)
flatiron (ferro de passar roupa)
take the garbage out (levar o lixo para fora)
sweep (varrer)
housework (serviço doméstico)
cleaner (faixineira)
maid (empregada doméstica)

Ex.: **Do you help your wife with the housework?**
(Você ajuda sua esposa com o serviço doméstico?)
Sure, I always do the dishes and take the garbage out.
(Claro, eu sempre lavo os pratos e levo o lixo para fora.)

HOUSEHOLD APPLIANCES

refrigerator/ fridge (geladeira)
stove (fogão)
oven (forno)
microwave (micro-ondas)
coffeemaker (máquina de café)
washing-machine (máquina de lavar)
dishwasher (lava-pratos)
vacuum cleaner (aspirador de pó)

Ex.: **Does Sally have a dishwasher?**
(A Sally tem um lava-pratos?)
Derek always heats food in the microwave.
(O Derek sempre esquenta a comida no micro-ondas.)
Sarah is baking a cake in the oven.
(A Sarah está fazendo um bolo no forno.)

PRACTICE SET 11

44 I. Listen to the questions and circle the right answer.

1. a) Yes, I do.
   b) Yes, I am.
   c) Yes, she is.

2. a) No, she doesn't have time.
   b) Yes, I did.
   c) Yes, I do. I always do the dishes.

3. a) She's making a chocolate cake.
   b) She has a backache.
   c) She's twenty-five years old.

4. a) Yes, it does.
   b) Yes, Paul lives in an apartment.
   c) No, it isn't.

5. a) The maid is.
   b) My wife isn't home.
   c) Kate is talking to Nick.

6. a) Yes, she is.
   b) No, I'm older than he is.
   c) Yes, I have one sister and two brothers.

7. a) She's cleaning the house now.
   b) She's shorter than I am.
   c) She's thirty-three years old.

8. a) He's taller than Fred.
   b) He's taking the garbage out.
   c) He takes the subway to work every day.

9. a) She likes to get up early.
   b) Yes, she does.
   c) About three times a week.

10. a) No, I don't.
    b) Yes, she does.
    c) No, I'm not.

ıılıl 45 II. Dictation: listen to the sentences and write them.

1. _____

2. _____

3. _____

4. _____

5. _____

III. Circle the right answer.

1. Who's that guy over there?
   a) That's a good idea.
   b) That's our friend Joe, he's thinner now!
   c) That's an interesting story.

2. Is this cell phone cheaper than that one?
   a) No, this cell phone is more expensive than that one.
   b) Yes, I have an expensive cell phone.
   c) No, it's a new cell phone.

3. Why don't you buy a new dishwasher?
   a) No, I don't usually do the dishes. My wife does.
   b) Yes, I use my dishwasher every day.
   c) I really need a new one, but I don't have money for that now.

4. Don't you have a bigger bag?
   a) Yes, I need a very big bag.
   b) Not really, this is the only one I have.
   c) Yes, they sell all kinds of bags there.

5. Does your husband help you clean the house?
   a) Sometimes he does, but not very often.
   b) No, he is taller than I am.
   c) Yes, he would like to go out tonight.

IV. Write questions/ phrases for the following answers.

1. _____?
   Yes, Melissa has a very good maid.

2. _____?
   We clean the house about twice a week.

3. _____?
   No, Bill is taller than Jason.

4. _____?
   He'd prefer to stay home tonight.

5. _____?
   No, I don't have a dishwasher. I do the dishes myself.

V. Circle the word or expression that is different from the group.

1. microwave – washing-machine – oven – kitchen – coffeemaker – fridge
2. wash the dishes – iron the clothes – take the garbage out – sweep – do the homework – clean the house
3. fingers – knee – toes – wrist – stove – head
4. shrimp – onion – carrot – wine – cucumber – cod
5. living-room – laundry – bathroom – oven – dining-room – bedroom

LESSON 12

DIALOGUE 12
You're a terrific classmate!

Paul: What's that on your face?
Daniel: Oh, nothing, I cut myself shaving this morning.
Paul: Ok, but just take a look at yourself in the mirror again, that looks awful, you should do something about it.
Daniel: Oh, don't worry! That's happened before, I'm a **lousy** shaver, you know?
Paul: All right! Listen, how about getting together tomorrow to finish our history **assignment**?
Daniel: There's no need for that.
Paul: No need for that? Are you **kidding** me?
Daniel: No, I've already done it, that's why!
Paul: You mean you finished it all by yourself?
Daniel: Yeah, I guess I was inspired last night, I **came up with** some interesting ideas and I **jotted** them **down**. I just need to rewrite it into a nice and clean text, but I can do that **in no time**, so **chill out pal**!
Paul: Wow Dan, what can I say? You're a **terrific** classmate!

▶ Veja a tradução desse diálogo na p. 295.

FOCUS ON VOCABULARY, PHRASES AND EXPRESSIONS 12

Lousy = bad (ruim)
Assignment = work that you must do as part of a course; task (trabalho escolar; tarefa)

Kidding = joking (brincando)
Come up with = think of a plan, idea etc. (ter uma ideia, plano etc.)
Jot down = write down (anotar)
In no time = very quickly or soon (em pouco tempo; "rapidinho")
Chill out = relax (relaxar)
Pal = close friend (amigo)
Terrific = very good; wonderful (muito bom; maravilhoso; sensacional)

ıı|ıı 47 DIALOGUE 12 – COMPREHENSION QUESTIONS

1. What's the matter with Daniel's face?
2. Is Daniel worried about it?
3. Why isn't it necessary for Paul and Daniel to get together tomorrow?
4. How does Paul feel about it?

APPLIED GRAMMAR 12
adjectives – comparison of superlative

A comparação de superlativo dos adjetivos curtos é feita de forma diferente dos adjetivos longos. Veja abaixo a comparação de superlativo para os adjetivos curtos:

Superlative: the + short adjective+**est**
Ex.: *the tallest* (o mais alto); *the youngest* (o mais jovem); *the newest* (o mais novo); *the biggest* (o maior); *the easiest* (o mais fácil); *the prettiest* (a mais bonita)

Obs.: Quando um adjetivo terminar em consoante, vogal, consoante (CVC) – por exemplo, big, hot – dobra-se a última letra do adjetivo antes de acrescentar -est, na comparação de superlativo. No caso dos adjetivos que terminam em "y" (por exemplo, happy, easy, pretty, busy, heavy etc.) é preciso substituir o "y" por "i" antes de acrescentar -est, na comparação de superlativo.

Veja alguns exemplos em frases contextualizadas:

Samuel is the youngest student in the classroom.
(Samuel é o aluno mais jovem na sala de aula.)
Which is the tallest building in the world?
(Qual é o edifício mais alto do mundo?)
Bob is the funniest guy I've ever met.
(Bob é o cara mais engraçado que eu conheci.)
That's the biggest house in the neighborhood.
(Aquela é a maior casa do bairro.)

Agora veja a comparação de superlativo para os adjetivos longos:

Superlative: the + **most** + long adjective
Ex.: *the most interesting* (o mais interessante); *the most famous* (o mais famoso); *the most expensive* (o mais caro); *the most difficult* (o mais difícil)

Exemplos em frases contextualizadas:

History is the most interesting subject in Mike's opinion.
(História é a matéria mais interessante na opinião do Mike.)
Did you do the most difficult exercise?
(Você fez o exercício mais difícil?)
Who's the most famous person you've ever met?
(Quem é a pessoa mais famosa que você já conheceu?)

Obs.: Os adjetivos *good* (bom, boa, bons, boas) e *bad* (ruim, ruins) são considerados irregulares. Veja no quadro abaixo as comparações de igualdade, superioridade e o superlativo desses adjetivos.

As good as = tão bom/ boa quanto; tão bons/ boas quanto
Better than = melhor do que; melhores do que

The best = o melhor/ a melhor; os melhores/ as melhores

As bad as = tão ruim quanto; tão ruins quanto
Worse than = pior do que; piores do que
The worst = o pior/ a pior; os piores/ as piores

Veja alguns exemplos contextualizados abaixo:

Who's the best soccer player in the world in your opinion?
(Quem é o melhor jogador de futebol do mundo na sua opinião?)
The weather is better now than yesterday.
(O tempo está melhor agora do que ontem.)
That was the worst movie that I ever saw.
(Aquele foi o pior filme que eu já vi.)
Living in San Francisco is as good as living in New York in Harry's opinion.
(Viver em San Franciso é tão bom quanto viver em Nova York na opinião de Harry.)
The best products are not necessarily the most expensive ones.
(Os melhores produtos não são necessariamente os mais caros.)

USUAL VOCABULARY 12

KEEPING IN SHAPE

do physical exercise (fazer exercício físico)
go jogging/ running (correr)
work out (fazer exercício físico; "malhar")
do aerobics (fazer aeróbica)
go swimming/ swim (nadar)
ride a bike (andar de bicicleta)
gym/ fitness center (academia)
fit/ in shape (em boa forma física)
push-up (flexão)

sit-up (abdominal)
go on a diet (fazer dieta)
put on weight/ gain weight (aumentar o peso; ganhar peso)
lose weight (perder peso, emagrecer)

Ex.: **You look like you are in shape/ fit.**
(Você parece estar em forma.)
How often do you work out?
(Com que frequência você malha?)
How often do you go jogging/ running?
(Com que frequência você corre?)
What do you do to keep in shape/ fit?
(O que você faz para manter-se em forma?)
I ride my bike for about an hour every day.
(Eu ando de bicicleta por aproximadamente uma hora todos os dias.)
I go jogging in the park every morning.
(Eu corro no parque todas as manhãs.)
I work out at the gym three times a week.
(Eu malho na academia três vezes por semana.)

PRACTICE SET 12

48 I.   Listen to the questions and circle the right answer.

1. a) Tony does.
    b) Tony is.
    c) Tony has.

2. a) No, I only did the easiest ones.
    b) Yes, he likes difficult exercises.
    c) Yes, I do.

3. a) Yes, I do.
    b) I enjoy working out.
    c) About four times a week.

4. a) I think so, he looks fatter, doesn't he?
   b) Yes, he was.
   c) No, he won't.

5. a) I prefer swimming.
   b) No, I'm not.
   c) Not really, only on weekends.

6. a) Yes, I'm in shape.
   b) I go jogging every morning and I also go swimming on Saturdays.
   c) I don't see them very often.

7. a) Me? No, I'm not.
   b) No, I'm vegetarian.
   c) No, I'd prefer to do that tomorrow.

8. a) No, he wasn't.
   b) Yes, he did.
   c) He bought the cheapest one.

9. a) No, he didn't.
   b) Yes, sometimes he does.
   c) Yes, he did.

10. a) I don't know, I don't really like soccer very much.
    b) Yes, he's the worst.
    c) No, he's not the best soccer player in my opinion.

〜〜 49 II. Dictation: listen to the sentences and write them.

1. _____

2. _____

3. _____

4. _____

5. _____

III. Circle the right answer.

1. Why does Phil need to go on a diet?
   a) He's on a diet.
   b) He needs to lose weight.
   c) He likes to ride his bike.

2. What do you do to keep in shape?
   a) I ride my bike for about an hour every day.
   b) I watch cartoons in the afternoon.
   c) Yes, I am.

3. Why don't you go jogging more often?
   a) About twice a week.
   b) I'd like to, but I don't have time now.
   c) Yes, I like to go jogging in the morning.

4. Which car would you prefer to buy?
   a) I'd prefer to stay home tonight.
   b) The fastest one, of course.
   c) Yes, I love fast cars.

5. How often do you go jogging?
   a) I like to go jogging.
   b) I went jogging yesterday.
   c) Three times a week.

IV. Write questions/ phrases for the following answers.

1. _____?
   No, he's not on a diet.

2. _____?
   Stephanie is the youngest student in my class.

3. _____?
   I go to the gym about twice a week.

4. _____?
   I go jogging every day and I also ride my bike on weekends.

5. _____?
   Yes, I'd love to go swimming today.

V. Circle the word or expression that is different from the group.

1. go jogging – work out – do physical exercise – go swimming – clean the house – do aerobics
2. sunny – rainy – turkey – windy – snowy – cloudy
3. engaged – single – family – married – divorced – separated
4. tuna – chicken – fish – meat – cod – tea
5. butter – basketball – tennis – golf – baseball – soccer

▌ 50

DIALOGUE 13
She looks cute, doesn't she?

Bill: You're not **dating** anyone now, are you?
Steve: No, not really. How about you?
Bill: Well, I **went out** with this girl **a couple of** times, but I'm not sure we **get along** so well together.
Steve: Really? What's her name?
Bill: Sarah.
Steve: Sarah? You mean the girl who works at the Ritz Café?
Bill: That's right. She looks **cute**, doesn't she?
Steve: I guess you could say so, but she's not really my type.
Bill: I see. Hey, don't you **feel like** going to a club tonight? You sure like dancing, don't you?
Steve: Yeah, sounds like a great idea to me, I really wouldn't mind **checking out** the **chicks** there, if you know what I mean.
Bill: Good! How about if I **pick** you **up** at 9?
Steve: **Deal!** See you at 9 then **pal!**

▶ Veja a tradução desse diálogo na p. 295.

FOCUS ON VOCABULARY, PHRASES AND EXPRESSIONS 13

Date/ dated/ dated = spend time with someone you have a romantic relationship with (namorar)

Go out = go somewhere for fun (sair para se diverter)
A couple of = a small number of; a few (alguns; algumas)
Get along = have a good relationship with (dar-se bem com)
Cute = pretty ("bonitinha")
Feel like = desire or want to do something (sentir vontade de, ter vontade de, "estar a fim de")
Check out = look at someone or something (olhar para alguém ou algo)
Chick = a young attractive woman (mulher jovem e atraente; "mina"; "gata")
Pick up = collect someone especially by car (pegar alguém especialmente de carro)
Deal = an agreement (de acordo; "fechado")
Pal = close friend (amigo)

〽️ 51 **DIALOGUE 13 – COMPREHENSION QUESTIONS**

1. Is Steve dating anyone at the moment? What about Bill?
2. Who's Bill dating and what does she do?
3. Does Steve think Sarah looks cute?
4. What do they plan to do tonight?

APPLIED GRAMMAR 13
tag questions

Veja as frases abaixo:

You're American, aren't you?
(Você é americano, não é?)
You work here, don't you?
(Você trabalha aqui, não trabalha?)
You don't smoke, do you?
(Você não fuma, fuma?)

Observe que ao final das frases acima temos sempre uma mini-pergunta que é empregada para a confirmação do que é dito. As sentenças acima são exemplos de *tag questions* e são muito frequentes na conversação cotidiana. Quando a sentença for afirmativa, a minipergunta ao final é negativa. Já quando a sentença for negativa, a minipergunta ao final é afirmativa. Veja mais alguns exemplos:

You came here yesterday, didn't you?
(Você veio aqui ontem, não veio?)
You can ride a bike, can't you?
(Você sabe andar de bicicleta, não sabe?)
Barry isn't tired, is he?
(O Barry não está cansado, está?)
Josh has a sister, doesn't he?
(O Josh tem uma irmã, não tem?)
You didn't see Tony yesterday, did you?
(Você não viu o Tony ontem, viu?)
You have to go now, don't you?
(Você tem que ir agora, não tem?)
That new computer wasn't so expensive, was it?
(Aquele computador novo não foi tão caro, foi?)
Sarah can't speak Japanese, can she?
(A Sarah não sabe falar japonês, sabe?)

USUAL VOCABULARY 13

DRIVING

driver's license (carteira de motorista)
traffic lights (semáforo)
one-way street (rua de mão única)
two-way street (rua de mão dupla)
traffic jam (congestionamento)
rush hour (hora do rush)

lane (pista, faixa)
toll (pedágio)
toll road (rodovia pedagiada)
fine/ ticket (multa)
exit (saída)
intersection (cruzamento)
detour (desvio)
bump (lombada, quebra-molas)
car crash (colisão, batida de veículo)
fender-bender (batida sem maiores consequências; "batidinha"; "arranhão")
short-cut (atalho)
shoulder (acostamento)
speed limit (limite de velocidade)

Ex.: **Do you know any short-cuts from here?**
(Você conhece algum atalho daqui?)
Watch out for the bump ahead!
(Cuidado com a lombada à frente!)
We need to get some cash for the toll.
(Precisamos pegar algum dinheiro para o pedágio.)
That's a four-lane road.
(Aquela estrada tem quatro pistas.)
We need to take exit 34. I think it's the next one.
(Precisamos pegar a saída 34. Acho que é a próxima.)

THE AUTOMOBILE

steering wheel (volante)
dashboard (painel)
speedometer (velocímetro)
trunk (porta-malas)
jack (macaco)
headlights (faróis dianteiros)
bumper (para-choque)
tire (pneu)
flat tire (pneu furado)

spare tire (estepe)
seatbelt (cinto de segurança)
power steering (direção hidráulica)
horn (buzina)
wheel (roda)
hood (capô)
fuel (combustível)

Ex.: **We need to rent a car with a big trunk.** (Precisamos alugar um carro com um porta-malas grande.)
We need to stop at a gas station. We're running out of fuel.
(Precisamos parar em um posto de gasolina. O combustível está acabando.)

AT THE GAS STATION

We're running out of gas. (Estamos ficando sem gasolina.)
Can you fill it up please? (Pode completar, por favor?)
Can you check the oil please? (Pode checar o óleo, por favor?)
Can you check the tires please? (Pode checar os pneus, por favor?)
Can you wash the windshield please? (Pode lavar o para-brisa, por favor?)

PRACTICE SET 13

🔊 52   I.   Listen to the questions and circle the right answer.

1.   a) Yes, I did.
     b) No, I don't.
     c) Yes, he does.

2.   a) No, she isn't.
     b) Yes, she does.
     c) No, she didn't

3. a) My brother's name is Joe.
   b) Yes, I am.
   c) Yes, I do. Her name is Sandra.
4. a) Yes, he's fluent in Spanish.
   b) Yes, he does.
   c) No, he isn't.

5. a) No, I can't.
   b) Yes, I did.
   c) Yes, she did.

6. a) Yes, you are.
   b) No, I don't.
   c) No, I'm not.

7. a) Yes, he is.
   b) Yes, he does.
   c) Yes, he did.

8. a) No, he didn't.
   b) No, I didn't.
   c) Yes, he does.

9. a) Yes, I am.
   b) No, I didn't.
   c) Yes, I do.

10. a) Yes, he does.
    b) Yes, he is.
    c) Yes, I am.

〽 53 II. Dictation: listen to the sentences and write them.

1. _____

2. _____

3. _____

4. _____

5. _____

III. Circle the right answer.

1. Is this a toll road?
   a) Yes, it was.
   b) Yes, it is.
   c) Yes, it does.

2. What's the traffic like in the rush hour?
   a) It's very bad.
   b) It's a two-way street.
   c) It's a four-lane road.

3. Your dad is a doctor, isn't he?
   a) Yes, he does.
   b) That's right. He works in a hospital near here.
   c) No, he didn't.

4. You're going to the party tonight, aren't you?
   a) Yes, you are.
   b) Yes, I do.
   c) Yes, I am.

5. Did you rent a car when you went to Florida?
   a) Yes, I rented a car with a big trunk.
   b) Yes, you did.
   c) Yes, I drive every day.

IV. Write questions/ phrases for the following answers.

1. _____?
   Rachel is twenty-five years old.

2. _____?
   He'd like to go swimming on Saturday.

3. _____?
   Gary has two brothers.

4. _____?
   Sabrina went to the movies with Tony.

5. _____?
   No, Mike doesn't smoke.

V. Fill in the blanks with an appropriate word/ expression from the box.

rush hour	speed limit	trunk	driver's license
	fine/ ticket	tires	

1. We need to rent a car with a big _____ . We have many bags.
2. "Can you check the _____ please?", said Greg at the gas station.
3. Is my _____ valid here?
4. Traffic is always bad like this in the _____ .
5. Watch out for the _____ on this road. You don't want to get a _____, do you?

So, the amusement parks there are huge, aren't they?

They are!

🎵 54 **DIALOGUE 14**
I heard you went to the Disney resorts

Tony: Hey Neil, **long time no see**. How are you?

Neil: Just fine Tony. How about you?

Tony: Very well. I heard you went to the Disney resorts on your vacation. So, how was it?

Neil: Great! I always have a wonderful time when I go there. Have you ever been to any of the **amusement parks** in that complex?

Tony: No, never, but I'm planning to go there sometime soon.

Neil: Yeah, you should do that. I'm sure your kids are **gonna** love it.

Tony: I know, they've been **begging** me to go there for a while now. So, the amusement parks there are **huge**, aren't they?

Neil: They are! You can actually get lost inside them if you're not careful.

Tony: Wow, sounds **exciting**. What do you usually do when you go there?

Neil: Well, we often get up early and have a **hearty** breakfast, you need a lot of energy to enjoy the **rides**, so you'**d better avoid** going there on an empty stomach. We also try to **get** to the parks just before they open so we can be the first ones to get inside.

Tony: Don't you sometimes feel tired after so many rides?

Neil: You do a little, but after a short rest you **feel like** starting all over **again**!

▶ Veja a tradução desse diálogo na p. 296.

FOCUS ON VOCABULARY, PHRASES AND EXPRESSIONS 14

Long time no see = I haven't seen you for a long time (há quanto tempo a gente não se vê)
Amusement park = a park with many rides and other attractions (parque de diversão)
Gonna = going to (vai; vão)
Beg/ begged/ begged = implore (implorar; suplicar)
Huge = enormous (enorme)
Exciting = stimulating (emocionante)
Hearty = large; substantial (grande; substancial)
Ride = mechanical device ridden for amusement (brinquedo em parque de diversões)
'd better = had better (seria melhor); veja *Applied grammar 19* na p. 170
Avoid/ avoided/ avoided = try to prevent something from happening (evitar)
Get: veja Usos do verbo *get* na p. 275
Feel like = desire or want to do something (sentir vontade de, ter vontade de, "estar a fim de")

ılılı 55 DIALOGUE 14 - COMPREHENSION QUESTIONS

1. Where did Neil go on vacation? Did he enjoy himself there?
2. Has Tony ever been to any of the amusement parks at the Disney resorts?
3. What does Neil usually do when he goes there?
4. Doesn't Neil sometimes feel tired after so many rides?

APPLIED GRAMMAR 14
adverbs of frequency + how long does it take?

Os principais advérbios de frequência são: **sometimes** (às vezes), **always** (sempre), **never** (nunca), **usually** (geralmente) e **often** (frequentemente). Veja abaixo alguns exemplos de uso:

I sometimes go to the park with my son on Sundays.
(Às vezes vou ao parque com o meu filho nos domingos.)
Do you always get up early?
(Você sempre levanta cedo?)
Tony never goes to bed before midnight.
(O Tony nunca vai se deitar antes da meia-noite.)
What do you usually do on weekends?
(O que você normalmente faz nos finais de semana?)
Harry and Liz often go to the club to play tennis on Saturdays.
(O Harry e a Liz frequentemente vão ao clube jogar tênis aos sábados.)

Veja agora alguns exemplos dos advérbios de frequência com o verbo *to be*. Observe a posição deles após o verbo *to be*:

Sally is always happy.
(A Sally está sempre feliz.)
I'm usually tired at the end of the week.
(Eu geralmente estou cansado no final da semana.)
Brian is never late for work.
(O Brian nunca está atrasado para o trabalho.)
Are you sometimes late for appointments?
(Você às vezes está atrasado para compromissos?)

Empregamos as construções "How long does it take..." e "It takes..." para perguntar e dizer quanto tempo alguma ação leva para ser feita. Veja abaixo alguns exemplos:

How long does it take you to go to work in the morning?
(Quanto tempo leva para você ir ao trabalho de manhã?)
It takes me about half an hour to go to work if the traffic is light.
(Eu levo aproximadamente meia hora para ir ao trabalho se o trânsito estiver bom.)
How long does it take Bob to shave and shower in the morning?
(Quanto tempo o Bob leva para fazer a barba e tomar banho de manhã?)

It takes him about twenty minutes.
(Ele leva uns vinte minutos.)

No tempo passado empregamos as construções "How long did it take..." e "It took...". Veja os exemplos:

How long did it take you to go from Miami to Orlando by car?
(Quanto tempo você levou para ir de Miami até Orlando de carro?)
It took me about four hours.
(Eu levei aproximadamente quatro horas.)

USUAL VOCABULARY 14

AT THE AIRPORT

departure (partida)
arrival (chegada)
bag/ suitcase (mala)
luggage/ baggage (bagagem)
scale (balança)
carry-on luggage/ hand luggage (bagagem de mão)
visa (visto)
fly/ flew/ flown (voar)
flight (voo)
time zone (fuso horário)
customs (alfândega)
locker (armário; guarda-volumes)
window seat (assento da janela)
aisle seat (assento do corredor)
seatbelt (cinto de segurança)
boarding-pass (cartão de embarque)
board/ boarded/ boarded (embarcar)
gate (portão)
take off/ took off/ taken off (decolar)

take-off (decolagem)
land/ landed/ landed (aterrissar)
landing (aterrissagem)
delay (atraso)
on schedule (no horário previsto)
flight attendant (comissário/a de bordo)
crew (tripulação)
stopover (escala)
jet lag (sensação de desconforto após longas viagens de avião)

Ex.: **Brazilian citizens need a visa to travel to the U.S.** (Cidadãos brasileiros precisam de visto para viajar para os Estados Unidos.)
Has flight 5171 landed yet?
(O voo 5171 já aterrissou?)
Do you know if there are lockers at this airport?
(Você sabe se há guarda-volumes neste aeroporto?)
Can you put your bag on the scale please?
(O senhor pode colocar a mala na balança, por favor?)
Can I take this one as carry-on luggage?
(Posso levar esta aqui como bagagem de mão?)
Will there be any delay? (Vai haver algum atraso?)
You will board at gate 12. (Você vai embarcar no portão 12.)
Fasten your seatbelts please. (Apertem os cintos, por favor.)
Crew prepare for take-off. (Tripulação, preparar para decolagem.)

PRACTICE SET 14

56 I. Listen to the questions and circle the right answer.

1. a) About twice a week.
   b) About five years.
   c) About half an hour.

2. a) Sure, no problem.
   b) We have a big bag here.
   c) It will take off in a few minutes.

3. a) Richard went from New York to Boston by car.
   b) It took him about four hours.
   c) He drove from New York to Boston.

4. a) No, the plane will take off on schedule.
   b) Yes, it was.
   c) No, it didn't.

5. a) Yes, she does.
   b) Yes, you do.
   c) Yes, you did.

6. a) Yes, they did.
   b) No, they didn't.
   c) Sorry, I don't know. Why don't you ask that man over there?

7. a) A window seat.
   b) Yes, I do.
   c) No, I don't.

8. a) Yes, he does.
   b) No, only on weekdays.
   c) Yes, I did.

9. a) She does, about four times a week.
   b) Yes, she will.
   c) No, she wouldn't.

10. a) Yes, I shave every day.
    b) No, I don't shave every day.
    c) About ten minutes.

ı|ı||ı 57 II. Dictation: listen to the sentences and write them.

1. _____

2. _____

3. _____

4. _____

5. _____

III. Circle the right answer.

1. Can you put your bags on the scale please?
   a) Sure!
   b) Sure, I'm fine!
   c) Yes, I do.

2. How long did it take you to do the homework?
   a) Yes, I did the homework.
   b) About an hour.
   c) About twice a week.

3. What time is your flight?
   a) Once a month.
   b) Yes, I do, I love to fly.
   c) 11 p.m.

4. Does Helen always work on Saturdays?
   a) No, only sometimes.
   b) Yes, she did.
   c) No, she won't.

5. You're not late for school, are you?
   a) Yes, I do.
   b) Yes, I am.
   c) Yes, I will.

IV. Write questions/ phrases for the following answers.

1. _____?
   It takes me about half an hour to drive to work.

2. _____?
   Yes, Karen always gets up early.

3. _____?
   Sophie visits her mother about twice a week.

4. _____?
   They went to a party last night.

5. _____?
   It took me about five minutes to write that e-mail.

V. Fill in the blanks with an appropriate word/ expression from the box.

| window seat   board   flight attendant |
| take off   aisle seat   delays |

1. What time is the plane going to _____?
2. "You will _____ at gate 41", the check-in agent told us.
3. We got to our final destination as scheduled. There were
   no _____ .
4. Caroline is a _____ in an American airline company.
5. Would you like a _____
   or an _____ ?", the check-in agent asked me.

So, you're into winter sports, right?

Oh, yeah!

LESSON 15

🎵 58 **DIALOGUE 15**
Watch out for slips, trips and falls!

Terry: So, what are you doing tonight?
Phil: I plan to go skating at the local park. They have a real nice **rink** there, very **smooth.**
Terry: Cool! I've never **been into** skating myself, but I have some friends who love it. Watch out for **slips, trips** and **falls!**
Phil: Oh don't worry, I'm always extra careful when I have my skates on. By the way, I'm teaching my twelve-year-old nephew how to skate. It's **amazing** how kids **pick** things **up** so quickly. He's just been to the rink twice and he's already **getting the hang of** it.
Terry: I know, kids are fast learners my friend! So, you**'re into** winter sports, right?
Phil: Oh, yeah! Besides skating I love to go skiing and snowboarding.
Terry: Skiing and snowboarding? Wow, I think I'd be afraid to do that. I guess it must be really difficult to keep your balance.
Phil: Well, it takes a lot of practising and you do have to **overcome** your **fear,** but once you learn how to do it it's a lot of **fun.**
Terry: I see, I prefer to have both my feet on the ground, if you know what I mean. Anyway I hope you enjoy yourself tonight at the rink.
Phil: I will, thanks! How about you? Are you doing anything tonight?
Terry: Yeah, I'm meeting some friends at a pub. I love to **hang out with** friends and **shoot the breeze** over beer.
Phil: Sounds good! **Have fun!**

▶ Veja a tradução desse diálogo na p. 297.

FOCUS ON VOCABULARY, PHRASES AND EXPRESSIONS 15

Rink = enclosed place for skating (rinque de patinação)
Smooth = flat; plane (liso, macio)
Cool = excellent; very good (ótimo; "legal")
Be into = be interested in; like (estar interessado em; gostar de)
Slips, trips and falls = the action of sliding, stumbling and falling (escorregões, tropeços e quedas)
Amazing = surprising and impressive (incrível)
Pick up = learn through observation and practice (aprender; "pegar")
Get the hang of = learn how to do something (aprender a fazer algo; "pegar o jeito")
Overcome/ overcame/ overcome = prevail over; defeat (superar)
Fear = the feeling that you have when you are frightened (medo)
Fun = enjoyable; amusing (divertido)
Hang out with = spend time with someone (passar tempo com alguém)
Shoot the breeze = chat; talk about things of little importance ("bater papo"; "jogar conversa fora")
Have fun = have a good time; enjoy yourself (divirta-se)

ı|ı|ı 59 **DIALOGUE 15 – COMPREHENSION QUESTIONS**

1. What's Phil doing tonight?
2. Does Terry like skating?
3. What does Terry advise Phil to do?
4. Does Phil think kids are fast learners?
5. What does Phil enjoy doing besides skating?
6. What's Terry doing tonight?

APPLIED GRAMMAR 15
reflexive pronouns

Veja na tabela abaixo os pronomes reflexivos:

Pronome pessoal	Pronome reflexivo
I	myself
you	yourself
he	himself
she	herself
it	itself
we	ourselves
you	yourselves
they	themselves

Agora veja alguns exemplos de uso em frases contextualizadas:

I cut myself shaving this morning.
(Eu me cortei fazendo a barba hoje de manhã.)
Don't blame yourself for what happened. It wasn't your fault!
(Não se culpe pelo o que aconteceu. Não foi sua culpa!)
Jeff and Bob are old enough to take care of themselves.
(O Jeff e o Bob já têm idade suficiente para cuidarem de si mesmos.)
This is no reason for Amy to be so angry. She needs to learn to control herself!
(Isto não é motivo para a Amy ficar tão brava. Ela precisa aprender a se controlar!)
Jim is always looking at himself in the mirror. He's so vain!
(O Jim está sempre se olhando no espelho. Ele é tão vaidoso!)
We don't need any help. We can solve the problem ourselves.
(Não precisamos de ajuda. Podemos resolver o problema nós mesmos.)

É também muito comum em inglês o uso de um **pronome reflexivo** precedido pela preposição **by**, com o significado de "sozinho, sem companhia, sem ajuda".

Ex.: **by myself; by yourself; by himself; by ourselves.** Veja alguns exemplos abaixo:

Did you do your homework by yourself?
(Você fez a lição de casa sozinho?)
Barry traveled to Australia by himself.
(Barry viajou à Austrália sozinho.)
Thanks, I don't need any help. I can do that by myself.
(Obrigado, não preciso de ajuda. Posso fazer isso sozinho.)

USUAL VOCABULARY 15

LEISURE AND ENTERTAINMENT

rest/ rested/ rested (descansar)
vacation (férias)
amusement park (parque de diversão)
ride (brinquedo em parque de diversão)
roller coaster (montanha russa)
go camping (acampar)
tent (barraca)
go fishing (pescar)
go hiking (fazer trilha)
bike lane (ciclovia)
waterfall (cachoeira)
go on a cruise (fazer um cruzeiro)
gamble/ gambled/ gambed (jogar em cassinos)
sunbathe/ sunbathed/ sunbathed (tomar banho de sol)
sunscreen (protetor solar)
RV Recreational Vehicle (trailer)
tan (bronzeado)
sightseeing tour (passeio turístico)
museum (museu)
gift shop (lojinha de presentes)

play (peça teatral)
go to the theater (ir ao teatro)
go to the movies (ir ao cinema)

Ex.: **How often do you go on vacation?**
(Com que frequência você sai de férias?)
Do you like to visit museums?
(Você gosta de visitar museus?)
We'd like to do some sightseeing. Can you recommend any places?
(Gostaríamos de fazer um passeio. Você pode recomendar alguns
lugares?)
You have a nice tan. Have you been sunbathing?
(Você está com um bronzeado bonito. Esteve tomando banho de sol?)
Tourists from all over the world go to Vegas to gamble.
(Turistas do mundo inteiro vão a Las Vegas para jogar nos cassinos.)

PRACTICE SET 15

🔊 60 I.   Listen to the questions and circle the right answer.

1.   a) Yes, I do that in my free time.
     b) Yes, I do.
     c) I like to read and watch movies.

2.   a) About once a year.
     b) Yes, he does.
     c) No, he isn't.

3.   a) Yes, she does.
     b) Yes, she did.
     c) No, she usually makes a cake on Saturday.

4.   a) Me? Oh, no, I prefer to stay at hotels.
     b) Yes, I did.
     c) No, I wouldn't.

5. a) Yes, I do.
    b) No, he doesn't really.
    c) Yes, he is.

6. a) No, thanks. I can do that by myself.
    b) Yes, I always help them.
    c) No, they didn't help me.

7. a) No, he isn't.
    b) No, he doesn't.
    c) Yes, he will.

8. a) No, she didn't.
    b) I think she was busy.
    c) Yes, she will.

9. a) About an hour.
    b) No, I have dinner at my mother's house on weekends.
    c) Yes, I love vegetables.

10. a) Yes, it was.
    b) Five bucks.
    c) Sorry, I only have ten dollars now.

ıllıl 61 II. Dictation: listen to the sentences and write them.

1. _____

2. _____

3. _____

4. _____

5. _____

III. Circle the right answer.

1. Does your wife like to go to museums?
   a) Yes, she did.
   b) Yes, she will.
   c) Yes, she loves to go to museums.

2. How many countries did you visit in Europe?
   a) Five times a month.
   b) Seven countries.
   c) Twice a year.

3. Did Mary write that letter by herself?
   a) No, she doesn't.
   b) No, Mike helped her write it.
   c) Yes, she likes to read letters.

4. Who's that woman over there?
   a) Yes, she likes to meet new people.
   b) No, I don't have any sisters.
   c) I have no idea.

5. What's the matter with Sam?
   a) I think he has a cold.
   b) He's at home now.
   c) No, he went to school.

IV. Write questions/ phrases for the following answers.

1. _____?
   Yes, Tony washed his car by himself.

2. _____?
   That's my friend Amy.

3. _____

   I prefer to watch action movies and sometimes love stories.

4. _____?

   No, Tim doesn't have any brothers. He's an only child.

5. _____?

   No, thanks. I think I can do it by myself.

V. Fill in the blanks with an appropriate word/expression from the box.

sunscreen	tan	vacation	rest	go camping

1. Magda is very tired. She wants to go home and _____ .
2. What do you like to do on _____ ?
3. You have a nice _____ . Did you go to the beach last weekend?
4. It's important to always wear _____ to protect your skin when you go to the beach.
5. Rita and Joe don't like to _____ . They prefer to stay at hotels when they travel.

62 **DIALOGUE 16**
We can try to cheer him up!

Ray: Poor Dave, he's been feeling **miserable** since his girlfriend **dumped** him.

Don: I know just how it feels. It took me a long time to **get over** my **breakup** with Sally. I wonder if there's anything we can do for him.

Ray: Maybe there is. We can try to **cheer** him **up**. What if we invite him to go somewhere **fun** tonight?

Don: Somewhere fun? You mean a place where we can meet some **hot chicks**, like a club?

Ray: That's right! Dave needs to meet a new girl. It will do him good.

Don: Great idea! I'd love to go to a place like that myself. Can you call him later and check if he'd like to join us?

Ray: Sure, I'll do that. We can also stop by Jimmy's for a burger and some beers. I'm sure Dave would like that.

Don: Sounds good to me! Hum, I just remembered something, my car is at the **repair shop**, can we take your car tonight?

Ray: No problem. I can **pick** you **up** at your place.

Don: Great! **Keep** me **posted** after you talk to Dave. I really hope he likes the idea. As for myself I'm really **in the mood** for some fun tonight!

▶ Veja a tradução desse diálogo na p. 298.

FOCUS ON VOCABULARY, PHRASES AND EXPRESSIONS 16

Miserable = very unhappy (muito infeliz)
Dump/ dumped/ dumped = end a relationship with someone ("dar o fora em alguém")
Get over = overcome emotional situations (superar problemas emocionais)
Breakup = the end of a relationship (separação)
Cheer up = make someone happy (animar alguém)
Fun = enjoyable; amusing (divertido)
Hot = sexually attractive (atraente)
Chick = a young attractive woman (mulher jovem e atraente; "mina"; "gata")
Repair shop = a shop specializing in repairs and maintenance (oficina de conserto)
Pick up = collect someone especially by car (pegar alguém especialmente de carro)
Keep posted = keep informed (manter informado)
In the mood = disposed to do something (com disposição para; "a fim de")

◀||▶ 63 **DIALOGUE 16 – COMPREHENSION QUESTIONS**

1. Why has Dave been feeling miserable?
2. How do they plan to cheer Dave up?
3. What does Ray think Dave needs to do?
4. What does Don think of the idea of going to a club tonight?
5. What else do they plan to do?
6. Whose car are they going to take?

APPLIED GRAMMAR 16
verbos modais *can* e *could*

Assim como o verbo *to be,* os verbos modais não necessitam dos ver-

146

bos auxiliares (*do, does, did, will* e *would*). O verbo modal **can** expressa habilidade, "saber fazer algo". **Can** também é usado para expressar possibilidade ou permissão. A forma negativa de **can** é **can't** ou **cannot**. Veja alguns exemplos abaixo:

Harry can play tennis very well.
(O Harry sabe jogar tênis muito bem.)
Can you speak Spanish?
(Você sabe falar espanhol?)
I can pick you up at the airport tomorrow.
(Posso te pegar no aeroporto amanhã.)
Can I borrow your pen for a minute?
(Posso pegar sua caneta emprestada por um minuto?)
Can you see Josh and Mike from here?
(Você consegue ver o Josh e o Mike daqui?)
We cannot go with you to the movies. We are busy.
(Não podemos ir com vocês ao cinema. Estamos ocupados.)
I need to make a call. Can I use your cell phone?
(Preciso fazer uma ligação. Posso usar seu celular?)
I can't understand what you're saying. Can you speak slowly please?
(Não consigo entender o que você está dizendo. Você pode falar devagar, por favor?)
What can I do for you?
(Como posso ajudá-lo?)
Where can I find a drugstore near here?
(Onde posso encontrar uma farmácia aqui perto?)
How can I help you?
(Como posso ajudá-lo?)
Can't you understand what he's saying?
(Você não consegue entender o que ele está dizendo?)

Could é o passado e condicional de **can**. Também é empregado para expressar habilidade, possibilidade ou permissão no tempo passado ou condicional. A forma negativa de **could** é **couldn't**. Veja os exemplos abaixo:

Could you do me a favor?
(Você poderia me fazer um favor?)
Jeff could ride a bike when he was just four years old.
(O Jeff sabia andar de bicicleta quando tinha apenas quatro anos de idade.)
I couldn't understand what she said. Could you?
(Não consegui entender o que ela disse. Você conseguiu?)

USUAL VOCABULARY 16

STORES AND SERVICES

mall/ shopping center (shopping)
department store (loja de departamentos)
gift shop (loja de presentes)
post office (correios)
laundromat (lavanderia autosserviço)
drugstore (farmácia)
newsstand (banca de jornal)
library (biblioteca)
bookstore (livraria)
ATM: Automated Teller Machine (caixa eletrônico)
toy store (loja de brinquedos)
deli/ delicatessen (mercadinho)
locksmith (chaveiro)
police station (delegacia de polícia)
garage (oficina)

Ex.: **Is there a mall near here?**
(Tem um shopping aqui perto?)
What time do the banks open?
(Que horas os bancos abrem?)
Do you close for lunch?
(Vocês fecham para o almoço?)

Where can I find a drugstore near here?
(Onde posso encontrar uma farmácia aqui perto?

PRACTICE SET 16

64 I. Listen to the questions and circle the right answer.

1. a) No, she doesn't.
   b) No, she can't.
   c) Yes, she is.

2. a) She has to study for a test.
   b) She loves parties.
   c) She's feeling all right.

3. a) Sure, it's very easy.
   b) Yes, you can.
   c) Yes, I do.

4. a) Yes, I can.
   b) No, I can't.
   c) Turn right on the next street and walk one block.

5. a) There's one on the next block.
   b) Yes, I can.
   c) No, he can't.

6. a) No, I don't.
   b) No, not really.
   c) Yes, I am.

7. a) At the gift shop.
   b) Yes, I can.
   c) At the laundromat.

8. a) Yes, you can.
   b) No, I don't.
   c) Sure!

9. a) Yeah, I think so.
   b) Yes, I do.
   c) No, you can't.

10. a) Yes, there's one on main street.
    b) No, she isn't.
    c) Yes, I can.

🔊 65 II. Dictation: listen to the sentences and write them.

1. _____

2. _____

3. _____

4. _____

5. _____

III. Circle the right answer.

1. Can you do me a favor?
   a) Yes, I do.
   b) Sure, what do you need?
   c) Yes, I am.

2. Could you understand what David said?
a) Yes, I think so.
b) Yes, I can.
c) No, I didn't.

3. Is there a mall near here?
a) Yes, I go to the mall very often.
b) No, the nearest mall is about twenty miles from here.
c) No, I didn't go to the mall yesterday.

4. Can I use your cell phone for a minute?
a) Sure!
b) Yes, I use my cell phone all the time.
c) Yes, you are.

5. When can we go there?
a) Yes, we can.
b) Maybe next Friday.
c) I go there very often.

IV. Write questions/ phrases for the following answers.

1. _____?
Yes, there's a bank on the next block.

2. _____?
Yes, my brother can speak Italian fluently.

3. _____?
No, she can't go with us to the movies.

4. _____?
You can buy souvenirs at the gift shop.

5. _____?

I go swimming twice a week.

V. Circle the word or expression that is different from the group.

1. bookstore – laundromat – newsstand – living-room – drugstore – gift shop
2. Italian – Spanish – Japanese – French – German – England
3. vacuum cleaner – trunk – stove – washing-machine – oven – microwave
4. bigger – happiest – taller – prettier – cheaper – smaller
5. cloudy – windy – rainy – snowy – delay – sunny

Speech bubbles: "Hey Ingrid! What's up?" "Nothing much."

66 **DIALOGUE 17**
What are friends for?

Ralph: Hey Ingrid! **What's up**?
Ingrid: Nothing much. I just decided to **stop by** to see you **guys**.
Ralph: Great idea. Thanks! How's your friend Dana? Is she still looking for a job?
Ingrid: Yeah, I guess so.
Ralph: I'll tell you what, the company I work for is **growing** very fast. We might have some **openings** soon. I guess I could **put in a word for** her with my boss.
Ingrid: Could you? That would be great!
Ralph: Does she have good computer skills?
Ingrid: She does. She loves using computers. She's actually taking an advanced course on some new software now that she's got some free time.
Ralph: Good, she could **definitely** get a better **position** in the company with good computer skills.
Ingrid: Great, I can't wait to tell her. I'm sure she's **gonna** be real **excited!**
Ralph: Right! I was thinking, maybe you could tell her to e-mail her résumé to me and then I can **forward** it to my boss and talk to him about her.
Ingrid: That's **super!** I'll talk to her this afternoon. Thanks a lot Ralph!
Ralph: It's okay, Ingrid. What are friends for?

▶ Veja a tradução desse diálogo na p. 298.

FOCUS ON VOCABULARY, PHRASES AND EXPRESSIONS 17

What's up? = what's new?; what's happening? (quais são as novidades?; "e aí?")

Nothing much = not much; nothing of importance (nada de importante)

Stop by = visit someone for a short time (fazer uma visita breve a alguém)

Guy = a man ("cara")

Grow/ grew/ grown = develop; increase (crescer)

Opening = position available (emprego, vaga disponível)

Put in a word for = speak favorably of; recommend (recomendar)

Definitely = absolutely (sem dúvida, com certeza)

Position = job (cargo)

Gonna = going to (vai; vão)

Excited = very happy and enthusiastic (animado/a; entusiasmado/a)

Forward/ forwarded/ forwarded = send something received to somebody else (encaminhar)

Super = very good; very nice (ótimo)

🎧 67 DIALOGUE 17 – COMPREHENSION QUESTIONS

1. Does Dana have a job?
2. What does Ralph offer to do?
3. Does Dana have good computer skills?
4. What does Ralph think Dana could do?
5. How does Ingrid feel about this situation?

APPLIED GRAMMAR 17
verbos modais *must* e *should*

O verbo modal **must** expressa obrigação, algo que deve ser feito. É usado também quando temos certeza sobre algo ou fazemos uma conclusão lógica. A forma negativa de **must, mustn't**, indica que algo é proibido e não deve ser feito. Veja os exemplos abaixo:

We must be at the airport at 6 a.m. tomorrow.
(Devemos estar no aeroporto às seis horas amanhã.)
That girl must be Jane's daughter. She looks just like her!
(Aquela garota dever ser filha da Jane. A menina é a cara dela!)
You mustsn't smoke here! Haven't you seen the no smoking sign?
(Você não deve fumar aqui! Você não viu o aviso de que é proibido fumar?)
You must finish that report tomorrow.
(Você deve terminar aquele relatório amanhã.)

O verbo modal **should** é usado para expressar conselhos e recomendações, algo que deveria ser feito. A forma negativa de **should** é **shouldn't**. Veja os exemplos abaixo:

You should put on a jacket. It's really cold out there.
(Você devia colocar uma jaqueta. Está muito frio lá fora.)
You shouldn't talk to her like that. It's not polite!
(Você não deveria falar com ela desta forma. Não é educado!)
I don't know what we should do about this situation. Do you have any ideas?
(Não sei o que deveríamos fazer a respeito desta situação. Você tem quaisquer ideias?)
Sam should explain to us what happened.
(O Sam devia explicar para nós o que aconteceu.)

USUAL VOCABULARY 17

GOING SHOPPING

sale/ clearance (liquidação)
aisle (corredor em supermercados, lojas etc.)
try on (experimentar, provar roupas ou calçados)

size (tamanho)
fit/ fit/ fit (servir)
bar code (código de barras)
scanner (scanner)
shelf (prateleira)
refund (reembolso)
fitting-room (provador)
mirror (espelho)
tight (apertado/a)
loose (folgado/a)
small (pequeno)
medium (médio)
large (grande)
extra large (extra grande)

Ex.: **They have a great sale today. Everything is at least 20% off.**
(Eles estão com uma liquidação ótima hoje. Tudo está com pelo menos 20% de desconto.)
Can I try on a larger size?
(Posso experimentar um tamanho maior?)
Where's the fitting-room please?
(Onde fica o provador, por favor?)
Did the shirt fit you?
(A camisa serviu?)
It's a little tight. Do you have a larger size?
(Está um pouco apertada. Você tem um tamanho maior?)
What size do you wear?
(Que tamanho você usa?)
I'm usually a medium.
(Geralmente uso tamanho médio)
How much is it?
(Quanto custa?)
It's $26.
(Custa vinte e seis dólares.)

PRACTICE SET 17

I. Listen to the questions and circle the right answer.

1. a) It's a big fitting-room.
    b) It's back there.
    c) Yes, we do.

2. a) Yes, you should.
    b) No, you shouldn't.
    c) Jeans and a t-shirt are okay.

3. a) Yes, I think so.
    b) No, you don't.
    c) Yes, you are.

4. a) Yes, you must be there.
    b) No, you mustn't.
    c) At 8 a.m.

5. a) It's a little tight.
    b) No, it's loose.
    c) I'm usually a small.

6. a) Sure!
    b) Yes, you do.
    c) I talk to him every day.

7. a) Yes, he did.
    b) He went to the mall with some friends.
    c) He was watching TV.

8. a) Yes, you can.
    b) We went to the mall last week.
    c) Sorry, I can't help. I'm not from around here.

9. a) I have no idea. Why don't you ask Brian?
   b) Yes, you should do that.
   c) No, you shouldn't.

10. a) Sure!
    b) Yes, it's small.
    c) No, it's bigger.

〽 69 II. Dictation: listen to the sentences and write them.

1. _____

2. _____

3. _____

4. _____

5. _____

III. Circle the right answer.

1. Did the shirt fit you?
   a) Yes, he does.
   b) No, I didn't.
   c) Not really, I think I need a larger size.

2. Who should we invite to the party?
   a) Yes, we invited them to the party.
   b) All our friends at school, of course!
   c) No, we shouldn't.

3. What size do you wear?
   a) A medium, please.
   b) Yes, I do.
   c) Jeans and a t-shirt.

4. Do you have a smaller size?
   a) Yes, I like that shirt.
   b) Yes, we do. I'll get it for you.
   c) No, we didn't.

5. How often do you buy clothes?
   a) Not very often.
   b) He likes to buy shoes.
   c) Yes, I do.

IV. Write questions/ phrases for the following answers.

1. _____?
I'm usually a medium.

2. _____?
It's $ 35.

3. _____?
Yes, I can swim very well.

4. _____?
No, Mary shouldn't invite Fred to the party.

5. _____?
No, I don't go to the mall very often.

V. Fill in the blanks with an appropriate word/ expression from the box.

fitting-room	size	try on	sale	how much

1. _____ is it? It's 37 dollars.
2. Can I _____ a larger size? This shirt is a little tight.
3. We have a _____ on men's shoes. They are 25% off.
4. Would you like to try it on? We have a _____ at the back.
5. "What _____ do you wear?", the store clerk asked Mike.

🎙 70 **DIALOGUE 18**
Check out that guy over there!

Tony: You must be **starving**, aren't you?
Neil: I am.
Tony: Do you **wanna** go **grab a bite to eat** at Rita's café?
Neil: Sure, let's go!

At the café

Sharon: Hello, what can I **get** you guys?
Tony: Umm, let me see, I guess I'll have the **tuna** sandwich and an orange juice.
Sharon: Good, how about you sir?
Neil: Uh, what does the DeLuxe burger come with?
Sharon: It comes with **mayo**, **lettuce** and tomatoes and fries on the side.
Neil: Great! I'll have one of those.

Sharon: Anything to drink?

Neil: Yeah, a regular coke please.

Sharon: Ok, I'll be right back with your drinks.

Tony: Hey Neil, **check out** that guy over there.

Neil: You mean the guy in the green shirt? What about him?

Tony: Doesn't he **remind** you of anyone?

Neil: Oh yeah, he **looks** a lot **like** Rick, doesn't he?

Tony: That guy **is the spitting image** of Rick! He must be Rick's brother or something.

Neil: Who knows? Maybe he is. Do you wanna ask him?

Tony: I guess so, I'll let him finish his sandwich first though.

Neil: All right!

▶ Veja a tradução desse diálogo na p. 299.

FOCUS ON VOCABULARY, PHRASES AND EXPRESSIONS 18

Starving = very hungry ("morrendo de fome")

Wanna = want to (querer)

Grab a bite to eat = eat some food or a small meal (comer algo)

Get: veja Usos do verbo *get*, p. 275

Tuna = the flesh of a large fish eaten as food (atum)

Mayo = mayonnaise (maionese)

Lettuce = a vegetable with large thin green leaves (alface)

Check out = take a look at (olhar para alguém ou algo)

Remind/ reminded/ reminded = cause to remember (lembrar alguém)

Look like = resemble (parecer-se com)

Be the spitting image = look exactly like someone (parecer-se exatamente com; "ser a cara de")

ılıl· 71 DIALOGUE 18 – COMPREHENSION QUESTIONS

1. What do Tony and Neil decide to do?
2. What does Tony order at the café?
3. What does the DeLuxe burger come with?
4. Who does Tony see at the café?

APPLIED GRAMMAR 18
verbos modais *may* e *might*

O verbo modal **may** é usado para pedir permissão e expressar possibilidade, algo que pode acontecer. A forma negativa de **may** é **may not**. Veja os exemplos abaixo:

May I talk to you for a minute?
(Posso falar com você por um minuto?)
I may go to the mall to watch a movie tonight.
(Talvez eu vá ao shopping assistir a um filme hoje à noite.)
We may not have time to visit Gary tomorrow.
(Talvez não tenhamos tempo de visitar Gary amanhã.)
May I smoke here?
(Posso fumar aqui?)
According to the weather forecast it may rain later today.
(De acordo com a previsão do tempo pode chover mais tarde.)

O verbo modal **might** é empregado para expressar possibilidade, assim como **may**. A forma negativa de **might** é **might not**. Veja os exemplos abaixo:

We might go to the beach this weekend.
(Nós talvez iremos à praia este final de semana.)
It might rain tomorrow.
(Talvez chova amanhã.)
They might not have time to visit Harry.
(Talvez eles não tenham tempo de visitar Harry.)
I might go to the gym tonight.
(Talvez eu vá à academia hoje à noite.)

USUAL VOCABULARY 18

SUPERMARKET AND DRUGSTORE ITEMS

toothpaste (pasta de dente)
toothbrush (escova de dente)
dental floss (fio dental)
shaving cream/ foam (creme de barbear)
razor blade (lâmina de barbear)
soap (sabão)
deodorant (desodorante)
cotton (algodão)
diaper (fralda)
toilet paper (papel higiênico)
napkin (guardanapo)
suntan lotion (bronzeador)
sunscreen (protetor solar)
nail clipper (cortador de unhas)
battery (pilha, bateria)
Q-tip/ cotton bud (cotonete)
first-aid kit (estojo de primeiros socorros)
tissue (lenço de papel)
condom (preservativo)
comb (pente)
scissors (tesoura)
nail polish (esmalte)
band aid (curativo adesivo)
lipstick (batom)
medicine (remédio)
painkiller (analgésico)

Ex.: **Where can I find batteries?**
(Onde encontro pilhas/ baterias?)
That's in aisle five.
(Fica no corredor cinco.)
Do you sell souvenirs here?
(Vocês vendem suvenires aqui?)

Excuse me, where's the fruit section please?
(Desculpe-me, onde fica a seção de frutas, por favor?
You can find dental floss and toothpaste in aisle four.
(Você encontra fio dental e pasta de dente no corredor quatro.)

PRACTICE SET 18

🔊 72 I. Listen to the questions and circle the right answer.

1. a) No, she may not.
    b) Sure!
    c) Yes, you do.

2. a) Yes, I brush my teeth every day.
    b) Yes, you can.
    c) That's in aisle four.

3. a) Yes, you may.
    b) Yes, you do.
    c) No, you didn't.

4. a) Yes, I am.
    b) Yes, we do, you can find sunscreen in aisle six.
    c) No, we won't.

5. a) Sure!
    b) Yes, he leaves early every day.
    c) No, I don't.

6. a) It's going to be very cold and it may snow.
    b) Yes, it is.
    c) I prefer the summer.

7. a) Yes, you do.
    b) No, you may not.
    c) No, you aren't.

8. a) Yes, you can.
   b) We need a larger size.
   c) I'm sorry, we don't sell diapers here.

9. a) I may go to the beach.
   b) Yes, I do.
   c) It's going to be sunny.

10. a) Yes, you may.
    b) Yes, you do.
    c) No, I don't.

〜 73 II. Dictation: listen to the sentences and write them.

1. _____

2. _____

3. _____

4. _____

5. _____

III. Circle the right answer.

1. May I leave earlier today?
   a) Yes, you do.
   b) Yes, you may.
   c) Yes, I will.

2. Where can I find shaving cream?
   a) No, he doesn't shave every day.
   b) Yes, you can.

c) That's in aisle two.

3. What's the weather forecast for today?
   a) It's going to be sunny but it may rain in the afternoon.
   b) Yes, I do. I prefer hot weather.
   c) Yes, it is.

4. Do you sell diapers here?
   a) Yes, I did.
   b) Sorry, I don't work here.
   c) No, it wasn't.

5. May I go now?
   a) No, I need to talk to you for a minute.
   b) Yes, I may.
   c) No, he may not.

IV. Write questions/ phrases for the following answers.

1. _____?
   No, you may not smoke here.

2. _____?
   It's going to be cold and it may rain later.

3. _____?
   You can find sunscreen in aisle five.

4. _____?
   No, I'm sorry, we don't sell lipstick here.

5. _____?
   Yes, you may.

V. Circle the word or expression that is different from the group.

1. diaper – lipstick – party – sunscreen – dental floss – toothbrush
2. flight attendant – crew – jet lag – pilot – aisle seat – nail clipper
3. herself – yourself – ourselves – her – myself – themselves
4. what – could – where – when – why – who
5. laundromat – cucumber – bookstore – newsstand – library – drugstore

> **LESSON 19**

🔊 74 **DIALOGUE 19**
It's freezing out there!

Gary: Are you going out like that?
Sean: I guess so. Why?
Gary: Nothing much, only I think you should **bundle up**. It's **freezing** out there!
Sean: Is it?
Gary: Yeah, I checked the **weather forecast** on my computer just now. Today should be even colder than yesterday. **Take a look** outside for yourself. You see all that **snow flurry** coming down?
Sean: Yeah, I guess you're right. Thanks for the **tip**! I'll **put on** a warmer coat and gloves. By the way, how's your history **assignment coming along**?
Gary: It's okay, we should have it finished by Thursday.
Sean: Really? My group is **behind schedule**. Actually we have **barely** started. We should have **gotten together** a few days ago but it never happened. It should take us at least one week to get it done.
Gary: I see. I'm really lucky I'm in a good group. They've all been very **helpful** contributing with ideas for the assignment.
Sean: Good for you! It does make a big difference when everyone cooperates.

▶ Veja a tradução desse diálogo na p. 300.

FOCUS ON VOCABULARY, PHRASES AND EXPRESSIONS 19

Nothing much = not much; nothing of importance (nada de importante)
Bundle up = put on warm clothes; wrap in something warm (agasalhar-se)
Freezing = very cold (muito frio; gelado)
Weather forecast = a report on weather conditions (previsão do tempo)
Take a look = look (olhar; "dar uma olhada")
Snow flurry = light snowfall (nevasca)
Tip = a piece of advice or information (dica)
Put on = put clothes on (vestir; colocar)
Assignment = work that you must do as part of a course; task (trabalho escolar; tarefa)
Come along = make progress (progredir)
Behind schedule = running late (atrasado)
Barely = hardly; scarcely (quase não; "mal")
Get together = meet (reunir-se)
Helpful = useful; providing help (útil)

ılı|ı 75 DIALOGUE 19 – COMPREHENSION QUESTIONS

1. What does Gary advise Sean to do?
2. What does Sean decide to do?
3. How's Sean's history assignment coming along?
4. Why does Gary think he's lucky?

APPLIED GRAMMAR 19
had better (seria melhor) + *would rather* (preferiria)

Usamos a estrutura **had better** (seria melhor) seguida de um verbo principal para dar conselhos. A forma contraída de **had** ('d) é frequentemente usada. Veja os exemplos abaixo:

170

You'd better tell them the truth.
(Seria melhor você dizer a verdade para eles.)
He'd better sleep earlier tonight.
(Seria melhor ele dormir mais cedo hoje à noite.)
They'd better do their homework now.
(Seria melhor eles fazerem a lição de casa agora.)
You'd better go on a diet.
(Seria melhor você fazer regime.)
She'd better not go out tonight.
(Seria melhor ela não sair hoje à noite.)
We'd better not miss the class tomorrow.
(Seria melhor não faltarmos à aula amanhã.)

Usamos a estrutura **would rather** para indicar preferência. A forma contraída de **would** ('d) é frequentemente usada. Veja os exemplos abaixo:

I'd rather stay home tonight.
(Preferiria ficar em casa hoje à noite.)
He'd rather live in a small city.
(Ele preferiria morar em uma cidade pequena.)
They'd rather go downtown by subway.
(Eles prefeririam ir à cidade de metrô.)
She'd rather watch a comedy show tonight.
(Ela preferiria assistir a uma comédia hoje à noite.)
I'd rather not eat pasta today.
(Preferiria não comer massas hoje.)
Would you rather drink tea or coffee?
(Você preferiria beber chá ou café?)

USUAL VOCABULARY 19

WORK AND CAREER

résumé (currículo)
apply for a job (candidatar-se a um emprego)
applicant (candidato)
openings (vagas, empregos disponíveis)
hire/ hired/ hired (contratar, empregar)
employ/ employed/ employed (contratar, empregar)
fire/ fired/ fired (despedir)
dismiss/ dismissed/ dismissed (despedir)
position (cargo)
employee (funcionário, empregado)
employer (empregador/a, empresa que emprega)
coworker/ colleague (colega de trabalho)
cafeteria (refeitório em empresa)
day off (dia de folga)
fringe benefits (benefícios adicionais)
perks (benefícios, "mordomias")
shift (turno de trabalho)
maternity leave (licença maternidade)
intern (estagiário)
internship (estágio profissional)
peer (par, pessoa do mesmo grupo profissional)
retire/ retired/ retired (aposentar-se)
retiree (aposentado)

Ex.: **The fringe benefits package include a company car and a cell phone.**
(O pacote de benefícios adicionais inclui um carro da empresa e um celular.)
How many employees work on the night shift?
(Quantos funcionários trabalham no turno da noite?)
The company has hired two new salesmen.
(A empresa contratou dois novos vendedores.)
Is that position still available?

(Aquele cargo ainda está disponível?)

PRACTICE SET 19

🔊 76　I.　Listen to the questions and circle the right answer.

1. a) Yes, I would.
   b) I think I'll go with them.
   c) No, I don't.

2. a) About one hundred people.
   b) Yes, it does.
   c) Yes, they work there.

3. a) No, I am not.
   b) No, I don't.
   c) Yes, I did.

4. a) I'm tired so I think I'll just stay home.
   b) Yes, I did.
   c) No, I didn't go out last night.

5. a) Yes, they did.
   b) Three new employees.
   c) Yes, they will.

6. a) Yes, I eat fish every week.
   b) He likes pasta.
   c) Fish, please.

7. a) Tuesday.
   b) I like to go jogging in the park.
   c) Yes, I am.

8. a) Yes, I did.
   b) I saw Mike yesterday.
   c) I went with Nick and Brian.
9. a) Yes, I do, we have lunch at the company cafeteria.
   b) Yes, I did. I had lasagna.
   c) Yes, we went to the mall for lunch.

10. a) No, I don't.
    b) No, it isn't.
    c) Yes, it does.

〰️ 77 II. Dictation: listen to the sentences and write them.

1. _____

2. _____

3. _____

4. _____

5. _____

III. Circle the right answer.

1. Would you rather stay home or go out tonight?
    a) Yes, I would.
    b) I think I'll stay home and watch a movie.
    c) Yes, I'd rather do that.

2. When is your day off?
    a) Usually on Friday.
    b) Yes, I go out on my day off.
    c) I usually stay home on my day off.

3. Where do you usually have lunch?
   a) I prefer salads.
   b) I like fish and vegetables.
   c) At the company cafeteria.

4. Would you rather eat meat or chicken?
   a) I'd rather not go.
   b) I'd rather eat chicken.
   c) Sure!

5. Why did Brian take a taxi to work?
   a) Because he was late.
   b) Yes, he did. He took a taxi.
   c) No, he prefers to go to work by subway.

IV. Write questions/ phrases for the following answers.

1. _____?
   They employ about two hundred people.

2. _____?
   Bob usually has lunch at the company cafeteria.

3. _____?
   I'd rather stay home tonight.

4. _____?
   Nancy goes jogging twice a week.

5. _____?
   No, I'm older than Barry.

V. Fill in the blanks with an appropriate word/expression from the box.

> **cafeteria   fringe benefits   employees   position**
> **coworkers   day off   apply for**

1. You have the qualifications required by the _____ .
   Why don't you _____ that job?
2. Rachel usually goes shopping and visit friends on her

   _____ .
3. How many _____ work in that factory?
4. Jeff usually has lunch with his _____ at the
   company _____ .
5. The _____ package includes a company car and a cell phone.

78 DIALOGUE 20

Do you have any plans for the weekend?

Fred: So Norma, do you have any plans for the weekend?

Norma: I may go to the beach, but I'm not **quite** sure yet. That will depend on what happens tonight.

Fred: What happens tonight? How do you mean?

Norma: I'm meeting some friends. We're supposed to talk about the weekend, we are planning to go to the beach together, a big group, you know.

Fred: Oh, yeah. Big groups are always a lot more **fun**. May I ask you a question?

Norma: Jesus Fred, you know there's no need for you to be so formal, just **shoot**!

Fred: Ok, are you still **dating** Brian?

Norma: Kind of.

Fred: Kind of?

Norma: Yeah, the thing is we **broke up** some time ago and then we **made up**, but ever since we got back together it's not been the same, you know, so I don't really know what's going to happen.

Fred: I see, and would Brian be going to the beach with you?

Norma: He may and he may not. He's usually busy with his band's **rehearsal** on Saturdays, so I'm still not sure what he plans to do.

Fred: Oh! I see.

▶ Veja a tradução desse diálogo na p. 300.

FOCUS ON VOCABULARY, PHRASES AND EXPRESSIONS 20

Fun = enjoyable; amusing (divertido)
Shoot = go ahead and start talking ("desembucha")
Date/dated/dated = spend time with someone you have a romantic relationship with (namorar)
Kind of = somewhat (mais ou menos)
Break up = end a relationship (terminar um relacionamento; romper)
Make up = reconcile after an argument (fazer as pazes)
Rehearsal = practice session (ensaio)

ılı|ı 79 ## DIALOGUE 20 – COMPREHENSION QUESTIONS

1. Is Norma sure where she's going for the weekend? Why not?
2. What's Fred's opinion of traveling with a big group?
3. Is Norma going steady with Brian?
4. Why is Brian usually busy on Saturdays?

APPLIED GRAMMAR 20
verbos seguidos de gerúndio

De uma forma geral, quando temos dois verbos na mesma sentença, eles aparecem separados pela partícula *to*. Veja o exemplo abaixo:

We need to go there tomorrow. (Precisamos ir lá amanhã.)

Observe na frase acima os verbos *need*, *go* e a partícula *to* entre eles. Veja mais alguns exemplos:

Fred wants to buy a new cell phone.
(Fred quer comprar um novo celular.)
I have to travel on business next week.
(Preciso viajar a negócios na próxima semana.)

178

Alguns verbos, no entanto, devem ser seguidos pela forma gerúndio *ing*. É o caso dos verbos *finish* (terminar), *enjoy* (gostar, apreciar), *mind* (importar-se) e *avoid* (evitar), entre outros. Veja os exemplos abaixo:

They have to finish doing their homework.
(Eles têm que terminar de fazer a lição de casa.)
Do you enjoy visiting museums?
(Você gosta de visitar museus?)
I don't mind getting up early.
(Não me importo de levantar cedo.)
Jeff avoids eating meat every day.
(Jeff evita comer carne todos os dias.)

Há também alguns verbos que podem ser seguidos pelo infinitivo (*to do, to go* etc.) ou pelo gerúndio *ing*. É o caso de *like* (gostar de), *begin* (começar) e *start* (começar, iniciar). Veja os exemplos abaixo:

I like to play soccer on Saturdays. = **I like playing soccer on Saturdays.**
(Gosto de jogar futebol aos sábados)
Nick began to study Spanish in July. = **Nick began studying Spanish in July.**
(Nick começou a estudar espanhol em julho.)
Cynthia starts to work at 9 a.m. = **Cynthia starts working at 9 a.m.**
(Cynthia começa a trabalhar às 9h.)

Obs.: O verbo **stop** (parar) pode ser seguido de infinitivo ou gerúndio, mas há mudança de significado. Compare os exemplos abaixo:

Carol stopped to talk to me. X **Carol stopped talking to me.**
Carol parou para falar comigo. X Carol parou de falar comigo.

USUAL VOCABULARY 20

MAKING PHONE CALLS

call/ called/ called (ligar, telefonar)
dial/ dialed/ dialed (discar, ligar)
operator (telefonista)
answer/ get the phone (atender o telefone)
answering machine (secretária eletrônica)
call back (ligar de volta, retornar a ligação)
hang up (colocar o telefone no gancho; desligar ao final de uma conversa)
extension number (ramal)
cell phone (telefone celular)
long distance call (interurbano)
speakerphone (viva-voz)
put through/ transfer (transferir a ligação)
hold on/ hang on (esperar, aguardar)
leave a message (deixar um recado)
the line is busy (a linha está ocupada)
area code (código de área)

Ex.: **I'm sorry, I'm busy right now. Can I call you back later?**
(Desculpe, estou ocupado no momento. Posso retornar a ligação mais tarde?)
Hold on a second please, I'll put you through to his department.
(Espere um segundo por favor, vou transferir você para o departamento dele.)
I left a message on your answering machine this morning.
(Deixei um recado na sua secretária eletrônica hoje de manhã.)
Please don't hang up.
(Por favor não desligue.)
Mr. Smith is not in at the moment. Would you like to leave a message?
(O sr. Smith não está no momento. O senhor gostaria de deixar um recado?)

PRACTICE SET 20

I. Listen to the questions and circle the right answer.

1. a) Yes, it is.
    b) No, thanks. I'll call back later.
    c) Yes, I do.

2. a) Yes, she talks to me every day.
    b) Yes, she loves talking to everyone.
    c) I don't know. I have no idea.

3. a) No, I don't.
    b) I get up early every day.
    c) I don't like to get up late on weekends.

4. a) Yes, he likes pasta.
    b) Yes, he does.
    c) No, he doesn't like cucumber.

5. a) She likes to go shopping and visit friends.
    b) She doesn't have any brothers or sisters.
    c) She gets up early on weekends.

6. a) I did. I asked her to call me.
    b) Yes, we talk on the phone about once a week.
    c) No, I don't have an answering machine.

7. a) Yes, he can.
    b) Yes, I do.
    c) Sure, hold on a second please.

8. a) No, not really.
    b) Yes, he does.
    c) No, I'm not.

9. a) Yes, she cleans the house twice a week.
   b) No, not yet.
   c) I usually clean the house on Saturday.

10. a) Yes, I did.
    b) No, it's okay.
    c) No, he doesn't smoke.

🔊 81 II. Dictation: listen to the sentences and write them.

1. _____

2. _____

3. _____

4. _____

5. _____

III. Circle the right answer.

1. Can you put me through to the sales department please?
   a) Yes, he works in the sales department.
   b) Sure, hold on a second please.
   c) Yes, I do.

2. Does Marylin enjoy going to parties?
   a) Yes, he went to a party with friends last night.
   b) Yes, she does. She loves parties!
   c) Yes, she will.

3. Does Nick mind getting up early every day?
   a) Yes, he gets up early every day.

b) No, he doesn't go there very often.
c) No, he doesn't.

4. Can I call you back later?
   a) Sure, no problem.
   b) Yes, you do.
   c) No, you didn't.

5. Would you like to leave a message?
   a) Yes, I do.
   b) Yes, please. Can you ask him to call me back?
   c) No, I won't.

IV. Write questions/ phrases for the following answers.

1. _____?
   No, Stephanie doesn't mind getting up early.

2. _____?
   Yes, he enjoys swimming.

3. _____?
   I usually go shopping and watch movies on Saturday.

4. _____?
   Yes, please. Can you ask her to call me back?

5. _____?
   No, Larry doesn't enjoy cooking.

V. Fill in the blanks with an appropriate word/ expression from the box.

> **dial   area code   call back**
> **answering machine   transfer   message**

1. Brian left a _____ on Rita's _____ yesterday.
2. Hang on a second. I'll _____ your call.
3. What's the _____ for Rio de Janeiro?
4. A: Would you like to leave a message? B: No, thanks I'll _____ later.
5. If you have an emergency _____ 911 for help.

I guess I'll have to change my plans then.

Why?

DIALOGUE 21

82

What's the weather forecast for the weekend?

Nancy: Have you heard the **weather forecast** for the weekend?

Ted: Yeah, I heard it on the radio on the way to work this morning. It seems we **are in for** some very cold days. The weatherman said it might even snow on Sunday.

Nancy: Really? I guess I'll have to change my plans then.

Ted: Why? What were you planning to do?

Nancy: I was supposed to go meet this friend who lives **about** a two-hour drive from here, but I always **get** a little **scared** to drive when it snows.

Ted: I see, but you**'re used to** very cold weather, aren't you? You lived in Canada for about two years, right?

Nancy: I did. It was **kind of tough** for me to adapt at first, but I had a great time while living there. So, are you doing anything this weekend?

Ted: Well, with all this cold weather coming our way I might just as well stay home and watch some DVDs by the **fireplace**.

Nancy: Sounds **cozy**! I guess I might just do the same.

▶ Veja a tradução desse diálogo na p. 301.

FOCUS ON VOCABULARY, PHRASES AND EXPRESSIONS 21

Weather forecast = a report on weather conditions (previsão do tempo)
Be in for = be certain to experience something unpleasant (estar certo de passar por algo desagradável)
About = approximately (aproximadamente; mais ou menos)
Get: veja Usos do verbo *get*, p. 275
Scared = frightened (assustado/a)
Be used to = be accustomed to (estar acostumado a)
Kind of = somewhat (mais ou menos)
Tough = hard; difficult (difícil)
Fireplace = a place in a room where a fire burns (lareira)
Cozy = comfortable (confortável; aconchegante)

ılıl 83 DIALOGUE 21 – COMPREHENSION QUESTIONS

1. What's the weather forecast for the weekend according to Ted?
2. Why is Nancy thinking of changing her plans?
3. Is Nancy used to cold weather?
4. What will Ted probably do this weekend?

APPLIED GRAMMAR 21
forma gerúndio do verbo após preposições

A forma gerúndio (*ing*) é empregada quando um verbo vier após uma preposição. Veja os exemplos abaixo:

I'm thinking about inviting Joe to go with us to the beach.
(Estou pensando em convidar o Joe para ir conosco à praia.)
He's not interested in studying French.
(Ele não está interessado em estudar francês.)
Jerry is good at making presentations.
(O Jerry é bom em fazer apresentações.)

Tony is tired of doing the same thing every day.
(O Tony está cansado de fazer a mesma coisa todos os dias.)
Amanda uses the internet for studying and talking to her friends. (Amanda usa a internet para estudar e conversar com os amigos.)
"How about going to a restaurant tonight?", Fred asked Sally.
("Que tal irmos a um restaurante hoje à noite?", Fred perguntou a Sally.)
What's the advantage of doing that?
(Qual é a vantagem de fazer isso?)

USUAL VOCABULARY 21

RELATIONSHIPS

fall in love (apaixonar-se)
be in love (estar apaixonado/a)
a date (um encontro)
date/ dated/ dated (namorar)
go steady with (namorar firme)
get along with (dar-se bem com, ter um bom relacionamento com)
break up (romper, terminar um relacionamento)
get over (superar o fim de um relacionamento, "esquecer")
make up (fazer as pazes)
get engaged (ficar noivo)
love at first sight (amor à primeira vista)
engagement (noivado)
get married (casar-se)
wedding (casamento, cerimônia)
anniversary (aniversário de casamento)
newlyweds (recém-casados)
honeymoon (lua de mel)
fiancé (noivo, durante o noivado)
fiancée (noiva, durante o noivado)

groom (noivo, no dia do casamento)
bride (noiva, no dia do casamento)

Ex.: **Is Sarah still dating Nick?**
(A Sarah ainda está namorando o Nick?)
Fred fell in love with Amanda as soon as he met her. It was love at first sight!
(Fred apaixonou-se pela Amanda assim que a conheceu. Foi amor à primeira vista!)
You have to get over your ex-girlfriend and move on with your life!
(Você precisar esquecer sua ex-namorada e tocar a vida!)
Betty and Sam decided to break up as they couldn't get along with each other.
(Betty e Sam decidiram se separar já que não conseguiam se entender.)
What time is your date tonight?
(A que horas é seu encontro hoje à noite?)
The newlyweds are going to Rio de Janeiro for their honeymoon.
(Os recém-casados vão passar a lua de mel no Rio de Janeiro.)

PRACTICE SET 21

ılıllı 84   I.   Listen to the questions and circle the right answer.

1.   a) Yes, they got married last week.
     b) They're going to Greece.
     c) Yes, they invited many people to their wedding.

2.   a) No, he doesn't.
     b) Yes, they do.
     c) Yes, he is.

3. a) My job.
   b) I'm going there tomorrow.
   c) Yes, I am.

4. a) He was very happy.
   b) He was twenty-seven.
   c) He was single.

5. a) I do. I use the internet very often.
   b) Yes, I have two computers.
   c) I use it for studying and entertainment.

6. a) I do. They are very friendly.
   b) Yes, I like to get up early.
   c) No, I don't go out very often.

7. a) Yes, I have a date tonight.
   b) No, she has blonde hair and green eyes.
   c) 8:00 p.m.

8. a) No, they aren't.
   b) I have no idea.
   c) Yes, they did.

9. a) Yes, he is.
   b) Yes, he does.
   c) He prefers to go to the movies.

10. a) I think it's at 7:00 p.m.
    b) I think it's on Friday.
    c) I think she has a sister.

🔊 85 II. Dictation: listen to the sentences and write them.

1. _____

2. _____

3. _____

4. _____

5. _____

III. Circle the right answer.

1. Do you get along with Harry?
    a) Oh, yeah, he's Rita's neighbor.
    b) Sure, we're good friends.
    c) Yes, I will.

2. Is Jim still dating Samantha?
    a) I think so.
    b) Yes, he does.
    c) He's coming from Boston tomorrow.

3. How old was Mark when he got married?
    a) Yes, he was very young.
    b) I think he was about thirty years old.
    c) No, he didn't get married last year.

4. Does Patricia have a date tonight?
    a) No, she doesn't.
    b) Yes, she is.
    c) Yes, she went to the mall last night.

5. What's your wife's name?
    a) She has a beautiful name.
    b) Her name is Betty.
    c) Her mother's name is Alice.

IV. Write questions/ phrases for the following answers.

1. _____?

   Yes, Rita is still dating Bob.

2. _____?

   Nick got married five years ago.

3. _____?

   I met Susan at the park.

4. _____?

   We went to a Greek restaurant last night.

5. _____?

   They are going to San Francisco on their honeymoon.

V. Fill in the blanks with an appropriate word/ expression from the box.

engagement honeymoon wedding newlyweds married love at first sight get over

1. Where are the _____ going for their _____ ?
2. Did you know Elaine and Steve are getting _____ ? They announced their _____ last week.
3. On the day they got engaged, Samuel gave her fiancée a beautiful _____ ring.
4. Gary fell in love with Magda immediately. It was _____ .
5. It took Anna a long time to _____ her ex-boyfriend.

Do you get along with all of them?

I do, they're very friendly indeed.

|▶ 86 **DIALOGUE 22**
Business is booming!

Nick: You seem to be enjoying your new job, aren't you?

Rachel: Oh yeah, it's been a great experience, a lot more interesting than I imagined. **Though** I've only been with this company for about a month, I've learned so many new things **so far**.

Nick: Wow, you do sound **excited**. How about your **coworkers**? Do you **get along with** all of them?

Rachel: I do, they're very friendly **indeed**.

Nick: Good. I guess you also have a good relationship with your boss, don't you?

Rachel: It's been great working with him **even though** he is very **demanding**. I mean, we sometimes have to work under pressure but he's also very **supportive** so I have nothing to complain about really.

Nick: Great! By the way, I heard your company is doing very well. It seems that it's growing really fast, isn't it?

Rachel: That's right. Business is **booming** and we're all excited about the **prospects**.

Nick: Good for you!

▶ Veja a tradução desse diálogo na p. 302.

FOCUS ON VOCABULARY, PHRASES AND EXPRESSIONS 22

Though: veja *Applied grammar 22*, p. 194
So far = until now (até agora)
Excited = very happy and enthusiastic (animado/a; entusiasmado/a)
Coworker = someone you work with, a colleague (colega de trabalho)
Get along with = have a good relationship with (ter um bom relacionamento com alguém, dar-se bem com)
Indeed = really (realmente)
Even though: veja *Applied grammar 22*, p. 194
Demanding = requiring a lot of attention, time or resources (exigente)
Supportive = that gives support (que dá apoio)
Boom/ boomed/ boomed = grow rapidly (crescer rapidamente, prosperar)
Prospects = the possibility of future success (perspectiva)

ılıll 87 DIALOGUE 22 – COMPREHENSION QUESTIONS

1. Why is Rachel enjoying her new job?
2. Does she get along with all her coworkers?
3. What does Rachel say about her boss?
4. How does Rachel feel about working for that company?

APPLIED GRAMMAR 22
although/ though/ even though + in spite of/ despite

Usamos as conjunções *although* (embora), *though* (embora) e *even though* (apesar de) para expressar contraste. Veja os exemplos abaixo:

Although Jack has a car, he goes to work by subway.
(Embora Jack tenha um carro ele vai ao trabalho de metrô.)
Obs.: Podemos também mudar a ordem da sentença acima para:

194

Jack goes to work by subway although he has a car.
(Jack vai ao trabalho de metrô embora tenha um carro.)

Veja mais um exemplo abaixo:

Although Nick is very rich, he still works hard = Nick still works hard although he is very rich.
(Embora o Nick seja muito rico, ele ainda trabalha bastante.)

Though tem o mesmo significado de **although,** mas é mais informal. Veja os exemplos abaixo.

Though it was very hot Howard didn't take off his jacket. = Howard didn't take off his sweater though it was very hot.
(Embora estivesse muito quente Howard não tirou a jaqueta.)
Though she liked the dress, Melissa decided not to buy it. = Melissa decided not to buy the dress though she liked it.
(Melissa decidiu não comprar o vestido embora ela tenha gostado dele.)

Obs.: *Though* também pode ser usado ao final da sentença. Veja o exemplo abaixo:

Melissa liked the dress. She decided not to buy it, though.

Even though tem o mesmo significado de **although**, mas é mais enfático. Veja os exemplos abaixo:

Even though Pierre had a strong French accent, we understood most of what he said. = We understood most of what Pierre said even though he had a strong French accent.
(Nós entendemos a maior parte do que o Pierre disse apesar de ele ter um sotaque francês forte.)
We decided to go swimming even though it was raining. = Even though it was raining we decided to go swimming.
(Embora estivesse chovendo nós decidimos ir nadar.)

As preposições **in spite of** (apesar de) e **despite** (apesar de) também são usadas para expressar contraste. Veja os exemplos abaixo:

In spite of the rain we had a good time on the beach.
 = Despite the rain we had a good time on the beach.
(Apesar da chuva nós nos divertimos na praia.)

Obs.: Podemos também inverter a ordem das sentenças acima para:
We had a good time on the beach in spite of the rain = We had a good time on the beach despite the rain.
(Nós nos divertimos na praia apesar da chuva.)

Veja agora mais dois exemplos com o uso dos verbos no gerúndio após **in spite of** e **despite**:

In spite of being tired we went to the movies. = Despite being tired we went to the movies.
(Apesar de estarmos cansados fomos ao cinema.)
Tony is thin in spite of eating a lot. = Tony is thin despite eating a lot.
(Tony é magro apesar de comer muito.)

USUAL VOCABULARY 22

COMPANIES AND BUSINESSES

headquarters/ head office (matriz, sede)
core business (atividade principal de uma empresa)
branch/ branch office (filial)
founder (fundador)
found/ founded/ founded (fundar)
advertise/ advertised/ advertised (anunciar, divulgar, fazer publicidade)
launch a product (lançar um produto)

competition (concorrência)
competitor (concorrente, empresa concorrente)
agenda (pauta de reunião, lista de assuntos)
manufacture/ manufactured/ manufactured (fabricar)
manufacturer (fabricante)
outsource/ outsourced/ outsourced (terceirizar)
outsourcement (terceirização)
trade show/ trade fair (feira comercial, feira de negócios)
booth/ stand (estande)
sample (amostra)
break even (alcançar o ponto de equilíbrio)
breakeven point (ponto de equilíbrio)
merger (fusão de empresas)
merge/ merged/ merged (fundir, unir)
market share (participação de mercado)
policy (política, norma de conduta)
shareholder (acionista)
boom/ boomed/ boomed (crescer rapidamente, prosperar)
boom (crescimento rápido, expansão econômica)
startup/ startup company (empresa iniciante)
plant/ factory (fábrica)

Ex.: **That company has branch offices in Miami and Boston.**
(Aquela empresa tem filiais em Miami e Boston.)
What's your company's core business?
(Qual é a atividade principal da sua empresa?)
There are over one hundred booths at this year's exhibition.
(Há mais de cem estandes na feira deste ano.)
The new sales strategy helped us increase our market share.
(A nova estratégia de vendas nos ajudou a aumentar a nossa
participação de mercado.)
Could you send us some samples of your products?
(Você poderia nos enviar algumas amostras de seus produtos?)

PRACTICE SET 22

🎵 88 I. Listen to the questions and circle the right answer.

1. a) It's very big.
    b) It's in Chicago.
    c) Yes, it is there.

2. a) They should launch it in September.
    b) Yes, they are going to launch a new product.
    c) Yes, they are.

3. a) Yes, I was there last year.
    b) Sure!
    c) No, I didn't see them last night.

4. a) They manufacture microwave ovens there.
    b) No, they don't.
    c) No, it's located in Ohio.

5. a) The fair will be in Dallas.
    b) Yes, the fair was very interesting.
    c) Oh yeah, we'll have a big one.

6. a) Yes, we have a new branch office.
    b) We have five branch offices.
    c) I work in one of the branch offices.

7. a) Sure, I'll show you some.
    b) Yes, they are working now.
    c) Yes, you can manufacture them.

8. a) About five times a month.
    b) Three hours and a half.
    c) About twenty miles from here.

9. a) They'll probably do it tomorrow.
   b) It took them about two weeks.
   c) They think the new product will be a hit.

10. a) About fifty people.
    b) No, they don't work here.
    c) Yes, all the employees are satisfied with the company.

ılı|l· 89 II. Dictation: listen to the sentences and write them.

1. _____

2. _____

3. _____

4. _____

5. _____

III. Circle the right answer.

1. Does your company have many branch offices?
   a) Yes, I do.
   b) No, it won't.
   c) Yes, it does.

2. How long did it take them to finish the project?
   a) About two weeks.
   b) Twice a month.
   c) Once a year.

3. How many people work in your department?
   a) Twelve days a month.
   b) Fifteen people.
   c) Yes, I enjoy working in the marketing department.

4. Are you attending the upcoming convention?
   a) I may attend, but I'm not sure yet.
   b) The convention was really good.
   c) A lot of people attended the convention.

5. Do you get along with your boss?
   a) Yes, he does.
   b) Yes, they do.
   c) Yes, I do.

IV. Write questions/ phrases for the following answers.

1. _____?
Oh yeah, although the weather wasn't so good we enjoyed the picnic.

2. _____?
It took them about a month to finish the project.

3. _____?
Yes, we have a branch office in New York.

4. _____?
Yes, Amanda enjoys working there.

5. _____?
The plant is about ten miles from here.

V. Fill in the blanks with an appropriate word/ expression from the box.

> **booth   advertise   launch   market share
> trade show   founder   samples**

1. They expect to increase their _____ after they _____ the new product.
2. Mr. Smith is the _____ and current president of the company.
3. Can you show us some _____ of your products?
4. Our company will have a big _____ at the international _____ in San Francisco this year.
5. Do they plan to _____ the new product on television?

Have you seen Jeff lately?

Not really. Why?

▌• 90 **DIALOGUE 23**
My congrats!

Don: Have you seen Jeff lately?

Ken: Not really. Why?

Don: I need to talk to him. I've been trying to **get in touch with** him, but I've had no luck **so far**.

Ken: I think you know he's been living at a new place for about a month now. Do you have his new phone number there?

Don: I do. I called him a couple of times but he was never there. I left two messages though, but he never **called** me **back**.

Ken: That's **weird**! It's not like Jeff to do something like that. I don't know, maybe he's been working too much or something.

Don: I guess so. I just hope he's okay. So, what have you **been up to** lately?

Ken: Me? Actually I've been doing a lot of new things. Did I tell you I started learning Spanish?

Don: Did you? How interesting! Why did you decide to **take up** Spanish now?

Ken: Well, I have a good reason, I've been dating this Mexican girl for about a month, that's why!

Don: Wow, I guess you will be fluent in Spanish **pretty** soon then. **My congrats!**

▶ Veja a tradução desse diálogo na p. 302.

FOCUS ON VOCABULARY, PHRASES AND EXPRESSIONS 23

Get in touch with = contact (entrar em contato com)
So far = until now (até agora)
Call back = return a phone call to someone (retornar uma ligação para alguém; "ligar de volta")
Weird = strange (estranho)
Be up to = be doing or planning (estar fazendo; "estar aprontando")
Take up = start doing something regularly (começar a fazer algo regularmente)
Pretty = very (muito)
My congrats = my congratulations (meus parabéns)

⑴⑴⑴ 91 DIALOGUE 23 – COMPREHENSION QUESTIONS

1. Has Ken seen Jeff lately?
2. Is Jeff living at the same place where he used to?
3. Why did Ken start learning Spanish?
4. Does Don think Ken will learn Spanish quickly?

APPLIED GRAMMAR 23
passive voice

Observe a sentença abaixo que está na *active voice* (voz ativa):

Paul wrote that e-mail.
(Paul escreveu aquele e-mail.)

Agora veja a mesma sentença na *passive voice* (voz passiva):

That e-mail was written by Paul.
(Aquele e-mail foi escrito pelo Paul.)

Observe que na *passive voice* (voz passiva) usamos o particípio passado do verbo principal. (Veja a terceira coluna na lista de verbos principais na p. 281.)

A *passive voice* (voz passiva) é bastante usada quando a pessoa que realizou a ação não é conhecida, veja o exemplo abaixo:

Someone stole Peter's bike.
(Alguém roubou a bicicleta do Peter)
Peter's bike was stolen.
(A bicicleta do Peter foi roubada)

Observe que, no exemplo acima, "someone" indica que a pessoa que realizou a ação, no caso, de roubar a bicicleta, não é conhecida. O uso da *passive voice* (voz passiva) nestes casos é bastante usual. Veja mais alguns exemplos de sentenças na *passive voice* (voz passiva) em destaque abaixo:

They will paint the house tomorrow.
(Eles pintarão a casa amanhã.)
The house will be painted tomorrow.
(A casa será pintada amanhã.)

Someone broke the vase yesterday.
(Alguém quebrou o vaso ontem.)
The vase was broken yesterday.
(O vaso foi quebrado ontem.)

They built that house in 1976.
(Eles construíram aquela casa em 1976.)
That house was built in 1976.
(Aquela casa foi construída em 1976.)

People don't use this road very often.
(As pessoas não usam esta estrada com muita frequência.)
This road isn't used very often.
(Esta estrada não é usada com muita frequência.)

They will have to cancel the flight because of the bad weather.
(Eles terão que cancelar o voo por causa do tempo ruim.)
The flight will have to be canceled because of the bad weather.
(O voo terá que ser cancelado por causa do tempo ruim.)

USUAL VOCABULARY 23

MONEY MATTERS

cash (dinheiro em espécie)
bill (1. nota, cédula; 2. conta de luz, telefone etc.)
coin (moeda)
currency (moeda corrente)
current account (conta corrente)
save/ saved/ saved (economizar)
savings (economias, poupança)
budget (orçamento)
earn/ earned/ earned (ganhar)
lend/ lent/ lent (emprestar)
loan (empréstimo)
borrow/ borrowed/ borrowed (pedir ou pegar emprestado)
buy/ bought/ bought (comprar)
purchase/ purchased/ purchased (comprar)
owe/ owed/ owed (dever)
pay/ paid/ paid (pagar)
payment (pagamento)
pay back (pagar de volta)
exchange rate (taxa de câmbio)
bank statement (extrato bancário)
interest rate (taxa de juros)
withdraw/ withdrew/ withdrawn (sacar dinheiro)
installment (prestação, parcela)
fee (taxa, preço de serviço)
spend/ spent/ spent (gastar)

income tax (imposto de renda)
buck (dólar - informal)
ATM Automated Teller Machine (caixa eletrônico)
cash or charge? (dinheiro ou cartão?)

Ex.: **What's the currency of Canada?**
(Qual é a moeda corrente do Canadá?)
It's the Canadian dollar.
(É o dólar canadense.)
Can you lend me twenty bucks? I'll pay you back tomorrow.
(Você pode me emprestar vinte dólares? Pago de volta amanhã.)
Paul needs to withdraw money from his account to make some payments.
(Paul precisa sacar dinheiro de sua conta para fazer alguns pagamentos.)
Do you know if there is an ATM near here? I need to withdraw some cash.
(Você sabe se tem um caixa eletrônico aqui perto? Preciso sacar algum dinheiro.)

PRACTICE SET 23

🎧 92 I. Listen to the questions and circle the right answer.

1. a) It's good.
    b) It's very expensive.
    c) It's the Australian dollar.

2. a) Sure, I love cash.
    b) Sure, do you have some cash?
    c) Sure, how much do you need?

3. a) Yes, Tony went there yesterday.
    b) Yes, Tony wrote it.
    c) Yes, Tony is at home right now.

4. a) They were built forty years ago.
   b) They were sold five years ago.
   c) They were bought ten years ago.

5. a) Yes, the flight was canceled.
   b) Because of the snow.
   c) No, my flight is at 11 p.m.

6. a) He'd like to spend some time by himself.
   b) He spent five days there.
   c) He spent fifty bucks.

7. a) Yes, there's one in that mall over there.
   b) Yes, I need to go to the bank.
   c) Yes, it is.

8. a) Yes, he does.
   b) Yes, he did.
   c) Yes, he is.

9. a) Yes, she saved the document.
   b) She saved my life.
   c) She saved twenty thousand dollars.

10. a) Because they were very busy.
    b) Because they were very young.
    c) Yes, they will come here tomorrow.

ılı|lı 93 II. Dictation: listen to the sentences and write them.

1. _____

2. _____

3. _____

4. _____

5. _____

III. Circle the right answer.

1. How much money did Alex borrow from you?
   a) Thirty months.
   b) Forty-five bucks.
   c) Yes, he borrowed money from me yesterday.

2. What's the currency of England?
   a) Yes, it's a lot of money.
   b) It's in London.
   c) It's the pound.

3. Does Sam earn a good salary there?
   a) Yes, he does.
   b) No, he isn't.
   c) Yes, he will.

4. When was the printer fixed?
   a) Yes, it was.
   b) Every day.
   c) Yesterday.

5. How much money do you have in your pocket?
   a) I have a credit card.
   b) Yes, I gave him some cash.
   c) I have ten dollars.

IV. Write questions/ phrases for the following answers.

1. _____?
   I lent him thirty bucks.

2. _____?
   The flight was canceled because of the snow.

3. _____?
   Jerry is planning to spend about one thousand dollars.

4. _____?
   Yes, there's an ATM in that mall over there.

5. _____?
   Deborah didn't come here yesterday because she was very tired.

V. Fill in the blanks with an appropriate word/expression from the box.

> **bucks   currency   payments   lend
> spend   ATM   withdraw   earn**

1. How much money did Jefferson _____ on his new car?
2. Do you know if there is an _____ near here?
   I need to _____ some money from my account to make some _____ .
3. Does James _____ a good salary working for that advertising agency?
4. Can you _____ me ten _____ I'll pay you back tomorrow.
5. The Australian dollar is the _____ in Australia.

🔊 94 **DIALOGUE 24**

I guess I just need to chill out for a while

Barry: Do you **feel like** going out tonight?

Tiffany: I don't know, I guess I**'d rather** stay home. I'm really tired.

Barry: Ok, we can order pizza if you like.

Tiffany: Good idea, I'm not **in the mood** for cooking either.

Barry: Good! So, how are things at work? You sounded **worried** when I talked to you on the phone this morning.

Tiffany: I am a little worried! We're **behind schedule** with our current project and we may need to **work overtime** if we are to finish it on time.

Barry: I see. Didn't you tell me the other day that your department is **short-staffed**?

Tiffany: It is. HR has been trying to find someone qualified but it hasn't been easy. Actually we need two new employees since Maggy will be going on **maternity leave** in a couple of weeks.

Barry: I hope they can find some new people soon. I hate to see you feeling so stressed like this.

Tiffany: It's okay Barry, I'd rather not talk about this subject anymore. I guess I just need to **chill out** for a while.

Barry: Sure, I have a bottle of your favorite white wine in the freezer. Do you want me to **get** you a glass?

Tiffany: I'd love that honey. Thanks!

▶ Veja a tradução desse diálogo na p. 303.

FOCUS ON VOCABULARY, PHRASES AND EXPRESSIONS 24

Feel like = desire or want to do something (sentir vontade de, ter vontade de, "estar a fim de")
'd rather = would rather = would prefer (peferiria)
In the mood = disposed to do something (com disposição para; "a fim de")
Worried = feeling concerned about something (preocupado)
Behind schedule = running late (atrasado)
Work overtime = work more than the usual time needed or expected in a job (fazer hora extra)
Short-staffed = without enough workers (com um número insuficiente de funcionários)
Maternity leave = a period of time a woman is legally allowed to be away from work in the weeks before and after she has a baby (licença maternidade)
Chill out = relax (relaxar)
Get: veja Usos do verbo *get*, p. 275

ılıılı 95 DIALOGUE 24 – COMPREHENSION QUESTIONS

1. Why doesn't Tiffany feel like going out tonight?
2. Why is Tiffany a little worried?
3. What does Tiffany think she needs to do now?
4. What does Barry offer Tiffany?

APPLIED GRAMMAR 24
unless + as long as

Veja abaixo alguns exemplos de uso de *unless* (a menos que):

You will miss the flight unless you hurry.
(Você vai perder o voo a menos que se apresse.)

I plan to go there on foot unless it rains.
(Planejo ir lá a pé a menos que chova.)
Unless you stop smoking you won't feel well.
(A menos que você pare de fumar não se sentirá bem.)
You cannot enter the stadium unless you have a ticket.
(Você não pode entrar no estádio a menos que tenha um ingresso.)

Veja abaixo alguns exemplos de uso de *as long as* (contanto que):

I'll lend you my car as long as you are careful.
(Emprestarei meu carro para você contanto que você seja cuidadoso.)
You can go and play with your friends as long as you finish your homework.
(Você pode ir brincar com seus amigos contanto que termine sua lição de casa.)
I don't mind if you go out tonight as long as you're back before 11 p.m.
(Eu não me importo que você saia hoje à noite contanto que você volte antes das 23h.)
We'll go to the beach on Sunday as long as it doesn't rain.
(Iremos à praia no domingo contanto que não chova.)

Obs.: Em outro contexto, *as long as* também pode significar "durante o tempo que". Veja os exemplos abaixo:

You can stay here as long as you want.
(Você pode ficar aqui durante o tempo que quiser.)
There's no hurry. You can work for as long as you want on the project.
(Não há pressa. Você pode trabalhar durante o tempo que quiser no projeto.)

USUAL VOCABULARY 24

USING COMPUTERS

application/ app (aplicativo)
flash drive (pen drive)
password (senha)
search engine (site de busca)
hit (visita a um site da internet, *hit*)
intranet (rede privada que interliga os departamentos de uma empresa)
spreadsheet (planilha eletrônica)
home page (primeira página de um site, página principal, *home page*)
attach/ attached/ attached (anexar)
attachment (anexo)
delete/ deleted/ deleted (deletar)
e-mail/ e-mailed/ e-mailed (enviar por e-mail)
back up/ backed up/ backed up (fazer *backup*)
backup copy (cópia de *backup*)
at = @ (arroba, usado em endereços de e-mail)
dot (ponto, usado em endereços de e-mail)
antivirus (antivírus)
database (banco de dados)
print/ printed/ printed (imprimir)
printer (impressora)
printout (cópia impressa)
WWW World Wide Web (a grande rede mundial de computadores)

Ex.: **Does your company have an intranet?**
(A sua empresa tem intranet?)
Harry saves all his files on a flash drive.
(O Harry salva todos seus arquivos em um pen drive.)
Sorry, I forgot to attach the document. I'll e-mail it to you again.
(Desculpe, esqueci de anexar o documento. Vou lhe enviar por e-mail de novo)

Don't forget to back up the file before turning off the computer.
(Não se esqueça de fazer *backup* do arquivo antes de desligar o computador.)
I need a printout of the document.
(Preciso de uma cópia impressa do documento.)
Our printer is out of ink. Can you get a new cartridge please?
(Nossa impressora está sem tinta. Você pode arrumar um cartucho novo, por favor?)
Their website has been getting an average of 500 hits a week.
(O site deles tem recebido uma média de 500 visitas por semana.)

PRACTICE SET 24

96   I.   Listen to the questions and circle the right answer.

1.   a) Yes, he did.
      b) No, I don't.
      c) Yes, I did.

2.   a) Yes, I worked on that spreadsheet.
      b) Sure!
      c) Yes, I like to work with spreadsheets.

3.   a) I don't know. I need to ask Mike.
      b) It's a new website.
      c) It's an interesting website.

4.   a) Yes, it is.
      b) No, Jeff doesn't check the intranet every day.
      c) No, it doesn't.

5.   a) About twice a month.
      b) About twenty thousand hits.
      c) About ten miles from here.

6. a) Sure, I saved it on my flash drive.
   b) Yes, I saved a lot of money.
   c) Yes, I'd like to see the document.

7. a) Yes, she uses it every day.
   b) Yes, he does.
   c) Yes, she was.

8. a) Yes, I do. I have a new printer.
   b) That new printer wasn't so expensive.
   c) I think it's out of ink.

9. a) They have a good memory.
   b) They do. I told them yesterday.
   c) They'd like to see that file.

10. a) I think he does.
    b) No, he isn't.
    c) I think he went to the mall.

🔊 97 II. Dictation: listen to the sentences and write them.

1. _____

2. _____

3. _____

4. _____

5. _____

III. Circle the right answer.

1. Doesn't Brian know the password?
   a) No, he isn't feeling very well today.
   b) Sure, he'd like to come with us.
   c) No, he's new here.

2. Do they have a website?
   a) They like websites.
   b) They do but I don't know the address.
   c) Yes, I like visiting websites.

3. Don't you check your e-mail every day?
   a) Sure, I check my e-mail all the time.
   b) No, she doesn't like to do that.
   c) Sure, I can call you later.

4. Did you save that file?
   a) We do that all the time.
   b) Yes, I checked the file.
   c) Sure, I saved it on my flash drive.

5. Doesn't Carol have a laptop?
   a) Yeah, she bought a new one last month.
   b) She loves to surf the Web.
   c) Yes, she checks her e-mail every day.

IV. Write questions/ phrases for the following answers.

1. _____?
   No, Jim doesn't check his e-mail every day.

2. _____?
   Yes, they have a website, but I don't know the address.

3. _____?
   Yes, I can print a copy for you.

4. _____?

No, he forgot to save the file.

5. _____?

No, I didn't check my e-mail yesterday. Why?

V. Fill in the blanks with an appropriate word/ expression from the box.

> **password   flash drive   delete   attach**
> **save   print   e-mail**

1. It's a lot easier and practical to _____ computer files on a _____ .
2. Can you _____ a copy of that document for me please?
3. You need a _____ to access the system.
4. Did you _____ any names from that list?
5. You forgot to _____ the document. Can you _____ it to me again?

DIALOGUE 25

What's the best way to get there?

Sean: So Ryan, what's the best way to **get** there?

Ryan: We can either take the subway or drive. In my opinion we'd better take the subway as the traffic is usually **heavy** at this time.

Sean: Good. We'll take the subway then. By the way, I didn't get a chance to talk to Derek yesterday.

Ryan: I didn't **either**.

Sean: Do you think he might still be interested in going with us?

Ryan: I guess so, but don't worry, I'll give him a call later.

Sean: Great! What about Jason? Do you think we should also invite him?

Ryan: I'm not sure, to be honest with you I don't like him very much.

Sean: Neither do I. You're right, he's always been a little arrogant, he's not my favorite kind of person either.

Ryan: Ok, so let's start **packing.** I want to get things ready **once and for all**.

Sean: Sure, let's do that now! I don't want to be late tomorrow.

Ryan: Me **neither!**

▶ Veja a tradução desse diálogo na p. 304.

FOCUS ON VOCABULARY, PHRASES AND EXPRESSIONS 25

Get: veja Usos do verbo *get*, p. 275
Heavy = bad (intenso; ruim)
Either: veja *Applied grammar 25*, nesta página
Pack/ packed/ packed = put something into a bag (fazer as malas)
Once and for all = finally; decisively (de uma vez por todas)
Neither: veja *Applied grammar 25*, nesta página

99 DIALOGUE 25 – COMPREHENSION QUESTIONS

1. Why do Sean and Ryan decide to take the subway?
2. Did they talk to Derek yesterday?
3. Do they intend to invite Jason to go with them? Why/ Why not?
4. Why do they start packing now?

APPLIED GRAMMAR 25
so do I; neither do I etc.

Usamos a estrutura *so* + **verbo auxiliar/ verbo to be/ verbo modal** + **sujeito** para demonstrar acordo com o que uma pessoa disse (frases afirmativas). Veja os exemplos abaixo:

Mary: "I get up early every day." (Acordo cedo todos os dias.)
Paul: "So do I." (Eu também.)

Karen: "I went to the mall on Saturday."
(Eu fui ao shopping center no sábado.)
Diane: "So did I." (Eu também.)

Walter: "I'm feeling cold." (Estou sentindo frio.)
Sam: "So am I." (Eu também.)

Mark: "I can speak two languages." (Eu sei falar duas línguas.)
Sue: "So can I." (Eu também.)

Podemos também, nesses casos, usar a palavra *too* (também) no final da frase, ou simplesmente dizer *"Me too"* (Eu também). Veja os exemplos abaixo:

Rob: "I go to the club on weekends."
(Eu vou ao clube nos finais de semana.)
Brian: "So do I." / "I do too." / "Me too." (Eu também.)

Sarah: "I talked to Harry yesterday." (Falei com o Harry ontem.)
Tina: "So did I." / "I did too." / "Me too." (Eu também.)

Derek: "I'm tired." (Estou cansado.)
Bob: "So am I." / "I'm tired too." / "Me too" (Eu também.)

Jeff: "I can swim very well." (Eu sei nadar muito bem.)
Tony: "So can I." / "I can too." / "Me too" (Eu também.)

Para demonstrar acordo com frases negativas, usamos a estrutura **neither + verbo auxiliar/ verbo to be/ verbo modal + sujeito**. Uma outra opção é usar *either* ao final da sentença, ou *"Me neither"* (Eu também não), que é bastante informal. Veja os exemplos abaixo:

Barry: "I don't speak Spanish." (Não falo espanhol.)
Ted: "Neither do I." / "I don't either." / "Me Neither."
(Eu também não.)

Sally: "I didn't see Barry yesterday." (Não vi Barry ontem.)
Melissa: "Neither did I." / "I didn't either." / "Me Neither."
(Eu também não.)

Joe: "I'm not ready yet." (Eu ainda não estou pronto.)
Larry: "Neither am I." / "I'm not either." / "Me Neither."
(Eu também não.)

Adam: **"I can't understand what he's saying."**
(Não consigo entender o que ele está dizendo.)
Tony: **"Neither can I." / "I can't either." / "Me Neither."**
(Eu também não.)

Sandra: **"I wouldn't like to live there."** (Não gostaria de morar lá.)
Celine: **"Neither would I." / "I wouldn't either." / "Me Neither."**
(Eu também não.)

IDIOMATIC EXPRESSIONS 1

a ballpark figure (um número aproximado, estimativa)
Ex.: **Can you give me a ballpark figure on how much you plan to spend?**
(Você pode me dar uma estimativa de quanto planeja gastar?)

a bed of roses ("um mar de rosas")
Ex.: **Life is not a bed of roses!**
(A vida não é um mar de rosas!)

a rip-off (muito caro, "um roubo")
Ex.: **Ten bucks for a cup of coffee? That's a rip-off!**
(Dez dólares por uma xícara de café? Isto é um roubo!)

around the clock (24 horas por dia, sem parar)
Ex.: **They'll need to work around the clock to meet the deadline.**
(Eles vão precisar trabalhar sem parar para cumprir o prazo.)

all set (pronto, preparado)
Ex.: **Is everything all set for the presentation tomorrow?**
(Está tudo pronto para a apresentação amanhã?)

in charge of (responsável por)
Ex.: **Who's in charge of the sales department in your company?**
(Quem é o responsável pelo departamento de vendas na sua empresa?)

in someone's shoes (no lugar de outra pessoa)
Ex.: **What would you do if you were in my shoes?**
(O que você faria se estivesse no meu lugar?)

be up to someone (ser a responsabilidade de alguém, caber a alguém)
Ex.: **It's up to you to decide.**
(Cabe a você decidir.)

beats me! (sei lá!)
Ex.: **A: What's the capital of Iceland? B: Beats me!**
(A: Qual é a capital da Islândia? B: Sei lá!)

bounce back (recuperar-se, "dar a volta por cima")
Ex.: **It's good to know you bounced back from the flu so quickly!**
(É bom saber que você se recuperou da gripe assim rapidamente!)

PRACTICE SET 25

100 I. Listen to the questions and circle the right answer.

1. a) Yes, I liked his new shoes. They are very nice.
   b) I have no idea.
   c) No, I don't need to buy shoes.

2. a) Yes, I'd like to do that.
   b) Yes, I'm watching the news.
   c) No, I'm not ready yet. I need some more time.

3. a) She thinks he's a nice guy.
   b) Beats me!
   c) She's a pretty girl.

4.   a) I didn't see him, that's why!
     b) I like to talk to Joe, he's a nice guy.
     c) I talk to him every day.

5.   a) They think they can start now.
     b) Yes, they are ready to go now.
     c) Yes, but they'll have to work around the clock to meet the deadline.

6.   a) Amanda likes to work here.
     b) A woman named Patricia Johnson.
     c) There are about ten people working in that department.

7.   a) About five hundred bucks.
     b) Yes, I do.
     c) They like to spend money on clothes.

8.   a) No, I wouldn't.
     b) Sure, what do you need?
     c) Yes, I do.

9.   a) About six miles from here.
     b) About four hours.
     c) About three times a year.

10. a) Yes, it does.
     b) Yes, it is.
     c) Yes, they do.

🔊 101   II.   Dictation: listen to the sentences and write them.

1. _____

2. _____

3. _____ .

4. _____

5. _____

III. Look at the examples and complete with *so* or *neither*.

Ex.: Bill goes to school in the morning. Tony goes to school in the morning too.
Bill goes to school in the morning. **So does Tony.**

Ex.: Jeff doesn't smoke. Bianca doesn't smoke either.
Jeff doesn't smoke. **Neither does Bianca.**

1. Josh bought a new computer. Sam bought a new computer too.
Josh bought a new computer. _____ .

2. Brian can't speak Spanish. Melissa can't speak Spanish either.
Brian can't speak Spanish. _____ .

3. Alex is sixteen years old. Nick is sixteen years old too.
Alex is sixteen years old. _____ .

4. Nancy didn't go to the party. Amanda didn't go to the party either.
Nancy didn't go to the party. _____ .

5. Bob enjoys swimming. Ron enjoys swimming too.
Bob enjoys swimming. _____ .

6. Mary doesn't have a sister. Carla doesn't have a sister either.
Mary doesn't have a sister. _____ .

7. Frank would prefer to live in a small city. Sandra would prefer to live in a small city too.
   Frank would prefer to live in a small city. _____ .

8. Michael isn't interested in art. Deborah isn't interested in art either.
   Michael isn't interested in art. _____ .

9. Ted loves chocolate. His brothers love chocolate too.
   Ted loves chocolate. _____ .

10. Michelle and Sonia weren't late for the show. Kate wasn't late either.
    Michelle and Sonia weren't late for the show. _____ .

IV. Write questions/ phrases for the following answers.

1. _____ ?
   I went to the mall because I needed to buy a new pair of sneakers.

2. _____ ?
   Yeah, everything is all set for the presentation tomorrow.

3. _____ ?
   No, I didn't see Fred last night.

4. _____ ?
   No, Linda can't speak French.

5. _____ ?
   No, Josh doesn't have a sister.

V. Fill in the blanks with an idiomatic expression from the box.

> **all set   around the clock   in charge of**
> **ballpark figure   in your shoes**

1. Elaine is _____ the financial department of a big company.
2. I don't know what I would do if I were _____ .
3. Can you give me a _____ on the number of people who will attend the event?
4. Everything seems to be _____ for the party tonight.
5. They had to work _____ to finish the project on time.

Thanks to a regular exercise program I feel a lot healthier than I used to.

Good for you!

▮▮▶ 102 **DIALOGUE 26**

How long have you been going to the gym?

Nick: Do you still go to bed very late at night?
Fred: Oh, no, I **used to** do that but now I always **make sure** I **turn in** by 10:00 pm. I have to get up early every morning to drive my kids to school now.
Nick: So no more late night movies for you, right?
Fred: Well, I can still watch the late night movies on weekends, but not on weekdays anymore.
Nick: Sure! You know, I was **meaning** to tell you something, you look really **slim**. Have you been on a diet or something?
Fred: You're right! I used to be fatter than I am now, but I haven't been on a diet. The thing is I've been **working out** at the gym four times a week now.
Nick: That's really good. How long have you been going to the gym?
Fred: About five months now. Thanks to a regular exercise program I feel a lot healthier than I used to.
Nick: Good for you!

▶ Veja a tradução desse diálogo na p. 304.

FOCUS ON VOCABULARY, PHRASES AND EXPRESSIONS 26

Used to: veja *Applied grammar 26*, p. 230
Make sure = make a point of doing something (fazer questão de)

Turn in = go to bed (ir para cama dormir)
Mean/ meant/ meant = intend (pretender; ter a intenção de)
Slim = thin in an attractive way (esbelto/a)
Work out = do physical exercise (fazer exercício físico; "malhar")

ılıllı 103 DIALOGUE 26 – COMPREHENSION QUESTIONS

1. Why doesn't Fred go to bed very late at night anymore?
2. Why does Fred look slim?
3. How long has Fred been going to the gym?
4. How does Fred feel now?

APPLIED GRAMMAR 26
used to / be used to / get used to

Usamos *used to* para se referir a algo que se costumava fazer no passado. Veja os exemplos abaixo:

I used to go to work by bus, but now I go by car.
(Eu ia ao trabalho de ônibus, mas agora vou de carro.)
Joe used to travel on business very often, but he doesn't anymore.
(Joe viajava a negócios com muita frequência, mas não viaja mais.)
Fred used to watch cartoons every day when he was a kid.
(Fred assistia desenho animado todos os dias quando era criança.)
Telma used to visit her aunt every week.
(Telma visitava sua tia todas as semanas.)

A forma interrogativa de *used to* é formada com **did** + **use to** e a negativa com **didn't** + **use to**. Veja os exemplos:

Did you use to play volleyball when you were at school?
(Você jogava voleibol quando estava na escola?)

230

Jeff didn't use to eat vegetables when he was a kid, but now he does.
(Jeff não comia legumes quando era criança, mas agora come.)
Did Tony use to smoke in the past?
(O Tony fumava no passado?)
I didn't use to travel abroad very often, but now I do.
(Eu não viajava ao exterior com muita frequência, mas agora viajo.)

Usamos *be used to* com o significado de "estar acostumado a algo". Os verbos seguidos de *be used to* devem vir na forma gerúndio. Veja os exemplos abaixo:

I'm not used to this cold weather.
(Não estou acostumado com este tempo frio.)
Jeff is used to getting up early.
(Jeff está acostumado a levantar cedo.)
Celine is used to having dinner late.
(Celine está acostumada a jantar tarde.)
Bob isn't used to driving in New York. He uses the subway every day.
(Bob não está acostumado a dirigir em Nova York. Ele usa o metrô todos os dias.)
Are you used to cooking?
(Você está acostumado a cozinhar?)

Usamos *get used to* com o significado de "acostumar-se a algo". Os verbos seguidos de *get used to* devem vir na forma gerúndio. Veja os exemplos abaixo:

Bob can't get used to working on weekends.
(Bob não consegue se acostumar a trabalhar nos finais de semana.)
Jane has been living in her new apartment for just about a month so she hasn't gotten used to the neighborhood yet.
(Jane está morando em seu novo apartamento há apenas um mês, então não se acostumou com o novo bairro ainda.)

It took Daniel a long time to get used to living in Canada since it's much colder than Florida, where he used to live.
(Levou bastante tempo para o Daniel se acostumar a viver no Canadá já que lá é muito mais frio do que a Flórida, onde ele morava antes.)
Kate can't get used to the noise in this city.
(Kate não consegue se acostumar ao barulho desta cidade.)

PHRASAL VERBS 1

ask out (convidar alguém para sair)
Ex.: **"Amanda is a pretty girl. Why don't you ask her out?", Brian asked Joe.**
("Amanda é uma garota linda. Por que você não a convida para sair?", Brian perguntou a Joe.)

be over (estar terminado, acabar)
Ex.: **Ok folks, the class is over. Don't forget to do your homework. See you tomorrow!**
(Ok, pessoal, a aula terminou. Não se esqueçam de fazer a lição de casa. Vejo vocês amanhã.)

break down (quebrar, parar de funcionar)
Ex.: **"Can you give me a ride to the subway station? My car broke down yesterday", Jim asked a friend.**
("Você pode me dar uma carona até o metrô? Meu carro quebrou ontem", Jim pediu a um amigo.)

break up (terminar um relacionamento, romper, separar-se)
Ex.: **"Did you know that Tom and Sally broke up?", Maggy asked a friend.**
("Você sabia que o Tom e a Sally se separaram?", Maggy perguntou a uma amiga.)

call off (cancelar)
Ex.: **Unfortunately we will have to call off the meeting.**
(Infelizmente teremos que cancelar a reunião.)

drop by (fazer uma visita breve, "dar um pulo na casa de")
Ex.: **Why don't we drop by Ted's house? I haven't seen him in a long time.**
(Por que não damos um pulo na casa do Ted? Não o vejo há muito tempo.)

fall apart (despedaçar-se, "cair aos pedaços")
Ex.: **It's no wonder your dictionary is falling apart. You've been using it for such a long time!**
(Não é de admirar que o seu dicionário esteja caindo aos pedaços. Você o usa há tanto tempo!)

feel like (sentir vontade de, "estar a fim de")
Ex.: **I feel like going to the movies tonight.**
(Estou com vontade de ir ao cinema hoje à noite.)

figure out (entender alguém ou algo; encontrar a solução de um problema)
Ex.: **"Arnold is a really weird guy. I can't figure him out!", said Jeff to his friends.**
("Arnold é um cara muito estranho. Não consigo entendê-lo", disse Jeff aos amigos.)

find out (descobrir)
Ex.: **"How did you find out her phone number?", Fred asked Josh.**
("Como você descobriu o telefone dela?", Fred perguntou a Josh.)

PRACTICE SET 26

I. Listen to the questions and circle the right answer.

1. a) Yes, she does. She goes to school in the morning.
    b) Yes, she is. She goes to school in the morning.
    c) Yes, she did. She got up very early.

2. a) No, they won't.
    b) No, I don't know where Trevor and Rita live.
    c) No, I don't.

3. a) Sure, I still watch them sometimes.
    b) They prefer to watch Woody Woodpecker and the Jetsons.
    c) Yes, I am.

4. a) She'd rather watch a movie.
    b) She went to the theater.
    c) She's talking to Joe on the phone now.

5. a) Yes, he dropped by my place last night.
    b) Good idea! Let's do that.
    c) Because I have time.

6. a) Yes, I have a new car.
    b) Yes, I'm planning to travel by car.
    c) No, not really.

7. a) I like to talk to Sheila.
    b) I talked to Brian.
    c) Yes, I did.

8. a) No, he didn't come to the meeting.
    b) Yes, they decided to call off the meeting.
    c) Beats me!

9. a) No, I'm kind of tired.
    b) Yes, I did.
    c) Yes, I went there yesterday.

10. a) His car broke down, that's why!
    b) He's taking a shower right now.
    c) Yes, we talked to him yesterday.

II. Dictation: listen to the sentences and write them.

1. _____

2. _____

3. _____

4. _____

5. _____

III. Circle the right answer.

1. What do you feel like doing tonight?
   a) Yes, I do. I need to talk to Margareth today.
   b) No, I don't know them.
   c) I'm tired. I think I'll stay home and go to bed early.

2. Did Steve use to smoke?
   a) No, he bought cigarettes.
   b) Yes, his brother likes to smoke.
   c) No, he didn't.

3. Why is Monica so late?
   a) Her car broke down on her.
   b) She's all set.
   c) No, I didn't ask her out.

4. Is Michelle used to cooking?
   a) Yes, she does. She cooks every day.
   b) No, she's not cooking now.
   c) Yes, she is. She cooks every day.

5. Did Jim figure out what's wrong with his car?
   a) Yes, he did.
   b) No, they don't.
   c) Yes, something's wrong.

IV. Write questions/ phrases for the following answers.

1. _____?
   He's reading a book.

2. _____?
   I feel like swimming.

3. _____?
   Yes, Nick told me what happened.

4. _____?
   No, they are not used to working on Saturday.

5. _____?
   No, Margareth can't come with us to the party.

V. Fill in the blanks with a phrasal verb from the box. Make sure you use the appropriate verb tense.

drop by	find out	break up	call off	feel like

1. Barry was surprised when I told him that Rita and Joe had _____ .
2. Do you know why they had to _____ the meeting?
3. It's so hot today! I _____ swimming.
4. "Can you _____ my place later today? I need to talk to you", Jim asked a friend over the phone.
5. Jane was very angry when she _____ that Nick had lied to her.

🔊 106 **DIALOGUE 27**

What would you do if you came into a fortune?

Larry: What would you do if you **came into** a fortune?

Ron: Gee, I don't know. I've never thought about that possibility, but I guess I'd probably buy a house first and stop paying rent.

Larry: Right! That would be a **wise** thing to do. What else do you think you would do?

Ron: I'm sure I'd also like to travel a lot, I love traveling!

Larry: Me too! There are so many countries that I want to visit. I hope I can still do that someday. Do you think you would also start a business?

Ron: Yeah, that's something I would consider doing. Maybe a franchise in the food industry.

Larry: Sure, I would **definitely set up** my own company too. You know, it would also be important to hire a financial consultant to **get** advice on how to invest the money properly.

Ron: I agree. You've just **reminded** me of something. Listen, are you going to see Harry later today?

Larry: I'm not sure, why?

Ron: I need to talk to him about some money he **borrowed** from me.

Larry: Sure, if I see him I'll let him know you want to talk to him.

Ron: Thanks! I guess we'd better stop **daydreaming** and get back to work now. Our boss is coming our way.

Larry: Okey-dokey!

▶ Veja a tradução desse diálogo na p. 305.

FOCUS ON VOCABULARY, PHRASES AND EXPRESSIONS 27

Come into = inherit (herdar)
Gee = used to express surprise or enthusiasm ("puxa")
Wise = having or showing wisdom or good judgement (sábio/a)
Definitely = absolutely (sem dúvida, com certeza)
Set up = establish or start a business (estabelecer, montar um negócio, etc.)
Get: veja Usos do verbo *get*, p. 275
Remind/ reminded/ reminded = cause to remember (lembrar alguém)
Borrow/ borrowed/ borrowed = receive and use something from someone and promise to give it back (pegar emprestado)
Daydream/ daydreamed/ daydreamed = have dreamlike fantasies while awake (sonhar acordado)
Okey-dokey = all right; okay (ok)

ılıllı 107 DIALOGUE 27 – COMPREHENSION QUESTIONS

1. What would Ron do if he came into a fortune?
2. What kind of business would Ron consider starting?
3. What does Larry believe it would be important to do if they came into a fortune?
4. What does Ron need to talk to Harry about?

APPLIED GRAMMAR 27
if clauses – conditional

Existem basicamente três estruturas condicionais empregadas em conjunto com ***if*** (se). Veja no quadro abaixo os tempos verbais empregados em cada estrutura:

Estrutura	If clause	Main clause
I	present	*will* (or modal + infinitive)
II	past	*would* + infinitive
III	past perfect	*would* + *have* + past participle

Agora veja os exemplos abaixo:

Estrutura	If clause	Main clause
I	**If I have money** (Se eu tiver dinheiro)	**I will travel to Miami.** (eu viajarei para Miami.)
II	**If I had money** (Se eu tivesse dinheiro)	**I would travel to Miami.** (eu viajaria para Miami.)
III	**If I had had money** (Se eu tivesse tido dinheiro)	**I would have traveled to Miami.** (eu teria viajado para Miami.)

Obs.: Podemos também inverter a ordem das frases acima, iniciando pela **main clause,** veja os exemplos abaixo:

I.   **I will travel to Miami if I have money.**
II. **I would travel to Miami if I had money.**
III. **I would have traveled to Miami if I had had money.**

Veja agora mais alguns exemplos:

If I see him I'll tell him you called.
(Se eu o vir falarei para ele que você ligou.)
You'll pass the test if you study.
(Você passará no teste se estudar.)
If I went to New York I would visit the Statue of Liberty.
(Se eu fosse a Nova York visitaria a estátua da liberdade.)
What would you do if you were a millionaire?
(O que você faria se fosse milionário?)
I would travel around the world if I were a millionaire.
(Viajaria ao redor do mundo se eu fosse milionário.)
I won't go to the club if it rains.
(Não irei ao clube se chover.)
If I hadn't spent all my money I could have gone to Italy as well.
(Se eu não tivesse gastado todo o meu dinheiro poderia também ter ido a Itália.)
Tony will move to a bigger apartment if he gets a promotion.
(Tony se mudará para um apartamento maior se receber uma promoção.)
Samantha could pick us up at the airport if she had a car.
(Samantha poderia nos pegar no aeroporto se tivesse um carro.)

IDIOMATIC EXPRESSIONS 2

break even (não ter lucro nem prejuízo, "empatar")
Ex.: **It took about a year for Nick's new business to break even.**
(Levou aproximadamente um ano para o novo negócio do Nick empatar.)

break the ice ("quebrar o gelo)
Ex.: **Barry is an outgoing person. He finds it easy to break the ice and get to know new people at social events.**
(Barry é uma pessoa extrovertida. Ele acha fácil quebrar o gelo e conhecer novas pessoas em eventos sociais.)

by heart (de cor)
Ex.: **Fred has an amazing memory. He knows all his friends' phone numbers by heart.**
(Fred tem uma memória incrível. Ele sabe os números dos telefones de todos seus amigos de cor.)

by oneself (sozinho)
Ex.: **Did you do your homework by yourself?**
(Você fez a lição de casa sozinho?)

call it a day (dar por encerradas as atividades, terminar)
Ex.: **It's nearly 7 pm and we're tired. Let's call it a day.**
(Já são quase 19h e estamos cansados. Vamos parar por aqui.)

catch one's eye (atrair a atenção de alguém, chamar a atenção)
Ex.: **"Pretty girls usually catch my eye", said Frank to a friend.**
(As garotas bonitas geralmente chamam a minha atenção.

change one's mind (mudar de opinião, mudar de ideia)
Ex.: **At first Larry wanted to go with us to the party, but he changed his mind later.**
(A princípio Larry queria ir conosco à festa, mas mudou de ideia mais tarde.)

couch potato (pessoa que não é ativa e passa muito tempo assistindo à TV)
Ex.: **All Bob does is watch TV all day. He's a real couch potato!**
(O Bob só assiste TV o dia inteiro. Ele é mesmo um vegetal!)

cross one's mind (passar pela cabeça)
Ex.: **"That idea has never crossed my mind", said Derek to his friends.**
("Essa ideia nunca passou pela minha cabeça", Derek disse aos amigos.)

down and out (em situação difícil, "na pior")
Ex.: **"Todd has been down and out since he lost his job. Let's drop by his place and cheer him up", said Mike to his friends.**
("Todd está na pior desde que perdeu o emprego. Vamos dar um pulo na casa dele para animá-lo", Mike disse aos amigos.)

PRACTICE SET 27

🎚 108 I.   Listen to the questions and circle the right answer.

1.   a) No, the party starts at 9 p.m.
b) Yes, he likes to do everything by himself.
c) No, Jeff is going with me.

2.   a) Sure!
b) Yes, he has a lot of time.
c) No, I didn't talk to Tony yesterday.

3.   a) About five miles from here.
b) About a year and a half.
c) About twice a year.

4.   a) Yes, I'm going to the mall tomorrow night.
b) I prefer comedies.
c) No, I won't.

5.   a) I guess so, I'm really tired.
b) No, they didn't call Sam.
c) Yes, I'd talk to them if I saw them.

6.   a) She bought a new car last month.
b) I think he doesn't have enough money.
c) Yes, he likes to drive.

7. a) I think he went to his parents' house.
   b) I think he needs to get up early.
   c) Sure!

8. a) Yes, I will.
   b) I met a girl named Carol.
   c) Yes, I like to meet new people.

9. a) I'm sorry, I'm late for work.
   b) His flight is at 11 p.m.
   c) I'm always on time for appointments.

10. a) I ate vegetables and fish.
    b) Yes, dinner was delicious.
    c) With my friend Nick.

◀‖▶ 109 II. Dictation: listen to the sentences and write them.

1. _____

2. _____

3. _____

4. _____

5. _____

III. Circle the right answer.

1. Would you buy a new car if you had money?
   a) Yes, I'd like to drive.
   b) Sure!
   c) Yes, I will.

2. Why didn't Josh talk to them?
   a) I think he didn't see them.
   b) I think he's on time for work.
   c) I think he wants to drink beer.

3. Would you visit them if you had time?
   a) Yes, I like to go to the theater.
   b) Yes, I would.
   c) Yes, they came here yesterday.

4. Who are you talking about?
   a) No, he's not here.
   b) We're talking about our vacation.
   c) Terry Williams, the guy we met at the party, remember?

5. Did he do that by himself?
   a) Sure, he did it alone.
   b) Sure, he likes to work here.
   c) No, he doesn't have time for that now.

IV. Write questions/ phrases for the following answers.

1. _____?
   If I had a lot of money I'd buy a new house.

2. _____?
   No, I didn't go there by myself. I went there with Mike.

3. _____?
   I had lunch with Rachel.

4. _____?
   Yes, Melissa has a younger sister.

5. _____?

Yeah, Karen made that cake by herself.

V. Fill in the blanks with an idiomatic expression from the box.

> **crossed my mind   call it a day   changed his mind
> by yourself   break the ice**

1. At first Mike planned to study medicine and become a doctor like his father, but he _____ later and decided to go to law school instead.
2. Dave's outgoing personality makes it easy for him to _____ and get to know people at parties.
3. After working all day long Frank decided to _____ and go home.
4. Did you really cook that wonderful meal _____ ?
5. Moving to another city never really _____ .

> 110 **DIALOGUE 28**
What has he been up to?

Stan: Have you seen Brian **lately**?

Tom: Yeah, I talked to him yesterday as a matter of fact.

Stan: Really? What has he **been up to**?

Tom: Well, he told me he's gone back to university, he's taking an MBA three times a week at night. He's also **broken up** with his girlfriend, Patty. Remember her?

Stan: Sure, wow, things seem to be changing all the time. I haven't talked to him in a long time, so I had no idea.

Tom: Ah, he's also **shaved off** his **goatee**, he looks very different now.

Stan: No kidding? His goatee was his **trademark**. It seems his life has changed a lot recently.

Tom: I guess you could say that. Hey, have you had dinner yet?

Stan: No, not yet. Why?

Tom: I'm **kind of** hungry so I thought maybe we could go to that **hamburger joint** on Main Street.

Stan: Sounds good to me. You know I love burgers. Let's go!

▶ Veja a tradução desse diálogo na p. 306.

FOCUS ON VOCABULARY, PHRASES AND EXPRESSIONS 28

Lately = recently (ultimamente; recentemente)
Be up to = be doing or planning (estar fazendo; "estar aprontando")
Break up = end a relationship (terminar um relacionamento; romper)
Shave off = shave (raspar a barba, bigode etc.)
Goatee = a small pointed beard (cavanhaque)
No kidding = really (sério; "é mesmo")
Trademark = something that you wear, do or say that is typical of you (marca registrada)
Kind of = somewhat (mais ou menos)
Hamburger joint = a snack bar that serves hamburgers (lanchonete que serve hambúrguer)

ılıllı 111   ## DIALOGUE 28 – COMPREHENSION QUESTIONS

1. Has Tom seen Brian lately?
2. How has Brian's life changed recently?
3. Has Stan had dinner yet?
4. Where do Tom and Stan decide to go?

APPLIED GRAMMAR 28
present perfect

A estrutura do **present perfect** é formada pelos verbos *have* ou *has* (no caso dos pronomes *he, she, it*) em conjunto com o particípio passado dos verbos principais. (Veja a terceira coluna na lista de verbos principais na p. 281.)

Veja abaixo cinco situações importantes em que o tempo verbal **present perfect** deve ser empregado:

1. O **present perfect** é usado para descrever uma ação iniciada há algum tempo (minutos, horas, dias, meses, anos etc.) e que

250

ainda não terminou. O uso das preposições "for" (há) e "since" (desde) é muito frequente nesta situação. Veja o exemplo abaixo:

I've known them for about two years.
(Eu os conheço há aproximadamente dois anos.)

Obs. 1: Seria incorreto dizer "I know them for about two years", embora a frase equivalente em português esteja no tempo presente.
Obs. 2: As contrações I've (I have); you've (you have); he's (he has); she's (she has); we've (we have) e they've (they've) são bastante usuais na conversação.

Agora veja mais alguns exemplos de uso dessa mesma situação que descreve uma ação que se iniciou no passado e continua até o presente:

Tony's worked for that company for six years.
(Tony trabalha naquela empresa há seis anos.)
How long have you been a teacher?
(Há quanto tempo você é professora?)
James and Sarah have been married since 1987.
(James e Sarah são casados desde 1987.)
How long has Joe lived in Miami?
(Há quanto tempo Joe mora em Miami?)

2. Quando a ênfase for na ação e não no tempo da frase. Nesses casos o tempo não é mencionado. Quando perguntamos, por exemplo: "Você conversou com o Paul?", o que importa é saber se o interlocutor conversou ou não com o Paul, e não quando conversou com ele. Assim, em inglês, a pergunta equivalente seria "Have you talked to Paul?", ou seja, usando a estrutura do *present perfect*. Nas frases em que o tempo passado estiver explícito (pelo uso de expressões como "yesterday", "last week", "last month", "last year", "some days ago" etc.), emprega-se a estrutura do passado simples com o verbo auxiliar *did*. (por exemplo: Did you talk to Paul yesterday?). Veja abaixo mais alguns exemplos:

Have you seen Amanda?
(Você viu a Amanda?)
I've read an interesting article about how to lose weight.
(Li um artigo interessante sobre como perder peso.)
Has Kate finished her homework?
(A Kate terminou a lição de casa?)
Mike's bought a new car.
(O Mike comprou um carro novo.)

3. Em frases que descrevem um período de tempo que não terminou ("today", "this week", "this month", "this year" etc.) e durante o qual a mesma ação pode voltar a acontecer. Quando dizemos, por exemplo, "Comprei dois livros novos este mês", a ação "comprar livros" poderá voltar a acontecer antes de o mês terminar. Nesse caso, a frase equivalente em inglês deve ser estruturada no *present perfect*: "I've bought two new books this month". Veja mais alguns exemplos:

I haven't seen Barry today. Have you?
(Não vi Barry hoje. Você o viu?)
Ted's played soccer three times this week.
(O Ted jogou futebol três vezes esta semana.)
Have you bought any new CDs this month?
(Você comprou algum CD novo este mês?)
Mr. Harrison has traveled to New York twice this year.
(O sr. Harrison viajou para Nova York duas vezes este ano.)

4. Para expressar uma situação que acabou de acontecer. Nestes casos, usamos em conjunto com o *present perfect* a palavra *just*. Veja os exemplos:

Brian's just bought a new car.
(Brian acabou de comprar um carro novo.)
"I'm sorry. Pam and Kate are not in. They've just left", Mike told Susan.

("Sinto muito. Pam e Kate não estão. Elas acabaram de sair", Mike disse para Susan.)

"I've just talked to Sam on the phone", said Linda to a friend.

("Acabei de falar com o Sam no telefone", disse Linda a uma amiga.)

5. O ***present perfect*** também é muito usado com as palavras *ever* ("já", no sentido de alguma vez na vida), *already* ("já", para ações cotidianas), *yet* (com o significado de "ainda", no final de frases negativas), *lately* (ultimamente) e *recently* (recentemente). Confira os exemplos:

I've worked a lot lately.
(Tenho trabalhado muito ultimamente.)
Have you ever been to Japan?
(Você já esteve no Japão?)
Tom and Diane have already had breakfast.
(Tom e Diane já tomaram o café da manhã.)
Have you seen Jack recently?
(Você tem visto o Jack recentemente?)
I haven't read that book yet. Is it any good?
(Ainda não li esse livro. É bom?)

PHRASAL VERBS 2

get off (sair, descer de ônibus, metrô, trem, avião etc., desembarcar)
Ex.: **"We're getting off at the next station", said Gary to a friend on the subway.**
("Vamos descer na próxima estação", disse Gary a um amigo no metrô.)

get on (entrar, subir em ônibus, metrô, trem, avião, etc., embarcar)
Ex.: **"The train is just about to leave, you'd better get on quickly", said the security guard at the platform.**
("O trem está prestes a partir, é melhor vocês entrarem rápido", disse o segurança na plataforma.)

get up (levantar-se da cama)
Ex.: **What time do you usually get up?**
(A que horas você geralmente acorda?)

give up (desistir)
Ex.: **"You've asked Linda out twice and she turned down both your invitations. Why don't you give up?", said Tony to a friend.**
("Você convidou a Linda para sair duas vezes e ela recusou ambos os convites. Por que você não desiste?", disse Tony a um amigo.)

grow up (crescer, referindo-se a pessoas)
Ex.: **Fred was born in England but he grew up in New York.**
(O Fred nasceu na Inglaterra mas cresceu em Nova York.)

hurry up (apressar-se)
Ex.: **"You'd better hurry up or you won't arrive at the airport in time", said Luke to a friend.**
("É melhor você se apressar ou não vai chegar ao aeroporto a tempo", disse Luke a um amigo.)

let down (desapontar, decepcionar)
Ex.: **"Don't worry. I won't let you down", Mark told Greg.**
("Não se preocupe. Não vou te desapontar", Mark disse a Greg.)

look after (cuidar de)
Ex.: **"Can you look after my dog while I'm away?", Rita asked a friend.**
("Você pode cuidar do meu cachorro enquanto eu estiver fora?", Rita pediu a uma amiga.)

look for (procurar)
Ex.: **"I'm looking for my cell phone. Have you seen it around?", Jeff asked a friend.**
("Estou procurando meu celular. Você o viu por aí?", Jeff perguntou a um amigo.)

look forward to (aguardar ansiosamente)

Ex.: **"I'm looking forward to my trip to Miami. I really need to take a few days off and relax a little", said Brian to a coworker.** ("Estou ansioso pela minha viagem a Miami. Preciso mesmo tirar alguns dias de folga e relaxar um pouco", disse Brian a um colega de trabalho.)

PRACTICE SET 28

112 I.   Listen to the questions and circle the right answer.

1.   a) Yes, I think he's a nice guy.
     b) Yes, I saw him last week.
     c) Yes, I know him.

2.   a) For eleven years.
     b) I do. I like to be an architect.
     c) I'd rather be an architect.

3.   a) Yes, I have some Chinese friends.
     b) No, she hasn't.
     c) Yes, she'd like to visit them.

4.   a) Yes, it's today's newspaper.
     b) Yes, I think so.
     c) No, not yet.

5.   a) She's lived there since 2007.
     b) She's living there for about a year.
     c) She's lived with her mom for two years now.

6.   a) She likes to travel abroad.
     b) She went to Boston last year.
     c) She grew up in Denver.

7. a) Yes, we had lunch together.
   b) Yes, he does. He has many friends.
   c) Yes, he'd like to go now.

8. a) My friend has a daughter.
   b) My friend Mike.
   c) My friend is a vet.

9. a) Yes, I'd like to know the news.
   b) Yes, I have.
   c) Yes, she has.

10. a) No, he hasn't done it.
    b) No, I haven't either.
    c) No, they have never read it.

⑊ 113 II. Dictation: listen to the sentences and write them.

1. _____

2. _____

3. _____

4. _____

5. _____

III. Circle the right answer.

1. Why did Stanley give up studying Japanese?
   a) Yes, he gave up.
   b) Because he thought it was too difficult.
   c) No, he talked to them in English, not Japanese.

2. Did Joe grow up in Dallas?
   a) Yes, he was born in Dallas.
   b) No, he wasn't.
   c) No, he grew up in Detroit.

3. Has Mike ever let you down?
   a) No, he's never let me down before.
   b) No, he always gets up early.
   c) Yes, he's already told me what happened.

4. What are you looking for?
   a) Yes, I am.
   b) My cell phone. Have you seen it?
   c) I'm not looking at you.

5. How long has she worked here?
   a) For just about a month.
   b) About twice a month.
   c) Yes, she's worked here before.

IV. Write questions/ phrases for the following answers.

1. _____?
   Yes, Nancy likes to look after children.

2. _____?
   Alice has been married for six years.

3. _____?
   Yes, I've seen that movie before.

4. _____?
   Josh has lived there since 2009.

5. _____?

I'm looking for my car keys. Have you seen them?

V. Fill in the blanks with a phrasal verb from the box. Make sure you use the appropriate verb tense.

grow up	look after	let down	hurry up	look for

1. "I'm _____ my car keys. Do you know where they are?", Magda asked Tim.
2. "_____! We're late for school", Bob told Josh.
3. You can trust James. He's a reliable guy. He won't _____ you _____ .
4. "I was born in Boston, but I _____ in Miami", Gary told Sean.
5. Amanda could be a baby-sitter. She loves to _____ kids.

DIALOGUE 29

It seems like you've been having a great time!

Jeff: Have you been enjoying yourself lately?

Greg: Yeah, I guess I can really say I've been having a lot of fun!

Jeff: Oh, really? You do sound excited. Tell me about it, what have you been doing?

Greg: Well, **for starters** I joined a gym recently so I've been doing regular physical exercise in the past few weeks.

Jeff: No kidding? I've been thinking of doing the same myself. What else have you been doing?

Greg: Well, I always make sure I go out with my friends at least once a week, you know, we go to movies, shows or sometimes just stay at some friend's place and **shoot the breeze** over beer. It's a great way to **unwind**!

Jeff: Oh, yeah, I bet it is. I like doing that too. Have you seen Ted lately?

Greg: Not really. I **lost touch** with him ever since he started **dating** Dana. I guess he's been **going steady** with her, that's what I heard.

Jeff: I heard that too. I haven't talked to him for a while now. What about at work? Have you been doing anything different?

Greg: As a matter of fact I've been given some new tasks and it's been exciting, it's great to have new challenges. I also feel like the opportunity for a promotion is **coming up** soon, so I'm really excited about the **prospects**.

Jeff: Well my friend, it seems like you've been having a great time. My congrats!

▶ Veja a tradução desse diálogo na p. 306.

FOCUS ON VOCABULARY, PHRASES AND EXPRESSIONS 29

For starters = to begin with; initially (para começar)
No kidding = really (sério; "é mesmo")
Shoot the breeze = chat; talk about things of little importance ("bater papo"; "jogar conversa fora")
Undwind/ unwinded/ unwinded = relax (relaxar)
Lose touch = stop communicating with someone (perder contato)
Date/ dated/ dated = spend time with someone you have a romantic relationship with (namorar)
Go steady = date one person exclusively and regularly (namorar firme)
Come up = become available; appear (surgir, aparecer)
Prospects = the possibility of future success (perspectiva)

〰️ 115 **DIALOGUE 29 – COMPREHENSION QUESTIONS**

1. What has Greg been doing lately?
2. Does Jeff also go to a gym?
3. Has Greg been in touch with Ted lately?
4. What's Greg excited about?

APPLIED GRAMMAR 29
present perfect progressive/ continuous

Assim como o **present perfect**, o **present perfect progressive/ continuous** descreve ações que foram iniciadas no passado e ainda não estão concluídas, ou seja, estão em progresso. A diferença básica entre esses dois tempos verbais é que o **present perfect progressive/**

continuous dá uma ênfase maior à continuidade da ação. Compare os dois exemplos abaixo:

Jeff has studied Spanish for two years.
(Jeff estuda espanhol há dois anos.)
Jeff has been studying Spanish for two years.
(Jeff está estudando espanhol há dois anos.)

As duas frases acima têm o mesmo significado, mas a frase no *present perfect progressive/ continuous* dá mais ênfase ao progresso (continuidade) da ação: "está estudando". Veja abaixo mais alguns exemplos com o *present perfect progressive/ continuous*:

I've been working a lot recently.
(Tenho trabalhado muito recentemente.)
How long has Paul been dating Rita?
(Há quanto tempo o Paul namora a Rita?)
What have you been doing lately?
(O que você tem feito ultimamente?)

O *present perfect progressive/ continuous* também é empregado para falar de uma ação que se iniciou no passado e acabou de terminar. Veja os exemplos abaixo:

Have you been smoking?
(Você esteve fumando?)
Your eyes are so red. Have you been crying?
(Seus olhos estão tão vermelhos. Você esteve chorando?)

IDIOMATIC EXPRESSIONS 3

for a change (para variar)
Ex.: **"I'm tired of pizza and sandwiches. Can we have a real meal for a change?", Mark asked his wife.**

("Estou cansado de pizza e sanduíches. Podemos ter uma refeição de verdade para variar?", Mark perguntou à esposa.)

for good (para sempre)
Ex.: **Arnold doesn't plan to be a taxi driver for good.**
(Arnold não planeja ser motorista de táxi para sempre.)

get rid of (livrar-se de)
Ex.: **Why don't you get rid of that old sofa and buy some new furniture?**
(Por que você não se livra daquele sofá velho e compra mobília nova?)

get the hang of (pegar o jeito)
Ex.: **Josh thought he would never learn how to play tennis, but he soon got the hang of it.**(Josh achava que nunca aprenderia a jogar tênis, mas logo pegou o jeito.)

have to do with (ter a ver com)
Ex.: **I have nothing to do with what happened. I swear!**
(Não tenho nada a ver com o que aconteceu. Eu juro!)

in a hurry (com pressa)
Ex.: **Sorry, I can't talk to you now. I'm in a hurry.**
(Desculpe, não posso falar com você agora. Estou com pressa.)

make believe (fazer de conta, fingir)
Ex.: **Children sometimes like to make believe they are superheroes.**
(As crianças às vezes gostam de fazer de conta que são super-heróis.)

make up one's mind (decidir-se)
Ex.: **Anna has not made up her mind yet as to which course she will take at college.**
(A Anna ainda não se decidiu qual curso vai fazer na faculdade.)

once and for all (de uma vez por todas)
Ex.: **Let's try and solve this problem once and for all.**
(Vamos tentar resolver este problema de uma vez por todas.)

ring a bell (fazer lembrar algo, soar familiar)
Ex.: **"Does the name Lola ring a bell?", Sam asked a friend.**
("O nome Lola lhe soa familiar?", Sam perguntou a um amigo)

PRACTICE SET 29

‖ 116 I. Listen to the questions and circle the right answer.

1. a) Since July.
   b) Yes, she's worked there before.
   c) Yes, she has.

2. a) Yes, we'd like to eat that.
   b) I'm sorry, she can't cook.
   c) Good, maybe we can go to that new restaurant downtown.

3. a) No, he wasn't.
   b) No, he hasn't made up his mind yet.
   c) Yes, he'd like to do that.

4. a) She's late for work.
   b) She goes to work by car.
   c) She is all right.

5. a) No, I didn't study last year.
   b) Three times a week.
   c) For about four years.

6. a) Yes, Michael's working at a new company.
   b) Yes, I have.
   c) No, I haven't seen Jeff recently.

7. a) She's been a good friend.
    b) She's not here right now.
    c) I don't know. I haven't seen her in the past few weeks.

8. a) I know it very well.
    b) I know I have to talk to them about it.
    c) I know I should. I'll probably buy a new one next month.

9. a) Yes, he loves to travel.
    b) Yes, I do.
    c) Yes, I've been to the U.S. and Canada.

10. a) She's been there with a friend.
    b) She's been there since October.
    c) She'll probably stay there for good.

🎵 117 II. Dictation: listen to the sentences and write them.

1. _____

2. _____

3. _____

4. _____

5. _____

III. Circle the right answer.

1. Has Jeniffer told you what happened?
   a) Yes, I have.
   b) No, she hasn't.
   c) Yes, she was.

2. How long has Dennis been an accountant?
   a) Since he graduated from university two years ago.
   b) Yes, he's been a very good accountant.
   c) Five times a year.

3. Do you have anything to do with that guy?
   a) I don't know what his name is.
   b) Me? Of course not! I don't even know that guy.
   c) Me? No, I haven't seen Joe lately.

4. Does the name Wallace ring a bell?
   a) Yes, I rang the bell.
   b) No, it doesn't. Who's this guy?
   c) No, he wasn't.

5. How long has Kate been a lawyer?
   a) Yes, she's studying law.
   b) For about five years.
   c) Yes, she has.

IV. Write questions/ phrases for the following answers.

1. _____?
He's been living there since last year.

2. _____?
No, Fred hasn't made up his mind yet.

3. _____?
Carla is in a hurry because she's late for work.

4. _____?
Jeff has been a teacher for about ten years.

5. _____?

No, Sarah doesn't have any brothers or sisters. She's an only child.

V. Fill in the blanks with an idiomatic expression from the box.

> **makes up his mind get the hang of**
> **for a change in a hurry had nothing to do with**

1. "We always go to the movies on Saturday. Why don't we do something different _____?
2. "I'm telling you the truth. I _____ what happened", Rick told Tony.
3. "I can't talk to you right now. I'm _____ . I'll call you later", said Nick to a friend.
4. Steve rarely changes his mind once he _____ about something.
5. "Don't worry, you'll soon _____ that new computer program", Ron told Jack.

LESSON 30

118 **DIALOGUE 30**
The finals are looming!

Ron: Did you get a chance to talk to Steve?
Frank: No, I didn't. He'd already left home when I **stopped by** his place, but I'll give him a call later, don't worry.
Ron: Good. I just want to make sure we get organized and start this new **assignment ASAP**.
Frank: Sure, but we have **plenty of** time. We're supposed to **hand** it **in** by September, 10th, right?
Ron: Yeah, but that's not all we have to worry about. The **finals** are **looming**, remember?
Frank: I know, I'll probably have to **burn the midnight oil** so I can **catch up** with my notes. By the way, I was wondering if you could give me some help with math.
Ron: No problem. Just let me know in advance when you want to meet.
Frank: Thanks Ron! So, what are you doing tonight?
Ron: No plans yet. How about you?
Frank: I'm not sure, but I might go downtown and catch an action movie or something. Do you **wanna come along**?
Ron: I don't think so, I'll probably **hit the sack** early tonight. I need to catch up on my sleep!

▶ Veja a tradução desse diálogo na p. 307.

FOCUS ON VOCABULARY, PHRASES AND EXPRESSIONS 30

Stop by = visit someone for a short time (fazer uma visita breve a alguém)

Assignment = work that you must do as part of a course; task (trabalho escolar; tarefa)

ASAP = as soon as possible (assim que possível)

Plenty of = a lot of (bastante)

Hand in = submit (entregar)

Finals = final exams (exames finais)

Loom/ loomed/ loomed = appear, especially when seeming threatening (aproximar-se, surgir ameaçadoramente)

Burn the midnight oil = stay up late studying or working (ficar estudando ou trabalhando até tarde)

Catch up = do what needs to be done in order to be up to date ("colocar em dia")

Wanna = want to (querer)

Come along = go somewhere with someone (ir junto)

Hit the sack = go to sleep (ir dormir)

ıı|ı|ı 119 **DIALOGUE 30 – COMPREHENSION QUESTIONS**

1. Why couldn't Frank talk to Steve?
2. What's Ron worried about?
3. What's Frank doing tonight?
4. Why does Ron want to go to bed early tonight?

APPLIED GRAMMAR 30
past perfect

O ***past perfect*** descreve uma ação que aconteceu antes de outra no passado. A estrutura do ***past perfect*** é formada pelo verbo *had* em conjunto com o particípio passado dos verbos principais. (Veja a terceira coluna na lista de verbos principais na p. 281.) Observe a seguinte sentença: Quando Amanda chegou em casa, o Fred já tinha saído. Observe que primeiro Fred saiu e depois Amanda chegou, ou seja, a ação de Fred sair aconteceu antes da ação de chegar de Amanda, portanto antes do tempo passado. A frase equivalente em inglês seria: When Amanda got home Paul had already left. Veja os outros exemplos abaixo:

Carol had done the dishes by the time her mother came home.
(Carol tinha lavado os pratos quando sua mãe chegou em casa.)
Jim had already taken a shower when we phoned him.
(Jim já tinha tomado banho quando ligamos para ele.)
Jason had never seen a roller coaster before he went to Disney World.
(Jason nunca tinha visto uma montanha-russa antes de ir ao Disney World.)
I had already had dinner when I met Chuck and Sam.
(Eu já tinha jantado quando encontrei o Chuck e o Sam.)

O *past perfect progressive/ continuous* é mais formal e por isso mesmo menos empregado na conversação cotidiana. É usado para enfatizar por quanto tempo uma ação aconteceu antes de outra ocorrer. A estrutura do *past perfect progressive/ continuous* é formada pelo verbo *had* em conjunto com *been* e o verbo principal no gerúndio. Veja os exemplos abaixo:

Harry had been watching TV for about half an hour when Susan arrived.
(Harry estava assistindo TV havia aproximadamente meia hora quando Susan chegou.)
How long had you been working in the company when you were promoted?
(Há quanto tempo você vinha trabalhando na empresa quando foi promovido?)
They had been living in Montreal for five years when they moved to Boston.
(Eles estavam morando em Montreal havia cinco anos quando se mudaram para Boston.)

PHRASAL VERBS 3

look like (parecer-se com)
Ex.: **Melissa looks like her mother.**
(A Melissa parece-se com a mãe.)

pick up (pegar alguém, especialmente de carro)
Ex.: **"Can you pick me up at the airport tomorrow?", Sally asked her mother.**
("Você pode me pegar no aeroporto amanhã?", Sally perguntou à mãe.)

show up (chegar, aparecer)
Ex.: **Nick didn't show up for class today.**
(Nick não apareceu para a aula hoje.)

take off (tirar roupas, sapatos etc.; decolar)
Ex.: **Why don't you take off your jacket? It's hot in here.**
(Por que você não tira a jaqueta? Está quente aqui dentro.)
Ex.: **"Did your plane take off on schedule?", Jerry asked a friend.**
("O seu avião decolou no horário previsto?", Jerry perguntou a um amigo.)

throw away (jogar fora)
Ex.: **That old armchair looks awful. Why don't you throw it away?**
(Aquela poltrona velha está com uma aparência horrível. Por que você não a joga fora?)

try on (experimentar, provar roupas, calçados etc.)
Ex.: **"This shirt is too tight. Can I try on a larger size please?", Jeff asked the clerk at the store.**
("Esta camisa está apertada demais. Posso experimentar um número maior por favor?", Jeff pediu ao atendente na loja.)

turn on (ligar rádio, TV, computador etc.; acender a luz)
Ex.: **Mike always turns on his computer as soon as he arrives at the office in the morning.**

(Mike sempre liga o computador assim que chega ao escritório de manhã.)

turn off (desligar TV, rádio, computador; apagar a luz)
Ex.: **"Can you please turn off the TV honey? I'm really tired and I need to sleep", Greg asked his wife.**
(Você pode, por favor, desligar a TV, querida? Estou muito cansado e preciso dormir.)

turn down (recusar, rejeitar)
Ex.: **"I can't believe Jack turned down such a good job offer!", said Clive to his friends.**
("Não acredito que o Jack recusou uma oferta de emprego tão boa", disse Clive aos amigos.)

work out (fazer exercício físico, "malhar")
Ex.: **"You look like you're in shape. How often do you work out at the gym?", Sam asked Tyler.**
("Você parece estar em boa forma. Com que frequência você malha na academia?", Sam perguntou a Tyler.)

PRACTICE SET 30

◀|||▶ 120 I. Listen to the questions and circle the right answer.

1. a) Yes, she had.
    b) No, I hadn't.
    c) Yes, I have.

2. a) Yes, I like to live in Europe.
    b) For about eight years.
    c) Yes, I had.

3. a) No, she doesn't see her mother very often.
    b) Yes, she talks to her father every day.
    c) No, she looks like her father.

4. a) Yes, he can drive really well.
   b) Sure, what time?
   c) Yes, I can pick them up at the airport later.

5. a) Yes, I talked to him yesterday.
   b) Three times a week.
   c) Yes, I think he's a nice guy.

6. a) No, he isn't.
   b) No, she prefers fish.
   c) No, she hasn't.

7. a) Sure, I'll get a smaller one for you.
   b) Yes, I can.
   c) Sure you can help me.

8. a) Yes, I read the newspaper yesterday.
   b) No, I prefer to read magazines.
   c) No, I didn't. Do you want to read it?

9. a) He took off his coat because he was feeling hot.
   b) It took off at half past eleven.
   c) It always takes off on time.

10. a) Sure!
    b) Yes, I watch the news every night.
    c) I'd rather watch an action movie.

ılıllı 121 II. Dictation: listen to the sentences and write them.

1. _____

2. _____

3. _____

4. _____

5. _____

III. Circle the right answer.

1. What time did he show up at the party?
    a) It's at nine o'clock.
    b) It starts later today.
    c) At about midnight.

2. Can you please take off your shoes before you enter the house?
    a) Sure, I'll do that, don't worry.
    b) Yes, he likes to take off his shoes when he arrives home at night.
    c) Yes, I'll buy new shoes tomorrow.

3. How often do you work out at the gym?
    a) I get up early and go to the gym.
    b) About three times a week.
    c) I'd rather go to the gym every day.

4. Can you pick me up at the airport?
    a) Sure you can.
    b) Sure I do.
    c) Sure, what time does your flight get in?

5. Did the plane take off on schedule?
    a) Yes, it would.
    b) No, there was a little delay.
    c) No, he didn't miss the plane.

IV. Write questions/ phrases for the following answers.

1. _____?
   No, Carol doesn't look like her father, she looks like her mother.

2. _____?
   Sure, I'll get a larger size for you.

3. _____?
   She's twenty-seven years old.

4. _____?
   Brian had been working there for four years when he was promoted.

5. _____?
   No, Dave didn't show up for class today.

V. Fill in the blanks with a phrasal verb from the box. Make sure you use the appropriate verb tense.

show up	pick up	turn off	look like	take off

1. Don't forget to _____ the lights before you leave.
2. Does Cynthia _____ her mother or her father?
3. Japanese people usually _____ their shoes before entering their houses.
4. "Can you _____ me _____ at school tonight?", Sandra asked her father.
5. David _____ late for work today because his car broke down.

USOS DO VERBO *GET*

O verbo ***get/got/gotten*** pode assumir vários significados e ser usado em diversos contextos. Esta seção apresenta os significados mais usuais desse verbo na conversação cotidiana. É importante lembrar que, além dos significados apresentados abaixo, muitos outros podem ser formados a partir do uso do verbo ***get*** em conjunto com preposições.

1. GET = OBTAIN: CONSEGUIR; ARRANJAR; ARRUMAR

Can you get me a copy of this document?
Você pode me arranjar uma cópia deste documento?

Where did you get those samples?
Onde você arrumou aquelas amostras?

How did Barry get Elaine's e-mail address?
Como o Barry conseguiu o endereço de e-mail da Elaine?

2. GET = RECEIVE: RECEBER

I got an e-mail from an old friend this morning.
Recebi um e-mail de um velho amigo hoje de manhã.

Did you get the post-card I sent you from Prague?
Você recebeu o cartão-postal que te enviei de Praga?

Rachel likes to get presents, doesn't she?
A Rachel gosta de ganhar presentes, não gosta?

3. GET = ARRIVE: CHEGAR

Tony got home very late last night.
O Tony chegou em casa muito tarde ontem à noite.

How long did it take you to get to the airport?
Quanto tempo você levou para chegar ao aeroporto?

What time do you usually get to the office?
A que horas você normalmente chega ao escritório?

4. GET = BECOME: TORNAR-SE; FICAR (NO SENTIDO DE MUDANÇA DE ESTADO OU SITUAÇÃO)

It's getting hot in here. Can you please turn on the air-conditioner?
Está ficando quente aqui dentro. Você pode, por favor, ligar o ar-condicionado?

Don't you get tired after a hard day's work?
Você não fica cansado depois de um dia duro de trabalho?

I think we should get going. It's getting dark.
Acho que devemos ir. Está ficando escuro.

5. GET = EARN: GANHAR (DINHEIRO, SALÁRIO)

Does Josh get a good salary working for that travel agency?
O Josh ganha um bom salário trabalhando para aquela agência de viagens?

All the employees got a good bonus as they reached the sales goals for the quarter.
Todos os funcionários ganharam um bom bônus porque conseguiram alcançar as metas de vendas do trimestre.

Sally is not getting enough money to pay her bills so she's looking for another job.
A Sally não está conseguindo ganhar dinheiro suficiente para pagar suas contas então está procurando um outro emprego.

6. **GET = BUY**: COMPRAR

Where did you get those shoes? They're really cool.
Onde você comprou esses sapatos? Eles são muito legais.

That's a really nice leather jacket. Where did you get it?
Essa jaqueta de couro é bonita mesmo. Onde você a comprou?

"Don't forget to get a present for Rita's birthday tomorrow!", Bill told a friend.
"Não se esqueça de comprar um presente para o aniversário da Rita amanhã!", Bill disse a um amigo.

7. **GET = UNDERSTAND**: ENTENDER

Why did he do that? I don't get it!
Por que ele fez aquilo? Eu não entendo!

Carol didn't get the joke when I told her for the first time.
A Carol não entendeu a piada quando eu contei para ela pela primeira vez.

That's what I wanted to tell you. Got it?
É o que eu queria te dizer. Entendeu?

8. **GET = ANSWER (THE PHONE, THE DOOR)**: ATENDER (O TELEFONE, A PORTA)

"Can you get the phone honey? I'm busy in the kitchen", Rita told her husband.
"Você pode atender o telefone querido? Estou ocupada na cozinha", Rita disse ao marido.

"I'll get it", said Ron to his wife as the phone rang.
"Eu atendo", disse Ron à esposa quando o telefone tocou.

"The bell is ringing. Can you get the door, please?", Diane asked Monica.
"A campainha está tocando. Você pode atender a porta, por favor?", Diane pediu a Monica.

9. **GET = FETCH:** IR BUSCAR; PEGAR ALGUÉM OU ALGUMA COISA

Do you want me to get you some coffee or anything?
Você quer que eu pegue um café para você ou alguma coisa?

Can you get the kids from school at noon today?
Você pode ir buscar as crianças na escola ao meio-dia hoje?

I'll get a glass of water. Would you like some?
Vou pegar um copo d'água. Você quer um?

10. **GET = TAKE (THE BUS, THE TRAIN, THE SUBWAY ETC.):** PEGAR (O ÔNIBUS, O TREM, O METRÔ ETC.)

What time will we arrive in Boston if we get the 7 a.m. train?
A que horas chegaremos a Boston se pegarmos o trem das 7 horas?

Why don't we get the subway on main street? I think it'll be faster.
Por que não pegamos o metrô na rua principal? Acho que vai ser mais rápido.

11. **GET = CATCH (A COLD, THE FLU, A DISEASE ETC.):** PEGAR (UM RESFRIADO, UMA GRIPE, UMA DOENÇA ETC.)

Bob got the flu. That's why he didn't come to school today.
O Bob pegou gripe. É por isso que ele não veio à escola hoje.

Don't worry! You can't get this disease from shaking hands with people.

Não se preocupe! Não se pega esta doença apertando as mãos das pessoas.

12. GET = PICK UP (TV CHANNELS, RADIO SIGNALS ETC.): SINTONIZAR, "PEGAR" (CANAIS DE TV, SINAIS DE RÁDIO ETC.)

Can you get the new sports channel where you live?
Você consegue pegar o novo canal de esportes onde você mora?

PRINCIPAIS VERBOS

A lista abaixo inclui os verbos principais (regulares e irregulares) mais utilizados na conversação cotidiana e seus significados. Os verbos regulares são aqueles cujo passado e particípio passado terminam em *ed*. Por exemplo: *to work/ worked/ worked* (trabalhar). Já os verbos irregulares são aqueles que possuem uma formação especial para o passado e particípio passado. Por exemplo: *to go/ went/ gone* (ir).

Infinitivo	Passado	Particípio	Significado
to agree	**agreed**	**agreed**	concordar
to answer	**answered**	**answered**	responder; atender (telefone, campainha)
to apply	**applied**	**applied**	candidatar-se a um emprego, vaga, bolsa de estudos etc. (apply for a job, position, scholarship etc.)
to arrive	**arrived**	**arrived**	chegar
to ask	**asked**	**asked**	pedir; perguntar
to attend	**attended**	**attended**	assistir (a uma aula, uma palestra etc.); participar (de uma reunião etc.)
to avoid	**avoided**	**avoided**	evitar
to be	**was/ were**	**been**	ser; estar (veja as conjugações desse verbo nas p. 18, 53)
to become	**became**	**become**	tornar-se
to begin	**began**	**begun**	começar
to believe	**believed**	**believed**	acreditar
to bet	**bet**	**bet**	apostar
to bite	**bit**	**bitten**	morder
to bleed	**bled**	**bled**	sangrar
to blow	**blew**	**blown**	soprar; assoprar
to borrow	**borrowed**	**borrowed**	pedir emprestado; pegar emprestado

to break	broke	broken	quebrar
to bring	brought	brought	trazer
to brush	brushed	brushed	escovar (dentes, cabelo)
to build	built	built	construir
to burn	burned	burned	queimar
to buy	bought	bought	comprar
to call	called	called	chamar; ligar; telefonar
to catch	caught	caught	apanhar; pegar (ônibus, metrô, avião)
to change	changed	changed	mudar; trocar
to choose	chose	chosen	escolher
to clean	cleaned	cleaned	limpar
to close	closed	closed	fechar
to come	came	come	vir
to complain	complained	complained	reclamar; queixar-se
to cook	cooked	cooked	cozinhar
to cost	cost	cost	custar
to count	counted	counted	contar (números, dinheiro etc.)
to cut	cut	cut	cortar
to dance	danced	danced	dançar
to date	dated	dated	namorar
to decide	decided	decided	decidir
to deserve	deserved	deserved	merecer
to die	died	died	morrer
to disturb	disturbed	disturbed	perturbar; incomodar
to do	did	done	fazer
to dream	dreamed	dreamed	sonhar
to drink	drank	drunk	beber
to drive	drove	driven	dirigir
to earn	earned	earned	ganhar (salário)
to eat	ate	eaten	comer
to e-mail	e-mailed	e-mailed	enviar por e-mail; mandar um e-mail
to enjoy	enjoyed	enjoyed	gostar de; divertir-se (enjoy oneself)
to expect	expected	expected	esperar; ter expectativa

to explain	explained	explained	explicar
to fall	fell	fallen	cair
to feed	fed	fed	alimentar
to feel	felt	felt	sentir
to fight	fought	fought	brigar; lutar
to find	found	found	achar; encontrar
to finish	finished	finished	terminar; acabar; concluir
to fix	fixed	fixed	consertar; preparar uma refeição (fix a meal)
to fly	flew	flown	voar; viajar de avião; pilotar (avião, helicóptero)
to forget	forgot	forgotten	esquecer
to forgive	forgave	forgiven	perdoar
to forward	forwarded	forwarded	enviar; remeter; encaminhar um e-mail (forward an e-mail)
to found	founded	founded	fundar
to freeze	froze	frozen	congelar
to get	got	gotten	conseguir; obter; adquirir; comprar; receber; ganhar; chegar; pegar; ir buscar; tornar-se (veja Usos do verbo *get*, p. 275)
to give	gave	given	dar
to go	went	gone	ir
to grow	grew	grown	crescer
to guess	guessed	guessed	achar; supor; adivinhar
to hang	hung	hung	pendurar
to happen	happened	happened	acontecer
to hate	hated	hated	odiar
to have	had	had	ter
to hear	heard	heard	ouvir
to help	helped	helped	ajudar
to hide	hid	hidden	esconder
to hire	hired	hired	contratar
to hit	hit	hit	bater em (agredir; chocar-se com); atingir

to hold	held	held	segurar; abraçar
to hope	hoped	hoped	esperar; ter esperança (que)
to hurt	hurt	hurt	machucar; ferir
to invite	invited	invited	convidar
to intend	intended	intended	pretender
to introduce	introduced	introduced	apresentar (pessoas); expor, apresentar (uma ideia, um assunto)
to join	joined	joined	juntar(-se); entrar, associar-se (a clube, academia etc.)
to keep	kept	kept	manter; ficar com; guardar
to know	knew	known	saber; conhecer
to lay	laid	laid	pôr; colocar; botar (ovos)
to lead	led	led	levar (conduzir); liderar
to learn	learned	learned	aprender; tomar conhecimento
to leave	left	left	sair; partir; deixar
to lend	lent	lent	emprestar
to let	let	let	deixar (permitir)
to lie	lied	lied	mentir
to lie	lay	lain	deitar-se
to like	liked	liked	gostar de
to listen	listened	listened	escutar
to live	lived	lived	viver; morar
to look	looked	looked	parecer; olhar para (look at); procurar (look for)
to lose	lost	lost	perder
to love	loved	loved	amar; adorar
to make	made	made	fazer; construir; fabricar; produzir
to mean	meant	meant	significar; querer dizer; ter a intenção de
to meet	met	met	encontrar pessoas; conhecer pessoas pela primeira vez
to mind	minded	minded	importar-se; incomodar-se com

to miss	missed	missed	perder (uma aula, uma reunião, o ônibus, uma oportunidade); sentir saudade ou falta de; errar, não acertar (um alvo etc.)
to move	moved	moved	mudar de casa; movimentar(-se); mexer
to open	opened	opened	abrir
to order	ordered	ordered	fazer o pedido (em restaurante, etc.)
to owe	owed	owed	dever (dinheiro, um favor)
to own	owned	owned	possuir; ter
to park	parked	parked	estacionar
to pay	paid	paid	pagar
to plan	planned	planned	planejar
to play	played	played	jogar (esportes); tocar (instrumentos musicais); brincar
to prefer	preferred	preferred	preferir
to pretend	pretended	pretended	fingir; fazer de conta
to prevent	prevented	prevented	impedir; evitar
to pull	pulled	pulled	puxar
to push	pushed	pushed	empurrar; apertar (botão, tecla)
to put	put	put	pôr; colocar
to quit	quit	quit	parar; largar
to rain	rained	rained	chover
to reach	reached	reached	entrar em contato com; alcançar; localizar
to read	read	read	ler
to receive	received	received	receber
to relax	relaxed	relaxed	relaxar; descansar; descontrair-se
to remember	remembered	remembered	lembrar-se de
to remind	reminded	reminded	fazer alguém lembrar de algo
to rent	rented	rented	alugar
to rest	rested	rested	descansar

to ride	rode	ridden	andar (de bicicleta, de moto, a cavalo etc.); andar (como passageiro de carro, ônibus etc.)
to ring	rang	rung	tocar (campainha, sino)
to run	ran	run	correr
to save	saved	saved	salvar; economizar
to say	said	said	dizer
to see	saw	seen	ver
to seem	seemed	seemed	parecer
to sell	sold	sold	vender
to send	sent	sent	enviar
to shake	shook	shaken	tremer; sacudir; abalar; apertar a mão (shake hands)
to share	shared	shared	dividir; compartilhar
to shave	shaved	shaved	fazer a barba; raspar
to shine	shone	shone	brilhar
to shoot	shot	shot	atirar (com arma de fogo); disparar
to show	showed	showed	mostrar; apresentar; exibir; demonstar
to shrink	shrank	shrunk	encolher
to shut	shut	shut	fechar
to sing	sang	sung	cantar
to sink	sank	sunk	afundar
to sit	sat	sat	sentar
to sleep	slept	slept	dormir
to smell	smelled	smelled	cheirar; sentir cheiro
to sneeze	sneezed	sneezed	espirrar
to snow	snowed	snowed	nevar
to sound	sounded	sounded	soar; parecer
to speak	spoke	spoken	falar
to spell	spelled	spelled	soletrar
to spend	spent	spent	gastar (dinheiro); passar (tempo, férias)
to spill	spilled	spilled	derramar
to spit	spat/ spit	spat/ spit	cuspir

to spoil	spoiled	spoiled	estragar(-se); mimar (uma criança)
to stand	stood	stood	estar/ ficar em pé; aguentar; tolerar; suportar
to start	started	started	começar; iniciar
to stay	stayed	stayed	ficar; permanecer
to steal	stole	stolen	roubar
to study	studied	studied	estudar
to swear	swore	sworn	jurar; xingar
to sweat	sweat	sweat	suar; transpirar
to swim	swam	swum	nadar
to take	took	taken	pegar (algum objeto); tomar (ônibus, táxi etc.); levar (alguém a algum lugar); tomar (remédio); tomar (um banho)
to talk	talked	talked	conversar
to teach	taught	taught	ensinar
to tell	told	told	contar; dizer
to think	thought	thought	pensar; achar
to throw	threw	thrown	atirar; arremessar; jogar
to travel	traveled	traveled	viajar
to try	tried	tried	tentar
to type	typed	typed	digitar
to understand	understood	understood	entender
to use	used	used	usar
to wait	waited	waited	esperar
to wake	woke	woken	despertar; acordar
to walk	walked	walked	andar
to want	wanted	wanted	querer
to wash	washed	washed	lavar
to watch	watched	watched	observar; assistir (TV, um jogo etc.)
to wear	wore	worn	usar (roupas, calçados, batom, brinco etc.)
to win	won	won	ganhar; vencer
to wonder	wondered	wondered	querer saber; perguntar-se

to work	worked	worked	trabalhar; funcionar
to worry	worried	worried	preocupar-se
to write	wrote	written	escrever

TRADUÇÃO DOS DIÁLOGOS

DIÁLOGO 1
O que você faz?

Brian: Prazer em conhecê-la Jane!
Jane: O prazer é todo meu.
Brian: E então, o que você faz?
Jane: Eu? Sou veterinária.
Brian: Sério? Você deve adorar os animais.
Jane: Adoro mesmo. Eu tenho dois cachorros e três passarinhos. E você? Você tem algum animal de estimação?
Brian: Não, não tenho tempo para cuidar deles.
Jane: Entendo. Nossa, já é quase meio-dia, desculpe, estou atrasada para o trabalho, tenho que ir. Te vejo por aí!
Brian: Claro, Jane. Se cuida!

DIÁLOGO 2
Por que não vamos acampar para variar?

Rita: Por que não fazemos alguma coisa diferente no próximo final de semana?
Joe: Claro, querida, em que você estava pensando?
Rita: Sei lá, talvez nós pudéssemos ir acampar para variar.
Joe: Parece emocionante. Ei, tive uma ideia. Por que você não liga para a sua amiga Karen e vê se ela e o Arnold gostariam de ir conosco? Você não acha que seria muito mais divertido?
Rita: Com certeza. Nós podíamos ir em apenas um carro e dividir as despesas. Olha, acho que vamos precisar comprar uma barraca nova.
Joe: Concordo, a nossa está muito velha e acho que é pequena demais. Não consigo nem lembrar a última vez que a usamos!
Rita: Eu também não! Legal, vou ligar para a Karen. Espero que eles possam se juntar a nós. Puxa, estou ansiosa pelo nosso final de semana!
Joe: Eu também, querida!

DIÁLOGO 3
O que o seu pai faz?

Mel: O que o seu pai faz?
Josh: Meu pai? Ele é advogado.
Mel: É mesmo? Ele trabalha em um escritório na cidade?
Josh: Trabalha, ele vai de metrô para o trabalho todos os dias.
Mel: Sei, e você só tem uma irmã, né?
Josh: Isso mesmo, a Helen, ela é mais jovem do que eu.
Mel: Quantos anos ela tem?
Josh: Ela acabou de fazer quinze anos.
Mel: Ela tem namorado?
Josh: Bom, não que eu saiba!

DIÁLOGO 4
Você tem uma memória ótima!

Tyler: Esse carro estacionado aí na frente é do seu pai?
Neil: Não, esse carro é do meu tio. Meu pai teve um problema com o carro e pegou o carro do irmão dele emprestado.
Tyler: Ah, eu pensei que talvez o seu pai tivesse comprado um outro carro. A propósito, eu vi sua irmã na escola hoje de manhã.
Neil: Viu?
Tyler: Vi, ela estava conversando com a Kate durante o intervalo.
Neil: Ah, sim, a Kate é uma das melhores amigas dela. Elas se dão muito bem. Você se lembra daqueles caras que encontramos no parque ontem?
Tyler: Claro.
Neil: Eu estava tentando lembrar os nomes deles.
Tyler: Josh e Oliver?
Neil: Isso mesmo! Você tem uma memória ótima!
Tyler: Mas o que tem eles? Por que você estava tentando lembrar os nomes deles?
Neil: Bom, eu acho que eles vão jogar no nosso time de basquete. Eu vi o treinador conversando com eles no ginásio hoje de manhã. É por isso!

DIÁLOGO 5
Você perdeu uma festa e tanto!

Sarah: E então, como foi a festa ontem à noite?
Dustin: Ótima, me diverti bastante.
Sarah: O Josh apareceu com a namorada nova?
Dustin: Ele foi, mas chegou muito tarde. Nós todos achávamos que ele não vinha mais. A propósito, sua amiga Dana também estava lá.
Sarah: Estava? Que pena que eu não pude ir!
Dustin: É, você perdeu uma festa e tanto, mas não se preocupe, nós estamos planejando organizar uma outra festa em breve.
Sarah: Ótimo! Me mantenha informada.
Dustin: Claro! Espero que você possa vir da próxima vez.

DIÁLOGO 6
É ótimo voltar para casa!

James: É ótimo voltar para casa!
Liz: Oi, querido. Como foi seu dia?
James: Muito bom! O que você está fazendo na cozinha, querida?
Liz: Estou fazendo um bolo de morango, seu favorito!
James: Oba, já estou ficando com água na boca. Onde estão a Pamella e o Jake?
Liz: A Pamella está tomando banho. Ela vai sair com o namorado hoje à noite. O Jake deve estar escutando música no quarto dele.
James: Bom, eu vou lá em cima falar um oi para ele. Na verdade, eu quero falar com ele sobre uma coisa.
Liz: Agora fiquei curiosa, qual é o assunto?
James: Ah, nada de importante! Eu comprei ingressos para o jogo de hóquei na sexta à noite.
Liz: O Jake vai adorar!
James: Eu sei!

DIÁLOGO 7
Uma festa de aniversário surpresa

Bill: Eu vi um cara muito parecido com você ontem!

Harry: Onde foi isso?

Bill: No shopping Bayshore, por volta das 16:00.

Harry: Deve ter sido eu. Eu estive lá à tarde. Estava comprando tênis. E você? O que estava fazendo no shopping ontem?

Bill: Eu fui comprar um presente para a Barbara. Hoje é o aniversário dela. A propósito, eu tentei entrar em contato com você ontem, eu liguei duas vezes, mas não deixei recado.

Harry: Eu me lembro que estava tomando banho quando o telefone tocou ontem, deve ter sido você, desculpe! Sobre o que você queria falar comigo?

Bill: Nós estamos planejando uma festa surpresa para a Barbara hoje à noite e eu queria saber se você gostaria de dar um pulo lá em casa e se juntar a nós.

Harry: Legal! A Barbara vai adora isso!

Bill: Eu realmente espero que sim. Eu cuidei de todos os preparativos e espero que tudo dê certo.

Harry: Vai dar, não se preocupe. A que horas eu devo aparecer então?

Bill: Por volta das 18:00 está ótimo. A Barbara vai chegar um pouco mais tarde.

Harry: Ótimo, vou estar lá antes das 18:00. E Bill?

Bill: O quê?

Harry: Muito obrigado por me convidar!

DIÁLOGO 8
Por que não damos uma festa?

Harry: Eu ouvi que a Jane não vai mais à praia conosco na próxima semana.

Sam: É, acho que ela vai estar muito ocupada cuidando do sobrinho. Tenho certeza que vamos sentir a falta dela, mas o que podemos fazer?

Harry: Bom talvez possamos parar para vê-la quando voltarmos.

Sam: Muito bom! Vamos fazer isso.

Harry: Claro. Escuta, nós vamos para a faculdade no próximo ano e eu estava pensando, por que não damos uma festa para comemorar?

Sam: É uma ótima ideia, Harry! Talvez pudesse ser em dezembro? O que você acha?

Harry: Ótimo! Vai ser uma boa oportunidade de ver todos os nossos colegas da escola novamente antes de nos mudarmos. Vou falar com o Steve, ele é muito bom em organizar eventos.

Sam: Tenho certeza que ele vai ficar animado com a festa. Me avise se vocês dois tiverem alguma ideia interessante.

Harry: Claro, Sam! Pode deixar.

DIÁLOGO 9
Você gostaria de ver um filme?

Mike: E então, o que você faria se estivesse no lugar dele?

Ray: Para ser sincero com você eu não tenho a mínima ideia.

Mike: Eu sei o que você quer dizer. Eu também sinto o mesmo. Tenho certeza de uma coisa, nunca gostaria de passar por uma experiência como essa.

Ray: É, é horrível.

Mike: Vou até a cozinha, você quer água ou café?

Ray: Não, obrigado. Ei, estava pensando, você não vai fazer nada hoje à noite, vai?

Mike: Não, por quê?

Ray: Você gostaria de ver um filme?

Mike: Boa ideia. Você sabe o que está passando no shopping Arcade?

Ray: Parece que tem um novo filme de ação, podemos dar uma olhada no site do shopping.

Mike: Ótimo, talvez também possamos ir comer alguma coisa na nova lanchonete do shopping.

Ray: Por mim tudo bem!

DIÁLOGO 10
Você tem feito regime?

Ben: Oi Rod, há quanto tempo a gente não se vê. Como você está?

Rod: Muito bem. Ei, você parece mais magro do que a última vez que te vi. Você tem feito regime?

Ben: Eu? Ah, não! Eu tenho malhado na academia três vezes por semana, é por isso, você está certo, eu realmente era mais gordo.

Rod: Puxa, você deve se sentir muito mais saudável agora, né?

Ben: Me sinto mesmo, é ótimo estar em forma. E então, ouvi falar que você se mudou para um apartamento maior, né? Como é o lugar novo?

Rod: Muito bom. Minha família está realmente contente com o apartamento novo, mais espaçoso e comfortável do que o anterior. Nós temos uma sala de estar maior e mais um dormitório agora, e isso faz toda a diferença.

Ben: Ótimo, você parece mesmo feliz. E a vizinhança, é mais silenciosa?

Rod: É sim, e a coisa boa é que temos ótimos vizinhos.

Ben: Puxa, parece que vocês mudaram para o lugar certo. Você também está morando mais perto da empresa agora, não está?

Rod: Estou sim. Consigo chegar mais rápido ao trabalho agora. Antes eu demorava por volta de meia hora, mas agora eu só levo uns quinze minutos.

Ben: Que bom!

DIÁLOGO 11
Como está a escola?

Jeff: Oi Brian, como foi o filme ontem à noite?

Brian: Uma droga!

Jeff: É mesmo?

Brian: É, acho que eu poderia dizer que foi o pior filme que já vi na minha vida.

Jeff: Puxa, estou surpreso! Esse filme recebeu uma crítica ótima. Alguns atores muito bons trabalham nele, não é?

Brian: É verdade, mas o enredo é horrível, bom, não quero nem falar sobre isso, é uma perda de tempo.

Jeff: Ok. E como está a escola?

Brian: Até agora tudo bem. Acho que poderia dizer que estou indo bem, a única coisa é que estou tendo dificuldade com física, é a matéria mais difícil para mim.

Jeff: Ah é? E qual é a matéria mais fácil para você?

Brian: Geografia, minha matéria preferida.

Jeff: A matéria mais difícil para mim sempre foi matemática, mas acho que estou me acostumando agora.

Brian: Que bom! Acho que não podemos reclamar, como você sabe nós estudamos em uma escola ótima e temos alguns dos melhores professores lá.

Jeff: É verdade!

DIÁLOGO 12
Você é um colega de classe sensacional!

Paul: O que é isso no seu rosto?

Daniel: Ah, nada, eu me cortei fazendo a barba hoje de manhã.

Paul: Ok, mas dê uma olhada no espelho de novo, isso está horrível, você deveria fazer algo a respeito.

Daniel: Não se preocupe! Isso já aconteceu antes, eu sou péssimo para fazer barba, sabe como é, né?

Paul: Tudo bem! Escuta, o que você acha de nos encontrarmos amanhã para terminar o trabalho de história?

Daniel: Não há necessidade disso.

Paul: Não há necessidade? Você está brincando comigo?

Daniel: Não, eu já fiz o trabalho, é por isso!

Paul: Você quer dizer que terminou tudo sozinho?

Daniel: Isso mesmo, acho que estava inspirado ontem à noite, eu tive umas ideias interessantes e as anotei. Só preciso passar o texto a limpo, mas consigo fazer isso rapidinho, então relaxa, camarada!

Paul: Puxa, Dan, o que eu posso dizer? Você é um colega de classe sensacional!

DIÁLOGO 13
Ela é bonitinha, não é?

Bill: Você não está namorando ninguém no momento, está?

Steve: Não, não estou não. E você?

Bill: Bom, eu sai com uma garota algumas vezes, mas não tenho certeza se combinamos bem juntos.

Steve: Ah é? Qual é o nome dela?

Bill: Sarah.

Steve: Sarah? Você está falando da garota que trabalha no Ritz Café?

Bill: Isso mesmo! Ela é bonitinha, não é?

Steve: Acho que sim, mas ela não faz o meu tipo.

Bill: Entendo. Ei, você não está a fim de ir a uma boate hoje à noite? Você deve gostar de dançar, não gosta?

Steve: É, parece uma ótima ideia. Eu realmente não me importaria de conferir as gatas lá, se você me entende.

Bill: Certo! Que tal se eu te pegar às 21h?

Steve: Combinado! Te vejo às 21h então, cara!

DIÁLOGO 14
Ouvi falar que você foi para a Disney

Tony: Ei Neil, há quanto tempo. Como você está?

Neil: Ótimo, Tony, e você?

Tony: Muito bem. Ouvi falar que você foi para a Disney nas suas férias. E então, como foi?

Neil: Ótimo! Eu sempre me divirto bastante quando vou lá. Você alguma vez já esteve em algum dos parques do complexo?

Tony: Não, nunca, mas estou planejando ir lá em breve.

Neil: É você devia fazer isso mesmo. Tenho certeza que seus filhos vão adorar.

Tony: Eu sei, já faz algum tempo que eles me pedem para ir lá. Os parques de diversão lá são enormes, não são?

Neil: São sim! Você pode até se perder dentro deles se não tomar cuidado.

Tony: Puxa, parece emocionante. O que você geralmente faz quando vai lá?

Neil: Bom, nós costumamos levantar cedo e tomamos um bom café da manhã, é preciso muita energia para aproveitar os brinquedos, então é bom evitar ir lá de barriga vazia. Nós também tentamos chegar aos parques um pouco antes de eles abrirem para sermos os primeiros a entrar.

Tony: Você às vezes não cansa depois de ir a tantos brinquedos?
Neil: Cansa um pouco, mas depois de descansar um pouco dá vontade de começar tudo de novo!

DIÁLOGO 15
Cuidado com escorregões, tropeços e quedas!

Terry: E então, o que você vai fazer hoje à noite?
Phil: Estou planejando ir patinar no parque local. Eles têm um rinque superlegal lá, bem liso.
Terry: Legal! Nunca gostei muito de patinar, mas tenho alguns amigos que adoram. Cuidado com escorregões, tropeços e quedas!
Phil: Ah, não se preocupe, sempre tomo mais cuidado quando estou com os meus patins. A propósito, estou ensinando o meu sobrinho de doze anos a patinar. É incrível como as crianças aprendem rápido. Ele só esteve no rinque duas vezes e já está pegando o jeito.
Terry: Eu sei, as crianças aprendem rápido mesmo meu amigo! Então você é chegado a esportes de inverno, né?
Phil: Ah sim! Além de patinar eu adoro esquiar e andar de prancha na neve também.
Terry: Esquiar e andar de prancha na neve? Nossa, acho que teria medo de fazer isso. Imagino que deve ser muito difícil manter o equilíbrio.
Phil: Bom, tem que treinar bastante e também precisa superar o medo, mas depois que você aprende é muito divertido.
Terry: Sei, prefiro manter os meus pés no chão, se me entende né? De qualquer forma, espero que você se divirta no rinque hoje à noite.
Phil: Vou me divertir sim, obrigado! E você? Vai fazer alguma coisa hoje à noite?
Terry: Sim, vou encontrar alguns amigos em um pub. Adoro tomar cerveja com amigos e jogar conversa fora
Phil: Que bom! Divirta-se!

DIÁLOGO 16
Podemos tentar animá-lo!

Ray: Coitado do Dave, ele está se sentindo arrasado desde que a namorada o largou.
Don: Eu sei bem como é. Eu levei um tempão para superar a minha separação da Sally. Não sei se há algo que possamos fazer por ele.
Ray: Talvez sim. Podemos tentar animá-lo. E se convidarmos ele para ir a algum lugar divertido hoje à noite?
Don: Algum lugar divertido? Você quer dizer um lugar onde possamos conhecer algumas gatas atraentes, como por exemplo uma boate?
Ray: Isso mesmo! Dave precisa conhecer uma garota nova. Vai fazer bem para ele.
Don: Ótima ideia! Adoraria ir a um lugar assim. Você pode ligar para ele mais tarde e ver se ele gostaria de se juntar a nós?
Ray: Claro, vou fazer isso. Podemos também dar um pulo no Jimmy's para comer uns hamburgueres e tomar umas cervejas. Tenho certeza que o Dave gostaria de fazer isso.
Don: Para mim está ótimo! Uhm, acabei de me lembrar de uma coisa, meu carro está na oficina, podemos ir com o seu carro hoje à noite?
Ray: Sem problemas. Posso te pegar em casa.
Don: Ótimo! Me mantenha informado depois que você falar com o Dave. Eu realmente espero que ele goste da ideia. Da minha parte eu estou super a fim de me divertir hoje à noite!

DIÁLOGO 17
Para que servem os amigos?

Ralph: Ei Ingrid! Quais são as novidades?
Ingrid: Não muitas. Só decidi dar um pulo aqui para vê-los.
Ralph: Ótima ideia. Obrigado! Como está sua amiga Dana? Ela ainda está procurando emprego?
Ingrid: Acho que sim.
Ralph: Sabe de uma coisa, a empresa em que eu trabalho está crescendo bem rápido. Talvez tenhamos algumas oportunidades de emprego em breve. Acho que poderia falar dela com o meu chefe.

Ingrid: É mesmo? Seria ótimo!

Ralph: Ela sabe usar bem computadores?

Ingrid: Sabe sim. Ela adora mexer com computadores. Ela está inclusive fazendo um curso avançado sobre um novo software agora que ela tem algum tempo livre.

Ralph: Que bom, com certeza ela pode conseguir um cargo melhor na empresa com bons conhecimentos de computação.

Ingrid: Ótimo, mal posso esperar para contar a ela. Tenho certeza que ela vai ficar super animada!

Ralph: Legal! Eu estava pensando, talvez você pudesse pedir para ela enviar o currículo para mim e aí eu encaminho para o meu chefe e falo com ele sobre ela.

Ingrid: Ótimo! Vou falar com ela hoje à tarde. Muito obrigada Ralph!

Ralph: Tudo bem, Ingrid. Para que servem os amigos?

DIÁLOGO 18

Olha só aquele cara ali!

Tony: Você deve estar morrendo de fome, né?

Neil: Estou mesmo.

Tony: Quer ir comer alguma coisa no Rita's café?

Neil: Claro, vamos lá!

Na lanchonete

Sharon: Oi, o que vocês gostariam de comer?

Tony: Hum, deixe me ver, acho que vou querer o sanduíche de atum e um suco de laranja.

Sharon: Ok, e o senhor?

Neil: Uh, o que vem no hambúrguer DeLuxe?

Sharon: Vem com maionese, alface e tomate, e acompanha batata frita.

Neil: Ótimo! Vou querer um.

Sharon: E para beber?

Neil: Uma coca normal por favor.

Sharon: Ok, volto já com as bebidas.

Tony: Ei Neil, olha só aquele cara ali.

Neil: O de camisa verde? O que tem ele?

Tony: Ele não te lembra ninguém?
Neil: Ah tá, ele parece bastante com o Rick, né?
Tony: Ele é a cara do Rick! Deve ser irmão dele.
Neil: Quem sabe? Talvez seja. Quer perguntar para ele?
Tony: Acho que sim, mas vou deixar ele terminar o sanduíche primeiro.
Neil: Tudo bem!

DIÁLOGO 19
Está um gelo lá fora!

Gary: Você vai sair assim?
Sean: Acho que sim. Por quê?
Gary: Por nada, eu só acho que você deveria se agasalhar. Está um gelo lá fora!
Sean: É mesmo?
Gary: É, eu acabei de checar a previsão do tempo no meu computador. Hoje deve ficar ainda mais frio do que ontem. Dá uma olhada lá fora. Tá vendo toda aquela nevasca caindo?
Sean: É, acho que você tem razão. Obrigado pela dica! Vou colocar um casaco mais quente e luvas. A propósito, como está caminhando o seu trabalho de história?
Gary: Tudo bem, devemos terminar até quinta-feira.
Sean: Sério? Meu grupo está atrasado. Nós mal começamos. Era para termos nos encontrado há alguns dias mas não deu certo. A gente deve levar pelo menos uma semana para terminar.
Gary: Sei. Tenho sorte de estar em um grupo bom. Todos têm sido muito úteis contribuindo com ideias para o trabalho.
Sean: Que bom! Realmente faz muita diferença quando todos cooperam.

DIÁLOGO 20
Você tem planos para o final de semana?

Fred: E então, Norma, você tem planos para o final de semana?
Norma: Talvez eu vá à praia, mas não tenho certeza ainda. Vai

depender do que acontecer hoje à noite.

Fred: O que acontecer hoje à noite? O que você quer dizer?

Norma: Vou encontrar alguns amigos. Nós ficamos de conversar sobre o final de semana, estamos planejando ir à praia juntos, uma turma grande, sabe.

Fred: Ah, sei. Turmas grandes são sempre mais divertidas. Posso te fazer uma pergunta?

Norma: Meu Deus, Fred, você sabe que não precisa ser assim tão formal, fala logo!

Fred: Ok, você ainda está namorando o Brian?

Norma: Mais ou menos.

Fred: Mais ou menos?

Norma: É que nós brigamos faz algum tempo e depois fizemos as pazes, mas desde que voltamos juntos não é a mesma coisa, sabe como é, e aí eu realmente não sei o que vai acontecer.

Fred: Sei, e o Brian iria para a praia com você?

Norma: Talvez sim, talvez não. Ele normalmente fica ocupado com o ensaio da banda dele nos sábados, então eu ainda não tenho certeza o que ele planeja fazer.

Fred: Ah! Entendi.

DIÁLOGO 21
Qual é a previsão do tempo para o final de semana?

Nancy: Você ouviu a previsão do tempo para o final de semana?

Ted: Sim, ouvi no rádio a caminho do trabalho hoje de manhã. Parece que vamos ter que enfrentar alguns dias muito frios. O homem do tempo falou que talvez até neve no domingo.

Nancy: É mesmo? Acho que vou ter que mudar meus planos então.

Ted: Por quê? O que você estava planejando fazer?

Nancy: Eu ia encontrar uma amiga que mora a umas duas horas de carro daqui, mas eu sempre fico com um pouco de medo de dirigir quando neva.

Ted: Entendo, mas você está acostumada a tempo bem frio, não está? Você morou no Canadá uns dois anos, não foi?

Nancy: Morei sim. Foi meio difícil para eu me adaptar no começo, mas foi muito bom enquanto eu morei lá. E você, vai fazer alguma coisa este final de semana?

Ted: Bom, com todo este tempo frio vindo em nossa direção eu devo mesmo é ficar em casa e assistir a alguns DVDs perto da lareira.

Nancy: Que aconchegante! Talvez eu faça o mesmo.

DIÁLOGO 22
Os negócios estão prosperando!

Nick: Você parece estar gostando do seu novo emprego, né?

Rachel: Ah sim, tem sido uma ótima experiência, muito mais interessante do que eu imaginava. Embora eu esteja há apenas um mês nesta empresa, já aprendi muitas coisas novas.

Nick: Puxa, você parece mesmo entusiasmado. E os seus colegas de trabalho? Você se dá bem com todos eles?

Rachel: Me dou sim, eles são super amigáveis.

Nick: Que bom. Acho que você também tem um bom relacionamento com o seu chefe, né?

Rachel: Embora ele seja bastante exigente, tem sido ótimo trabalhar com ele. Às vezes temos que trabalhar sob pressão, mas ele também dá muito apoio e realmente eu não tenho do que me queixar.

Nick: Ótimo! A propósito, ouvi falar que sua empresa está indo muito bem. Parece estar crescendo muito rápido, não é?

Rachel: É verdade. Os negócios estão prosperando e estamos todos animados com as perspectivas.

Nick: Que bom!

DIÁLOGO 23
Meus parabéns!

Don: Você tem visto o Jeff ultimamente?

Ken: Não. Por quê?

Don: Preciso falar com ele. Tenho tentado entrar em contato com ele, mas não tive sorte até agora.

Ken: Acho que você sabe que ele está morando em um outro lugar há aproximadamente um mês. Você tem o telefone novo dele?

Don: Tenho. Liguei para ele algumas vezes, mas ele nunca estava lá. Deixei dois recados, mas ele nunca me retornou.

Ken: Parece estranho! Não é do feitio do Jeff fazer uma coisa dessas. Não sei, talvez ele esteja trabalhando demais ou algo assim.

Don: Acho que sim. Só espero que ele esteja bem. E então, o que você tem feito?

Ken: Eu? Bom, tenho feito muitas coisas novas. Eu te contei que comecei a aprender espanhol?

Don: É mesmo? Que interessante! Por que você decidiu aprender espanhol agora?

Ken: Bom, eu tenho uma boa razão, estou namorando uma garota mexicana há mais ou menos um mês, é por isso!

Don: Puxa, acho que você vai ficar fluente em espanhol rapidinho então. Meus parabéns!

DIÁLOGO 24
Acho que só preciso relaxar um pouco

Barry: Você está a fim de sair hoje à noite?

Tiffany: Não sei, acho que preferiria ficar em casa. Estou muito cansada.

Barry: Ok, podemos pedir uma pizza se você quiser.

Tiffany: Boa ideia, também não estou com vontade de cozinhar.

Barry: Certo! Como estão as coisas no trabalho? Você parecia preocupada quando falei com você no telefone hoje de manhã.

Tiffany: Eu estou um pouco preocupada! Estamos atrasados com o nosso projeto atual e talvez tenhamos que fazer hora extra para terminarmos a tempo.

Barry: Entendi. Você não me falou outro dia que o seu departamento está desfalcado?

Tiffany: Está mesmo. O RH está tentando encontrar alguém qualificado, mas não tem sido fácil. Na verdade precisamos de dois funcionários novos já que a Maggy vai sair de licença maternidade em algumas semanas.

Barry: Espero que eles encontrem alguém logo. Odeio ver você estressada assim.

Tiffany: Está tudo bem, Barry, prefiro não falar mais sobre este assunto. Acho que só preciso relaxar um pouco.

Barry: Claro, tenho uma garrafa do seu vinho branco preferido no freezer. Quer que eu lhe traga um copo?

Tiffany: Adoraria, querido. Obrigada!

DIÁLOGO 25
Qual é a melhor maneira de chegar lá?

Sean: E então, Ryan, qual é a melhor maneira de chegar lá?

Ryan: Podemos pegar o metrô ou ir de carro. Na minha opinião é melhor irmos de metrô já que o trânsito é geralmente ruim nesse horário.

Sean: Certo. Vamos pegar o metrô, então. A propósito, não tive oportunidade de falar com o Derek ontem.

Ryan: Eu também não.

Sean: Você acha que ele talvez ainda tenha interesse em ir conosco?

Ryan: Acho que sim, mas não se preocupe, vou ligar para ele mais tarde.

Sean: Ótimo! E o Jason? Você acha que também devemos convidá-lo?

Ryan: Não tenho certeza, para ser sincero com você eu não gosto muito dele.

Sean: Eu também não. Você tem razão, ele sempre foi um pouco arrogante, ele também não é o meu tipo preferido de pessoa.

Ryan: Ok, então vamos começar a fazer as malas. Quero deixar tudo pronto de uma vez por todas.

Sean: Claro, vamos fazer isso agora! Não quero me atrasar amanhã.

Ryan: Eu também não!

DIÁLOGO 26
Há quanto tempo você está indo à academia?

Nick: Você ainda se deita bem tarde à noite?

Fred: Ah, não, eu fazia isso antes, mas agora eu sempre vou me deitar lá pelas 22h. Eu tenho que levantar cedo todas as manhãs agora para levar os meus filhos de carro para a escola.

Nick: Então você não assiste mais filmes de madrugada?

Fred: Bom, eu ainda posso assistir os filmes no final de semana, mas não mais durante a semana.

Nick: Ah sim! Sabe, eu queria te falar uma coisa, você parece que está bem magro. Você tem feito regime ou algo diferente?

Fred: Você tem razão! Eu era mais gordo antes, mas não estou fazendo regime. O que eu tenho feito é malhar na academia quatro vezes por semana agora.

Nick: Isso é muito bom. Há quanto tempo você está indo à academia?

Fred: Uns cinco meses. Graças a um programa regular de exercícios eu me sinto muito mais saudável do que antes.

Nick: Que bom!

DIÁLOGO 27
O que você faria se herdasse uma fortuna?

Larry: O que você faria se herdasse uma fortuna?

Ron: Puxa, não sei. Nunca pensei nessa possibilidade, mas acho que compraria uma casa primeiro e pararia de pagar aluguel.

Larry: Certo! Isso seria sensato. O que mais você acha que faria?

Ron: Tenho certeza que também gostaria de viajar bastante, eu adoro viajar!

Larry: Eu também! Há tantos países que eu quero conhecer. Espero que eu possa fazer isso algum dia. Você acha que também abriria um negócio?

Ron: É, isso é uma coisa que eu consideraria. Talvez uma franquia do ramo alimentício.

Larry: Claro, eu também certamente montaria minha própria empresa. Sabe, seria também importante contratar um consultor financeiro para se aconselhar como investir o dinheiro adequadamente.

Ron: Concordo. Você acabou de me lembrar de uma coisa. Escuta, você vai ver o Harry mais tarde hoje?

Larry: Não tenho certeza, por quê?

Ron: Preciso falar com ele sobre um dinheiro que ele pegou emprestado de mim.

Larry: Claro, se eu o vir aviso que você quer falar com ele.

Ron: Obrigado! Acho que é melhor pararmos de sonhar acordados e voltar ao trabalho agora. Nosso chefe está vindo.

Larry: Ok!

DIÁLOGO 28
O que ele tem feito?

Stan: Você tem visto o Brian ultimamente?

Tom: Sim, falei com ele ontem mesmo.

Stan: Ah é? O que ele tem feito?

Tom: Bom, ele me disse que voltou para a faculdade, ele está fazendo um MBA três vezes por semana à noite. Ele também terminou com a namorada, a Patty. Você se lembra dela?

Stan: Claro, nossa, as coisas parecem estar mudando o tempo todo. Não falo com ele há muito tempo e não fazia ideia.

Tom: Ah, ele também raspou o cavanhaque, ele está com uma aparência bem diferente agora.

Stan: Sério? O cavanhaque era a marca registrada dele. Parece que a vida dele mudou bastante recentemente.

Tom: Acho que sim. Ei, você já jantou?

Stan: Não, ainda não. Por quê?

Tom: Eu estou com um pouco de fome e pensei que talvez pudéssemos ir àquela lanchonete da rua principal.

Stan: Boa ideia. Você sabe que eu adoro hambúrguer. Vamos lá!

DIÁLOGO 29
Parece que você tem se divertido bastante!

Jeff: Você tem se divertido ultimamente?

Greg: É, acho que posso realmente dizer que tenho me divertido bastante!

Jeff: É mesmo? Você parece mesmo animado. Me conta, o que você tem feito?

Greg: Bom, para começar eu entrei em uma academia recentemente e tenho feito exercício físico regular nas últimas semanas.

Jeff: É mesmo? Eu tenho pensado em fazer o mesmo. O que mais você tem feito?

Greg: Bom, eu sempre dou um jeito de sair com meus amigos pelo menos uma vez por semana, a gente vai assistir filmes, shows ou às vezes ficamos na casa de algum amigo tomando cerveja e jogando conversa fora. É uma maneira ótima de relaxar!

Jeff: Ah, sim, tenho certeza que é. Também gosto de fazer isso. Você tem visto o Ted ultimamente?

Greg: Não. Perdi contato com ele desde que ele começou a namorar a Dana. Acho que ele está firme com ela, foi o que eu ouvi dizer.

Jeff: Também ouvi isso. Já faz um tempo que não falo com ele. E no trabalho? Você tem feito algo diferente?

Greg: De fato eu recebi algumas novas tarefas e tem sido estimulante. É ótimo ter novos desafios. Eu também sinto que a oportunidade de uma promoção vai surgir em breve e estou bastante animado com as perspectivas.

Jeff: Bom, meu amigo, parece que você tem se divertido bastante. Meus parabéns!

DIÁLOGO 30
Os exames finais já estão quase aí!

Ron: Você conseguiu falar com o Steve?

Frank: Não. Ele já tinha saído quando eu passei pela casa dele, mas vou ligar para ele mais tarde, não se preocupe.

Ron: Certo. Só quero ter certeza que vamos nos organizar e começar o trabalho novo assim que possível.

Frank: Claro, mas temos bastante tempo. Temos que entregar até 10 de setembro, não é?

Ron: É, mas não precisamos nos preocupar apenas com isso. Os exames finais já estão quase aí, lembra?

Frank: Eu sei. Eu provavelmente vou ter que ficar estudando até tarde para colocar em dia as minhas anotações. À propósito, eu estava pensando se você poderia me dar uma ajuda com matemática.

Ron: Sem problema. Só me avise com antecedência quando você quiser se encontrar.

Frank: Obrigado, Ron! E então, o que você vai fazer hoje à noite?

Ron: Ainda não sei. E você?

Frank: Não tenho certeza, mas talvez vá ao centro assistir a um filme de ação. Quer ir junto?

Ron: Acho que não, eu provavelmente vou dormir cedo hoje à noite. Preciso colocar o sono em dia!

LESSON 1

DIALOGUE 1 – COMPREHENSION QUESTIONS

1. She's a vet. / She's a veterinarian.
2. No, he doesn't.
3. She has five pets.
4. Because he doesn't have time to take care of them.
5. Because she's late for work.

PRACTICE SET 1

I. Listen to the questions and circle the right answer.
1. Do you work here? b) No, I don't.
2. Is Paul your friend? c) Yes, he is.
3. When do you have Spanish classes? a) On Mondays and Wednesdays.
4. Who's that man? c) That's Harry.
5. Do you smoke? a) No, I don't.
6. What's your phone number? b) It's 504-6571.
7. What do you do? c) Me? I'm a webdesigner.
8. How old is Pamella? b) She's twenty-three years old.
9. Where is Joe from? a) He's Australian.
10. How do you spell your name? c) It's Mike: M - I - K - E.

II. Dictation: listen to the sentences and write them.
1. What's your name?
2. How do you spell your name?
3. Where are you from?
4. How old are you?
5. What do you do for a living?

III. Rewrite the sentences with contractions.
1. Kate's a teacher.
2. What's your phone number?
3. It's hot today.

4. Sam's not American, he is from Canada.
5. I'm thirty-two years old.

IV. Write questions/ phrases for the following answers.
1. What do you do? / What's your occupation?
2. How are you?
3. How old is Victor?
4. Do you smoke?
5. Thank you! / Thanks!

V. Circle the word or expression that is different from the group.
1. April
2. Thursday
3. Saturday
4. Italy
5. Where are you from?

LESSON 2
DIALOGUE 2 – COMPREHENSION QUESTIONS

1. She wants to do something different, maybe go camping.
2. Yes, he does.
3. They plan to invite Karen and Arnold.
4. Because their tent is very old and too small.

PRACTICE SET 2

I. Listen to the questions and circle the right answer.
1. Who do you live with? c) I live with my wife and children.
2. Don't you speak Spanish? b) No, I don't.
3. How's it going? c) Very good, thanks!
4. Why don't you go to the club? a) I have to study.
5. Who's that woman? b) That's Mary.
6. What's your friend's name? b) It's Elizabeth.
7. Where is Melissa from? c) She's from Brazil.
8. How old is Joe? a) He's nineteen years old.
9. What's your telephone number? b) It's 539-6742.

10. Don't you go to the club on Sundays? c) Yes, I go to the club every Sunday.

II. Dictation: listen to the sentences and write them.
1. Don't you speak Spanish?
2. Is Kate married?
3. Where is Jeniffer from?
4. How old is Jack?
5. What's your telephone number?

III. Write the plural of the following words:
1. computers
2. boxes
3. families
4. wives
5. children

IV. Write questions/ phrases for the following answers.
1. Do you have a car? / Don't you have a car?
2. Are you married?
3. How old is Linda?
4. Is Rita married?
5. Nice to meet you.

V. Circle the word or expression that is different from the group.
1. child
2. webdesigner
3. uncle
4. husband
5. Italian

LESSON 3
DIALOGUE 3 – COMPREHENSION QUESTIONS

1. He's a lawyer.
2. He catches the subway to work. / He goes to work by subway.

3. He has only one sister.
4. It's Helen. / Helen.
5. She's fifteen.

PRACTICE SET 3

I. Listen to the questions and circle the right answer.
1. Does Sophie smoke? a) No, she doesn't.
2. Who's that woman? c) That's my sister-in-law.
3. How do you come to work? b) By bus.
4. Who's that boy? c) That's Bill.
5. Does your husband speak French? c) Yes, he does.
6. How old is your brother? a) He's nineteen years old.
7. Where does your husband work? a) He works in a bank.
8. Do you have kids? a) Yes, I do. I have a son and a daughter.
9. What does Susan do for a living? b) Susan? She's a dentist.
10. How does Victor come to work? c) He comes to work by car.

II. Dictation: listen to the sentences and write them.
1. What's your occupation?
2. Does Paul speak Italian?
3. John lives with his wife and kids.
4. What does your husband do?
5. Does Mary smoke?

III. Replace the underlined word(s) by a pronoun.
1. I don't understand him.
2. Susan likes us.
3. I see them every day.
4. Do you like her?
5. We don't know him.

IV. Write questions/ phrases for the following answers.
1. Does Rita smoke?
2. Where is Nick from?
3. How ols id your daughter?
4. Where does your brother work?

5. How does Barry come to work?

V. Circle the word or expression that is different from the group.
1. boy
2. husband
3. they
4. me
5. August

LESSON 4
DIALOGUE 4 – COMPREHENSION QUESTIONS

1. No, he didn't.
2. Because he had a problem with his car.
3. He saw Neil's sister.
4. Kate is one of Neil's sister's best friends.
5. Because he thinks they will play on their basketball team.

PRACTICE SET 4

I. Listen to the questions and circle the right answer.
1. Does Robert play soccer? b) Yes, he does.
2. Who are those people? c) Those are Jeff's friends.
3. Do you know her family? a) Yes, I do.
4. What's your sister's name? b) It's Sandra.
5. Who does Samantha play volleyball with? a) She plays volleyball with her friends.
6. How old is your brother's friend? b) He's twenty-six years old.
7. Does Susan have children? c) Yes, she has a son and two daughters.
8. Where is your sister? a) She's at school.
9. What does Mary's father do? c) Her father is a doctor.
10. What's your favorite sport? b) Volleyball.

II. Dictation: listen to the sentences and write them.
1. Joe and Nick are our friends.
2. Where does Paul live?

3. Jane is a nurse. She works in a hospital.
4. Where's Mike's sister?
5. What's your husband's occupation?

III. Write the following numbers.
a) 83 – eighty-three
b) 407 – four hundred and seven.
c) 6.354 – six thousand, three hundred and fifty-four.
d) 9.971 – nine thousand, nine hundred and seventy-one.
e) 729 – seven hundred and twenty-nine.

IV. Write questions/ phrases for the following answers.
1. Is that umbrella yours?
2. Whose is that cell phone?
3. Who's that girl/ woman?
4. Do you play soccer on Saturdays?
5. Where does Samantha work?

V. Circle the word or expression that is different from the group.
1. she
2. window
3. Monday
4. nephew
5. Canadian

LESSON 5
DIALOGUE 5 – COMPREHENSION QUESTIONS

1. Yes, he did. He had a lot of fun.
2. Yes, he did.
3. She's Sarah's friend.
4. Yes, she does.

PRACTICE SET 5

I. Listen to the questions and circle the right answer.
1. Did you and your friends play basketball yesterday? a) Yes, we did.

2. Was Joe late for the meeting yesterday? b) No, he wasn't.
3. How much did that dress cost? c) It cost two hundred dollars.
4. What does Bill need to do tomorrow? a) He needs to go to the bank.
5. Was it cold yesterday? b) No, it wasn't.
6. Where did David go last Sunday? b) He went to the club.
7. Did George and Kate come here last night? a) Yes, they did.
8. Where did Nelson go last week? c) He went to Miami.
9. What day is today? c) Today is Monday.
10. What did Tony do last Friday? b) He played soccer last Friday.

II. Dictation: listen to the sentences and write them.
1. What did you do yesterday?
2. Priscilla went to the club on Sunday.
3. Whose are those CDs?
4. Where did Mary go last night?
5. Does Tony like those brown shoes?

III. Complete the following questions.
1. Were you here yesterday? Yes, I was.
2. Whose are those socks? They're mine.
3. What color is it? It's blue.
4. Does Phillip smoke? No, he doesn't.
5. Did Susan come here last week? Yes, she did.

IV. Write questions/ phrases for the following answers.
1. Was David here last night?
2. Is that green shirt yours?
3. Who's that man/ guy/ boy?
4. Where did you go on Friday/ When did you go to the club?
5. What's her name?

V. Circle the word or expression that is different from the group.
1. his
2. hat
3. newspaper

4. sneakers
5. bowling

LESSON 6
DIALOGUE 6 – COMPREHENSION QUESTIONS

1. It was great. / Great.
2. She's making a strawberry cake.
3. Pamella is taking a shower and Jake is listening to music in his bedroom.
4. She's going out with her boyfriend tonight.
5. He wants to tell him that he bought tickets for the hockey game on Friday night.

PRACTICE SET 6

I. Listen to the questions and circle the right answer.
1. What's Tony doing now? a) He's reading a book.
2. Does Jeff read the newspaper every day? b) No, he doesn't.
3. Is Priscilla working today? c) No, she isn't. It's a holiday, remember?
4. How much was that tie? b) It cost forty-five dollars.
5. Were you here yesterday? c) No, I wasn't.
6. What time is it now please? a) It's noon.
7. Where did David go last night? b) He went to the movies with his friends.
8. How much were those sneakers? a) They cost eighty dollars.
9. What's your favorite day of the week? c) I think it's Friday.
10. When did Bill and Fred arrive from England? a) They arrived last Tuesday.

II. Dictation: listen to the sentences and write them.
1. Is Bob working today?
2. Where is Sandra going tonight?
3. Barbara is traveling to the beach next weekend.
4. Did Fred buy new sneakers?
5. What are you doing tomorrow?

III. Circle the right answer.

1. b   2. a   3. b   4. a   5. b

IV. Write questions/ phrases for the following answers.

1. Where are you going tonight?
2. Are those black shoes yours?
3. How much does that shirt cost? / How much is that shirt?
4. Where did you go last weekend?
5. What time is it?

V. Circle the word or expression that is different from the group.

1. daughter
2. that
3. New York
4. student
5. Tuesday

LESSON 7
DIALOGUE 7 – COMPREHENSION QUESTIONS

1. He was shopping for sneakers.
2. He went there to get Barbara a gift. / He went there to buy Barbara a present.
3. Because it's her birthday.
4. He wanted to invite Harry to the surprise party tonight.

PRACTICE SET 7

I. Listen to the questions and circle the right answer.

1. What were you doing when I called you this morning? c) I was taking a shower.
2. Does Jim have breakfast at home every morning? b) No, he doesn't.
3. How many bedrooms are there in your house? c) We have three bedrooms.
4. How much was that new dress? a) It cost one hundred and fifty-four dollars.

5. Was it raining when you left Susan's house last night? b) No, it wasn't.
6. What did you have for breakfast this morning? a) I had orange juice, bacon and eggs and coffee.
7. Where did James go last night? a) He went to the supermarket with his wife.
8. Does Jane drink milk every day? b) No, she doesn't like milk.9.   What time was it when Bill arrived last night? a) It was midnight.
10. How many bedrooms are there in Fred's apartment? c) There's just one bedroom.

II. Dictation: listen to the sentences and write them.
1. Fred was having dinner when I arrived.
2. There were many people at the party last night.
3. David's house has four bedrooms and a big living-room.
4. What were you doing when I called you?
5. Sophie lives in a small apartment. It has just one bedroom.

III. Circle the right answer.
1. b   2. c   3. b   4. a   5. c

IV. Write questions/ phrases for the following answers.
1. How many bedrooms are there?
2. What do you usually have for breakfast?
3. Is there a drugstore on the next block?
4. Is there any milk in the refrigerator?
5. Is the kitchen big?

V. Circle the word or expression that is different from the group.
1. neighbor
2. television
3. breakfast
4. friend
5. kitchen

LESSON 8
DIALOGUE 8 – COMPREHENSION QUESTIONS

1. Because she has to take care of her nephew.
2. They plan to stop by to see Jane.
3. Yes, he does.
4. They plan to throw the party in December.
5. Steve is.

PRACTICE SET 8

I. Listen to the questions and circle the right answer.
1. What are you planning to do today? b) I'll probably go to the club and play tennis.
2. Will you see Melissa tomorrow? a) I think so.
3. What's the weather like today? c) It's cold and rainy.
4. What do you usually have for lunch? b) I have pasta and sometimes just a hamburger.
5. Will you have time to finish your homework today? a) Yes, I will.
6. Does Priscilla like to play cards? b) No, not really.
7. When will you see Tom and Joe again? a) I'll see them tomorrow night.
8. What time is Rita going to arrive tonight? c) Around 10 pm.
9. What kind of food do you prefer? b) I like hamburgers and other kinds of sandwiches.
10. What did you do last night? a) I went to the mall to see a movie.

II. Dictation: listen to the sentences and write them.
1. I'll have lunch with Michael today.
2. My sister is going to arrive from Italy tomorrow.
3. Robert likes to eat vegetables and salads.
4. What kind of food does your wife like?
5. When will you see them again?

III. Circle the right answer.
1. c   2. b   3. a   4. c   5.a

IV. Write questions/ phrases for the following answers.
1. What's your favorite season? / What season do you prefer?
2. What do you like to eat? / What kind of food do you like?
3. Will you see him tomorrow?
4. What's the weather like?
5. Does Sheila have a brother?

V. Circle the word or expression that is different from the group.
1. spring
2. weather
3. pretty
4. she
5. England

LESSON 9
DIALOGUE 9 – COMPREHENSION QUESTIONS

1. A bad one.
2. No, they don't.
3. No, he doesn't.
4. He invites Mike to see a movie.
5. They plan to go grab a bite to eat at the hamburger joint in the mall. / They plan to eat something at the mall.

PRACTICE SET 9

I. Listen to the questions and circle the right answer.
1. What would you like to do tonight? c) I'd prefer to stay home.
2. Would you like some coffee? a) No, thanks, I'm ok.
3. What kind of movies do you prefer? b) I love action movies.
4. Where would Rita like to go next Saturday? a) She'd like to visit her brother.
5. Why didn't you do your homework yesterday? c) I didn't have time.
6. Does Sarah like love stories? a) No, she doesn't. She prefers comedies.
7. What would you like to drink? b) Passion fruit juice, please.

8. Do you like thrillers? c) No, I prefer sitcoms.
9. Where did you go last night? a) I went to a restaurant with friends.
10. How often do you go to the movies? b) About once a week.

II. Dictation: listen to the sentences and write them.
1. Would you like to go to the movies tonight?
2. She would buy that house if she had money.
3. How often do you go to the beach?
4. Mike loves comedies.
5. He'd prefer to stay home tonight.

III. Circle the right answer.
1. b   2. a   3. a   4. b   5. a

IV. Write questions/ phrases for the following answers.
1. How often does Rachel visit her sister?
2. Would you like to go to the beach next weekend?
3. Does Monica speak Japanese?
4. What would she prefer to do tonight?
5. Do you like war movies?

V. Circle the word or expression that is different from the group.
1. bacon
2. geography
3. his
4. woman
5. magazine

LESSON 10
DIALOGUE 10 – COMPREHENSION QUESTIONS

1. Because he's been working out at the gym three times a week.
2. Yes, he does.
3. It's more spacious and comfortable than the last one.
4. No, he doesn't. He has great neighbors.
5. It takes him about fifteen minutes.

PRACTICE SET 10

I. Listen to the questions and circle the right answer.
1. Is your sister as tall as you? b) No, she isn't.
2. Does Gary brush his teeth after every meal? c) Yes, he does.
3. What's the matter with Sheila? b) She has a stomachache.
4. Is this blue tie as expensive as the gray one? a) Yes, it is.
5. How often do you brush your teeth? b) Three times a day.
6. What would you like to do on Saturday? c) I'd prefer to play tennis.
7. Is Sam feeling all right? a) Yes, he is.
8. Why would she do that? b) I don't know. I have no idea.
9. How often do you shave? a) About four times a week.
10. Is Maggie feeling all right? c) No, she has a headache.

II. Dictation: listen to the sentences and write them.
1. Jack brushes his teeth after every meal.
2. What's the matter with Nick?
3. How often does Jeff play basketball?
4. What would you prefer to do tonight?
5. Is Tony feeling all right?

III. Circle the right answer.
1. b   2. a   3. c   4. b   5. a

IV. Write questions/ phrases for the following answers.
1. How often does Sabrina brush her teeth?
2. Is he feeling all right?
3. What would you prefer to do today?
4.Where did she go?
5. Does Sarah smoke?

V. Circle the word or expression that is different from the group.
1. backache
2. bread
3. foot
4. shoulder
5. beer

LESSON 11
DIALOGUE 11 – COMPREHENSION QUESTIONS

1. No, he didn't.
2. Because the movie got a rave review and some great actors work in it.
3. It's physics. / Physics.
4. It's geography. / Geography.
5. Yes, they are.

PRACTICE SET 11

I. Listen to the questions and circle the right answer.
1. Are you taller than your father? b) Yes, I am.
2. Do you help your wife with the housework? c) Yes, I do. I always do the dishes.
3. What's Carol doing? a) She's making a chocolate cake.
4. Is your apartment bigger than Paul's? c) No, it isn't.
5. Who's cleaning the house? a) The maid is.
6. Is your brother older than you? b) No, I'm older than he is.
7. How old is your wife? c) She's thirty-three years old.
8. What's Bob doing? b) He's taking the garbage out.
9. How often does the cleaner sweep the floor? c) About three times a week.
10. Do you have a maid? a) No, I don't .

II. Dictation: listen to the sentences and write them.
1. Steve helps his wife with the housework. He does the dishes and takes the garbage out every day.
2. Is your sister younger or older than you?
3. Does Carol have a maid?
4. Where did you buy your new microwave?
5. Bob is fatter than Mike.

III. Circle the right answer.
1. b   2. a   3. c   4. b   5. a

IV. Write questions/ phrases for the following answers.
1. Does Melissa have a good maid?
2. How often do you clean the house?
3. Is Bill shorter than Jason? / Is Jason taller than Bill?
4. What would he prefer to do tonight?
5. Do you have a dishwasher?

V. Circle the word or expression that is different from the group.
1. kitchen
2. do the homework
3. stove
4. wine
5. oven

LESSON 12
DIALOGUE 12 – COMPREHENSION QUESTIONS

1. He cut himself shaving.
2. No, he isn't.
3. Because Daniel has already finished their history assignment by himself.
4. He's very happy and he thinks Daniel is a terrific classmate.

PRACTICE SET 12

I. Listen to the questions and circle the right answer.
1. Who's the tallest player? b) Tony is.
2. Did you do the most difficult exercises? a) No, I only did the easiest ones.
3. How often do you work out at the gym? c) About four times a week.
4. Did Fred put on weight? a) I think so, he looks fatter, doesn't he?
5. Do you go swimming very often? c) Not really, only on weekends.
6. What do you do to keep in shape? b) I go jogging every morning and I also go swimming on Saturdays.
7. Are you on a diet? a) Me? No, I'm not.

8. Which watch did Barry buy? c) He bought the cheapest one.
9. Does Fred go jogging with you in the morning? b) Yes, sometimes he does.
10. Who's the best soccer player in your opinion? a) I don't know, I don't really like soccer very much.

II. Dictation: listen to the sentences and write them.
1. Mark bought the cheapest cell phone at the store.
2. Who's the youngest student in your class?
3. How often does Sandra go swimming?
4. Does Sam go jogging very often?
5. You look like you're in shape. Do you work out at the gym every day?

III. Circle the right answer.
1. b   2. a   3. b   4. b   5. c

IV. Write questions/ phrases for the following answers.
1. Is he on a diet?
2. Who's the youngest student in your class?
3. How often do you go to the gym?
4. What do you do to keep in shape?
5. Would you like to go swimming today?

V. Circle the word or expression that is different from the group.
1. clean the house
2. turkey
3. family
4. tea
5. butter

LESSON 13
DIALOGUE 13 – COMPREHENSION QUESTIONS

1. Steve isn't. Bill went out with a girl a couple of times, but he's not sure they get along so well together.

2. Sarah. She works at the Ritz Café.
3. He thinks so, but she's not really his type.
4. They plan to go to a club.

PRACTICE SET 13

I. Listen to the questions and circle the right answer.
1. You don't smoke, do you? b) No, I don't.
2. Priscilla isn't taller than you, is she? a) No, she isn't.
3. You have a sister, don't you? c) Yes, I do. Her name is Sandra.
4. Ronald can speak Spanish, can't he? a) Yes, he's fluent in Spanish.
5. You talked to Celine last night, didn't you? b) Yes, I did.
6. You're not tired, are you? c) No, I'm not.
7. Fred goes jogging every morning, doesn't he? b) Yes, he does.
8. Gary didn't tell you what happened, did he? a) No, he didn't.
9. You get up early every day, don't you? c) Yes, I do.
10. Harry is older than you, isn't he? b) Yes, he is.

II. Dictation: listen to the sentences and write them.
1. You go to work by subway, don't you?
2. Martha has a younger brother, doesn't she?
3. Brian isn't taller than you, is he?
4. Nick didn't tell his wife what happened, did he?
5. You don't see them very often, do you?

III. Circle the right answer.
1. b   2. a   3. b   4. c   5. a

IV. Write questions/ phrases for the following answers.
1. How old is Rachel?
2. What would he like to do on Saturday?
3. How many brothers does Gary have?
4. Where did Sabrina go?
5. Does Mike smoke?

V. Fill in the blanks with an appropriate word/ expression from the box.

1. We need to rent a car with a big trunk. We have many bags.
2. "Can you check the tires please?", said Greg at the gas station.
3. Is my driver's license valid here?
4. Traffic is always bad like this in the rush hour.
5. Watch out for the speed limit on this road. You don't want to get a fine/ ticket do you?

LESSON 14
DIALOGUE 14 – COMPREHENSION QUESTIONS

1. He went to the Disney resorts. He had a wonderful time there.
2. No, he hasn't.
3. He usually gets up early and has a hearty breakfast. He also tries to get to the parks just before they open.
4. He does a little, but after a short rest he feels like starting all over again.

PRACTICE SET 14

I. Listen to the questions and circle the right answer.
1. How long does it take you to get to work in the morning? c) About half an hour.
2. Can I take this small bag as carry-on luggage? a) Sure, no problem.
3. How long did it take Richard to drive from New York to Boston? b) It took him about four hours.
4. Will there be any delay? a) No, the plane will take off on schedule.
5. Do we need a visa to enter the U.S.? b) Yes, you do.
6. Excuse me, do you know if they have lockers at this train station? c) Sorry, I don't know. Why don't you ask that man over there?
7. Do you prefer a window seat or an aisle seat? a) A window seat.
8. Do you always get up early? b) No, only on weekdays.
9. Does Rachel visit her parents very often? a) She does, about four times a week.
10. How long does it take you to shave? c) About ten minutes.

II. Dictation: listen to the sentences and write them.
1. Gary is sometimes late for appointments.
2. How long did it take you to clean the house?
3. Do you always go to the mall on weekends?
4. Can you get me an aisle seat please?
5. It took me about an hour to get to work this morning.

III. Circle the right answer.
1. a   2. b   3. c   4. a   5. b

IV. Write questions/ phrases for the following answers.
1. How long does it take you to drive to work?
2. Does Karen always get up early?
3. How often does Sophie visit her mother?
4. Where did they go last night?
5. How long did it take you to write that e-mail?

V. Fill in the blanks with an appropriate word/ expression from the box.
1. What time is the plane going to take off?
2. "You will board at gate 41", the check-in agent told us.
3. We got to our final destination as scheduled. There were no delays.
4. Caroline is a flight attendant in an American airline company.
5. Would you like a window seat or an aisle seat?", the check-in agent asked me.

LESSON 15
DIALOGUE 15 – COMPREHENSION QUESTIONS

1. He plans to go skating at the local park.
2. No, not very much.
3. He advises Phil to watch out for slips, trips and falls.
4. Yes, he does.
5. He loves to go skiing and snowboarding.
6. He's meeting some friends at a pub.

PRACTICE SET 15

I. Listen to the questions and circle the right answer.
1. What do you like to do in your free time? c) I like to read and watch movies.
2. How often does Brian go on vacation? a) About once a year.
3. Did Rebecca make that cake by herself? b) Yes, she did.
4. Don't you sometimes go camping? a) Me? Oh, no, I prefer to stay at hotels.
5. Does your brother like to go to amusement parks? b) No, he doesn't really.
6. Do you need any help? a) No, thanks. I can do that by myself.
7. Does Jack like to go fishing? b) No, he doesn't.
8. Why didn't Rita call us? b) I think she was busy.
9. How long does it take you to cook dinner? a) About an hour.
10. How much was it? b) Five bucks.

II. Dictation: listen to the sentences and write them.
1. I'd like to do some sightseeing. Can you recommend any places?
2. This is no reason for you to be so angry. You have to learn to control yourself.
3. What kind of movies do you prefer to watch?
4. Amy would prefer to stay home and rest tonight.
5. Can you do that by yourself?

III. Circle the right answer.
1. c   2. b   3. b   4. c   5. a

IV. Write questions/ phrases for the following answers.
1. Did Tony wash his car by himself?
2. Who's that woman/ girl?
3. What kind of movies do you prefer to watch? / What kind of movies do you like?
4. Does Tim have any brothers? / Doesn't Tim have any brothers?
5. Do you need any help?

V. Fill in the blanks with an appropriate word/ expression from the box.

1. Magda is very tired. She wants to go home and rest.
2. What do you like to do on vacation?
3. You have a nice tan. Did you go to the beach last weekend?
4. It's important to always wear sunscreen to protect your skin when you go to the beach.
5. Rita and Joe don't like to go camping. They prefer to stay at hotels when they travel.

LESSON 16
DIALOGUE 16 – COMPREHENSION QUESTIONS

1. Because his girlfriend dumped him.
2. They plan to invite him to go somewhere fun tonight.
3. He thinks Dave needs to meet a new girl.
4. He loves the idea.
5. They also plan to stop by at Jimmy's for a burger and some beers.
6. They're going to take Ray's car.

PRACTICE SET 16

I. Listen to the questions and circle the right answer.

1. Can your sister speak Spanish? b) No, she can't.
2. Why can't Elaine come to the party with us tonight? a) She has to study for a test.
3. Can you tell me how to go to the bank from here? a) Sure, it's very easy.
4. How can I get to the subway station from here? c) Turn right on the next street and walk one block.
5. Do you know where I can find an ATM near here? a) There's one on the next block.
6. Could you understand what she said? b) No, not really.
7. Where can I buy souvenirs? a) At the gift shop.
8. Can you repeat that please? c) Sure!
9. Can you tell me what happened? a) Yeah, I think so.
10. Is there an ATM near here? a) Yes, there's one on main street.

II. Dictation: listen to the sentences and write them.
1. Can't Mike come with us to the beach?
2. There's an ATM on the next block.
3. Where can I find a laundromat near here?
4. Could you please tell us what happened?
5. How can I go to the airport from here?

III. Circle the right answer.
1. b   2. a   3. b   4. a   5. b

IV. Write questions/ phrases for the following answers.
1. Is there a bank near here? / Is there a bank on the next block?
2. Can your brother speak Italian?
3. Can she go with us to the movies?
4. Where can I buy souvenirs?
5. How often do you go swimming?

V. Circle the word or expression that is different from the group.
1. living-room
2. England
3. trunk
4. happiest
5. delay

LESSON 17
DIALOGUE 17 – COMPREHENSION QUESTIONS

1. No, she doesn't. She's looking for a job.
2. He offers to help Dana get a job in the company he works for. / He offers to put in a word for Dana with his boss.
3. Yes, she does.
4. He thinks she could e-mail her résumé to him so he can forward it to his boss and talk to him about her.
5. She's very happy and grateful to Ralph.

PRACTICE SET 17

I. Listen to the questions and circle the right answer.
1. Where's the fitting-room please? b) It's back there.
2. What should I wear? c) Jeans and a t-shirt are okay.
3. Should we tell them the truth? a) Yes, I think so.
4. What time must you be there? c) At 8 a.m.
5. What size do you wear? c) I'm usually a small.
6. Can I talk to you for a minute? a) Sure!
7. Where did Frank go? b) He went to the mall with some friends.
8. How can I get to the mall from here? c) Sorry, I can't help. I'm not from around here.
9. What should I do? a) I have no idea. Why don't you ask Brian?
10. Can I try on a smaller size? a) Sure!

II. Dictation: listen to the sentences and write them.
1. That boy must be Jeff's son. He looks just like him!
2. They have a great sale this week. Everything is at least 15% off.
3. In my opinion you should talk to them and explain what happened.
4. How can I get to the train station from here?
5. Do you think I should tell her what happened?

III. Circle the right answer.
1. c   2. b   3. a   4. b   5. a

IV. Write questions/ phrases for the following answers.
1. What size do you wear?
2. How much is it? / How much does it cost?
3. Can you swim?
4. Should Mary invite Fred to the party?
5. Do you go to the mall very often?

V. Fill in the blanks with an appropriate word/ expression from the box.
1. How much is it? It's 37 dollars.
2. Can I try on a larger size? This shirt is a little tight.
3. We have a sale on men's shoes. They are 25% off.

4. Would you like to try it on? We have a fitting-room at the back.
5. "What size do you wear?", the store clerk asked Mike.

LESSON 18
DIALOGUE 18 – COMPREHENSION QUESTIONS

1. They decide to go grab a bite to eat at Rita's Café as Tony is starving.
2. He orders the tuna sandwich and an orange juice.
3. It comes with mayo, lettuce and tomatoes and fries on the side.
4. He sees a guy who looks a lot like Rick.

PRACTICE SET 18

I. Listen to the questions and circle the right answer.
1. May I sit here? b) Sure!
2. Where can I find dental floss please? c) That's in aisle four.
3. May I go now? a) Yes, you may.
4. Do you sell sunscreen here? b) Yes, we do, you can find sunscreen in aisle six.
5. May I leave earlier today? a) Sure!
6. What's the weather forecast for tomorrow? a) It's going to be very cold and it may snow.
7. May I smoke here? b) No, you may not.
8. Where can I find diapers? c) I'm sorry, we don't sell diapers here.
9. What are your plans for the weekend? a) I may go to the beach.
10. May I borrow your pen? a) Yes, you may.

II. Dictation: listen to the sentences and write them.
1. I may go to the club later today.
2. It might rain tomorrow.
3. May I leave earlier today?
4. We might go to the beach this weekend.
5. It may rain later today.

III. Circle the right answer.
1. b   2. c   3. a   4. b   5. a

IV. Write questions/ phrases for the following answers.

1. May I smoke here?
2. What's the weather forecast for today?
3. Where can I find sunscreen?
4. Do you sell lipstick here?
5. May I use your pen/ cell phone/ etc.?/ May I go now?/ May I smoke?/ etc.

V. Circle the word or expression that is different from the group.

1. party
2. nail clipper
3. her
4. could
5. cucumber

LESSON 19
DIALOGUE 19 – COMPREHENSION QUESTIONS

1. He advises Sean to bundle up as it's very cold outside.
2. He decides to put on a warmer coat and gloves.
3. They are behind schedule.
4. Because he's in a good group and everyone cooperates.

PRACTICE SET 19

I. Listen to the questions and circle the right answer.

1. Would you rather stay here or go with them? b) I think I'll go with them.
2. How many people does that company employ? a) About one hundred people.
3. Do you have to work on Saturdays? b) No, I don't.
4. What would you rather do tonight? a) I'm tired so I think I'll just stay home.
5. How many new employees did they hire? b) Three new employees.
6. Would you rather eat pasta or fish? c) Fish, please.
7. When is your day off? a) Tuesday.
8. Who did you go to the club with? c) I went with Nick and Brian.

9. Do you usually have lunch with your coworkers? a) Yes, I do, we have lunch at the company cafeteria.
10. Is that position still available? b) No, it isn't.

II. Dictation: listen to the sentences and write them.
1. We'd better go. It's getting late.
2. I'd rather not go out tonight.
3. He'd better go on a diet.
4. What would you rather do tonight?
5. They'd better not go swimming today. It's cold.

III. Circle the right answer.
1. b   2. a   3. c   4. b   5. a

IV. Write questions/ phrases for the following answers.
1. How many people do they employ?
2. Where does Bob usually have lunch?
3. What would you rather do tonight?
4. How often does Nancy go jogging?
5. Are you younger than Barry? / Is Barry older than you?

V. Fill in the blanks with an appropriate word/ expression from the box.
1. You have the qualifications required by the position. Why don't you apply for that job?
2. Rachel usually goes shopping and visit friends on her day off.
3. How many employees work in that factory?
4. Jeff usually has lunch with his coworkers at the company cafeteria.
5. The fringe benefits package includes a company car and a cell phone.

LESSON 20
DIALOGUE 20 – COMPREHENSION QUESTIONS

1. No, she isn't, because she needs to talk to some friends about the

weekend first.

2. He thinks big groups are a lot more fun.
3. No, not really. They broke up some time ago and got back together, but it hasn't been the same like before.
4. Because of his band's rehearsal.

PRACTICE SET 20

I. Listen to the questions and circle the right answer.
1. Would you like to leave a message? b) No, thanks. I'll call back later.
2. Why did Rachel stop talking to you? c) I don't know. I have no idea.
3. Do you mind getting up early? a) No, I don't.
4. Does Jeff avoid eating meat? b) Yes, he does.
5. What does Sally enjoy doing on Sunday? a) She likes to go shopping and visit friends.
6. Did you leave a message on her answering machine? a) I did. I asked her to call me.
7. Can you put me through to Mr. Smith? c) Sure, hold on a second please.
8. Do you enjoy traveling on business? a) No, not really.
9. Did you finish cleaning the house? b) No, not yet.
10. Do you mind if I smoke? b) No, it's okay.

II. Dictation: listen to the sentences and write them.
1. I'm sorry, Mr. Brown is not in. Would you like to leave a message?
2. Don't you enjoy going to the beach in the summer?
3. Why did Linda stop talking to you?
4. Sorry, I can't talk to you right now. I'll call you back later.
5. Did Frank finish washing his car?

III. Circle the right answer.
1. b 2. b 3. c 4. a 5. b

IV. Write questions/ phrases for the following answers.
1. Does Stephanie mind getting up early?

2. Does he enjoy swimming?
3. What do you usually do on Saturday?
4. Would you like to leave a message?
5. Does Larry enjoy cooking?

V. Fill in the blanks with an appropriate word/ expression from the box.
1. Brian left a message on Rita's answering machine yesterday.
2. Hang on a second. I'll transfer your call.
3. What's the area code for Rio de Janeiro?
4. A: Would you like to leave a message? B: No, thanks I'll call back later.
5. If you have an emergency dial 911 for help.

LESSON 21
DIALOGUE 21 – COMPREHENSION QUESTIONS

1. It will be very cold and it might even snow on Sunday.
2. Because she always gets a little scared to drive when it snows.
3. Yes, she is.
4. He'll probably stay home and watch some DVDs by the fireplace.

PRACTICE SET 21

I. Listen to the questions and circle the right answer.
1. Where are they going on their honeymoon? b) They're going to Greece.
2. Is Fred still dating Sharon? c) Yes, he is.
3. What are you thinking about? a) My job.
4. How old was Mike when he got married? b) He was twenty-seven.
5. What do you use the internet for? c) I use it for studying and entertainment.
6. Do you get along with all your coworkers? a) I do. They are very friendly.
7. What time is your date tonight? c) 8:00 p.m.
8. Why did Sam and Deborah break up? b) I have no idea.

9. Is Greg going steady with Nancy? a) Yes, he is.
10. What time is the wedding? a) I think it's at 7:00 p.m.

II. Dictation: listen to the sentences and write them.
1. David fell in love with Patricia as soon as he met her. It was love at first sight!
2. Where are the newlyweds going on their honeymoon?
3. I have no idea why they broke up.
4. How old was Steve when he got married?
5. How about going to an Italian restaurant tonight?

III. Circle the right answer.
1. b 2. a 3. b 4. a 5. b

IV. Write questions/ phrases for the following answers.
1. Is Rita still dating Bob?
2. When did Nick get married? / How long ago did Nick get married?
3. Where did you meet Susan?
4. Where did you go last night?
5. Where are they going on their honeymoon?

V. Fill in the blanks with an appropriate word/ expression from the box.
1. Where are the newlyweds going for their honeymoon?
2. Did you know Elaine and Steve are getting married? They announced their wedding last week.
3. On the day they got engaged, Samuel gave her fiancée a beautiful engagement ring.
4. Gary fell in love with Magda immediately. It was love at first sight.
5. It took Anna a long time to get over her ex-boyfriend.

LESSON 22
DIALOGUE 22 – COMPREHENSION QUESTIONS

1. Because it has been a great experience and she has been learning many new things.

2. Yes, she does.
3. She says he's very demanding, but also very supportive.
4. She's happy and excited about the prospects.

PRACTICE SET 22

I. Listen to the questions and circle the right answer.
1. Where's your company's headquarters? b) It's in Chicago.
2. When is your company going to launch the new product? a) They should launch it in September.
3. Are you attending the upcoming tech expo? b) Sure!
4. What do they manufacture in that plant? a) They manufacture microwave ovens there.
5. Will your company have a booth at this year's fair? c) Oh yeah, we'll have a big one.
6. How many branch offices does your company have? b) We have five branch offices.
7. Can you show me some samples? a) Sure, I'll show you some.
8. Where is the plant located? c) About twenty miles from here.
9. How long did it take them to plan the marketing campaign? b) It took them about two weeks.
10. How many people work in the head office? a) About fifty people.

II. Dictation: listen to the sentences and write them.
1. Even though Nick eats a lot he isn't fat.
2. We enjoyed the trip in spite of the rain.
3. Although Ron is only twelve years old, he's taller than his mother.
4. In spite of the bad weather we had a good time at the beach.
5. Dave loves his apartment although it's very small.

III. Circle the right answer.
1. c   2. a   3. b   4. a   5. c

IV. Write questions/ phrases for the following answers.
1. Did you enjoy the picnic?
2. How long dit it take them to finish the project?
3. Do you have a branch office? / Do you have any branch offices?

4. Does Amanda enjoy working there?
5. Where is the plant located? / Where is the plant?

V. Fill in the blanks with an appropriate word/ expression from the box.
1. They expect to increase their market share after they launch the new product.
2. Mr. Smith is the founder and current president of the company.
3. Can you show us some samples of your products?
4. Our company will have a big booth at the international trade show in San Francisco this year.
5. Do they plan to advertise the new product on television?

LESSON 23
DIALOGUE 23 – COMPREHENSION QUESTIONS

1. No, he hasn't.
2. No, he isn't. He's been living at a new place for about a month now.
3. Because he's been dating a Mexican girl.
4. Yes, he does.

PRACTICE SET 23

I. Listen to the questions and circle the right answer.
1. What's the currency of Australia? c) It's the Australian dollar.
2. Can you lend me some cash? c) Sure, how much do you need?
3. Was that message written by Tony? b) Yes, Tony wrote it.
4. When were those houses built? a) They were built forty years ago.
5. Why was the flight canceled? b) Because of the snow.
6. How much did Frank spend yesterday? c) He spent fifty bucks.
7. Is there an ATM near here? a) Yes, there's one in that mall over there.
8. Did Joe pay back the money he owed you? b) Yes, he did.
9. How much money did Carla save? c) She saved twenty thousand dollars.

10. Why didn't they come here yesterday? a) Because they were very busy.

II. Dictation: listen to the sentences and write them.
1. How much money did you lend him?
2. There's an ATM in that mall over there.
3. Do you know why the flight was canceled?
4. Bill is planning to spend about three thousand dollars in Miami.
5. Can you lend me fifty bucks? I'll pay you back tomorrow.

III. Circle the right answer.
1. b   2. c   3. a   4. c   5. c

IV. Write questions/ phrases for the following answers.
1. How much money did you lend him?
2. Why was the flight canceled?
3. How much is Jerry planning to spend?
4. Is there an ATM near here?
5. Why didn't Deborah come here yesterday?

V. Fill in the blanks with an appropriate word/ expression from the box.
1. How much money did Jefferson spend on his new car?
2. Do you know if there is an ATM near here? I need to withdraw some money from my account to make some payments .
3. Does James earn a good salary working for that advertising agency?
4. Can you lend me ten bucks? I'll pay you back tomorrow.
5. The Australian dollar is the currency in Australia.

LESSON 24
DIALOGUE 24 – COMPREHENSION QUESTIONS

1. Because she's tired.
2. Because they are behind schedule with their current project at work and they may need to work overtime to finish it on time.

3. She thinks she just needs to chill out for a while.
4. He offers her a glass of her favorite white wine.

PRACTICE SET 24

I. Listen to the questions and circle the right answer.
1. Did you print that document? c) Yes, I did.
2. Can you e-mail that spreadsheet to me please? b) Sure!
3. What's their website address? a) I don't know. I need to ask Mike.
4. Does your company have an intranet? c) No, it doesn't.
5. How many hits did their website get last month? b) About twenty thousand hits.
6. Did you save that document? a) Sure, I saved it on my flash drive.
7. Does Carla have a laptop? a) Yes, she uses it every day.
8. What's the matter with the printer? c) I think it's out of ink.
9. Do they know the password? b) They do. I told them yesterday.
10. Doesn't Fred check his e-mail every day? a) I think he does.

II. Dictation: listen to the sentences and write them.
1. Can you print a copy of that letter for me please?
2. Gabriel won't buy that car unless they give him a good discount.
3. You forgot to attach the document. Can you e-mail it to me again please?
4. Unless it rains we'll go there tomorrow.
5. I'll lend you my car as long as you promise to be careful.

III. Circle the right answer.
1. c   2. b   3. a   4. c   5. a

IV. Write questions/ phrases for the following answers.
1. Does Jim check his e-mail every day? / Doesn't Jim check his e-mail every day?
2. Do they have a website? / Don't they have a website?
3. Can you print a copy for me?
4. Didn't he save the file? / Did he save the file?

5. Didn't you check your e-mail yesterday? / Did you check your e-mail yesterday?

V. Fill in the blanks with an appropriate word/ expression from the box.

1. It's a lot easier and practical to save computer files on a flash drive.
2. Can you print a copy of that document for me please?
3. You need a password to access the system.
4. Did you delete any names from that list?
5. You forgot to attach the document. Can you e-mail it to me again?

LESSON 25
DIALOGUE 25 – COMPREHENSION QUESTIONS

1. Because the traffic is usually heavy at that time.
2. No, they didn't.
3. No, they don't. Because they don't like him very much.
4. Because they want to get things ready once and for all and they don't want to be late tomorrow.

PRACTICE SET 25

I. Listen to the questions and circle the right answer.

1. What would you do if you were in his shoes? b) I have no idea.
2. Are you all set? c) No, I'm not ready yet. I need some more time.
3. Who's that guy over there? b) Beats me!
4. Why didn't you talk to Joe yesterday? a) I didn't see him, that's why!
5. Do you think they can meet the deadline? c) Yes, but they'll have to work around the clock to meet the deadline.
6. Who's in charge of the human resources department in your company? b) A woman named Patricia Johnson.
7. Can you give me a ballpark figure on how much you plan to spend? a) About five hundred bucks.
8. Could you do me a favor? b) Sure, what do you need?

9. How long did it take them to prepare the presentation? b) About four hours.
10. Is everything all set for the meeting tomorrow? b) Yes, it is.

II. Dictation: listen to the sentences and write them.
1. Our meal in that restaurant was a complete rip-off. We'll never go back there.
2. It's not up to us to decide. It's up to them.
3. Who's in charge of the I.T. department in your company?
4. We're glad Fred bounced back from his surgery so quickly.
5. Taking care of four kids is no bed of roses!

III. Look at the examples and complete with so or neither.
1. Josh bought a new computer. So did Sam.
2. Brian can't speak Spanish. Neither can Melissa.
3. Alex is sixteen years old. So is Nick.
4. Nancy didn't go to the party. Neither did Amanda.
5. Bob enjoys swimming. So does Ron.
6. Mary doesn't have a sister. Neither does Carla.
7. Frank would prefer to live in a small city. So would Sandra.
8. Michael isn't interested in art. Neither is Deborah.
9. Ted loves chocolate. So do his brothers.
10. Michelle and Sonia weren't late for the show. Neither was Kate.

IV. Write questions/ phrases for the following answers.
1. Why did you go to the mall?
2. Is everything all set for the presentation tomorrow?
3. Did you see Fred last night?
4. Can Linda speak French?
5. Does Josh have a sister?

V. Fill in the blanks with an idiomatic expression from the box.
1. Elaine is in charge of the financial department of a big company.
2. I don't know what I would do if I were in your shoes.
3. Can you give me a ballpark figure on the number of people who will attend the event?

4. Everything seems to be all set for the party tonight.
5. They had to work around the clock to finish the project on time.

LESSON 26
DIALOGUE 26 – COMPREHENSION QUESTIONS

1. Because he has to get up early to drive his kids to school in the morning.
2. Because he's been working out at the gym four times a week now.
3. He has been going to the gym for about five months.
4. He feels a lot healthier than before.

PRACTICE SET 26

I. Listen to the questions and circle the right answer.
1. Is Pamella used to getting up early? b) Yes, she is. She goes to school in the morning.
2. Do you know why Trevor and Rita broke up? c) No, I don't.
3. Did you use to watch cartoons when you were a kid? a) Sure, I still watch them sometimes.
4. What does Carol feel like doing tonight? a) She'd rather watch a movie.
5. Why don't we drop by Joe's tonight? b) Good idea! Let's do that.
6. Are you used to driving in this city? c) No, not really.
7. How did you find out what happened? b) I talked to Brian.
8. Why did they call off the meeting? c) Beats me!
9. Do you feel like going out tonight? a) No, I'm kind of tired.
10. Why is Gary so late? a) His car broke down, that's why!

II. Dictation: listen to the sentences and write them.
1. They will have to call off the game if the rain continues.
2. Did you find out what happened?
3. Mike's old car is falling apart. He'd better get a new one soon.
4. Bob's car broke down on him this morning. That's why he got to the office so late.
5. We need to figure out a way to help them.

III. Circle the right answer.

1. c   2. c   3. a   4. c   5. a

IV. Write questions/ phrases for the following answers.

1. What's he doing?
2. What do you feel like doing?
3. Did Nick tell you what happened?
4. Are they used to working on Saturday?
5. Can Margareth come with us to the party?

V. Fill in the blanks with a phrasal verb from the box. Make sure you use the appropriate verb tense.

1. Barry was surprised when I told him that Rita and Joe had broken up .
2. Do you know why they had to call off the meeting?
3. It's so hot today! I feel like swimming.
4. "Can you drop by my place later today? I need to talk to you", Jim asked a friend over the phone.
5. Jane was very angry when she found out that Nick had lied to her.

LESSON 27
DIALOGUE 27 – COMPREHENSION QUESTIONS

1. He would probably buy a house, travel a lot and start a business.
2. A franchise in the food industry.
3. He thinks it would be important to hire a financial consultant to get advice on how to invest the money properly.
4. He needs to talk to Harry about some money Harry borrowed from him.

PRACTICE SET 27

I. Listen to the questions and circle the right answer.

1. Are you going to the party by yourself? c) No, Jeff is going with me.
2. Will you drop by Tony's place if you have time? a) Sure!

3. How long did it take your new business to break even? b) About a year and a half.
4. Will you watch a movie if you go to the mall tonight? c) No, I won't.
5. Should we call it a day? a) I guess so, I'm really tired.
6. Why did Ron change his mind about buying a new car? b) I think he doesn't have enough money.
7. Do you think he'll pass the test if he studies hard? c) Sure!
8. Did you meet anyone at the party last night? b) I met a girl named Carol.
9. Can you drive us to the airport? a) I'm sorry, I'm late for work.
10. Who did you have dinner with? c) With my friend Nick.

II. Dictation: listen to the sentences and write them.
1. Do you find it easy to break the ice and meet new people at parties?
2. How long did it take Tony's new business to break even?
3. Rachel changed her mind about traveling after she heard the weather forecast on the radio.
4. I still can't believe Larry wrote that poem by himself.
5. It's already 7 p.m. and we're all tired. Let's call it a day.

III. Circle the right answer.
1. b   2. a   3. b   4. c   5. a

IV. Write questions/ phrases for the following answers.
1. What would you do if you had a lot of money?
2. Did you go there by yourself?
3. Who did you have lunch with?
4. Does Melissa have a younger sister?
5. Did Karen make that cake by herself?

V. Fill in the blanks with an idiomatic expression from the box.
1. At first Mike planned to study medicine and become a doctor like his father, but he changed his mind later and decided to go to law school instead.

2. Dave's outgoing personality makes it easy for him to break the ice and get to know people at parties.
3. After working all day long Frank decided to call it a day and go home.
4. Did you really cook that wonderful meal by yourself?
5. Moving to another city never really crossed my mind.

LESSON 28
DIALOGUE 28 – COMPREHENSION QUESTIONS

1. Yes, he has. He talked to him yesterday.
2. It has changed a lot. He's gone back to university, he's broken up with his girlfriend and he's also shaved off his goatee.
3. No, he hasn't.
4. They decide to go to a hamburger joint on Main Street.

PRACTICE SET 28

I. Listen to the questions and circle the right answer.
1. Have you seen Bob lately? b) Yes, I saw him last week.
2. How long have you been an architect? a) For eleven years.
3. Has Pamella ever been to China? b) No, she hasn't.
4. Have you read the newspaper today? c) No, not yet.
5. How long has Carol lived in that apartment? a) She's lived there since 2007.
6. Where did Mary grow up? c) She grew up in Denver.
7. Has Fred already had lunch? a) Yes, we had lunch together.
8. Who are you looking for? b) My friend Mike.
9. Has Kate told you the news? c) Yes, she has.
10. I haven't read that book yet, have you? b) No, I haven't either.

II. Dictation: listen to the sentences and write them.
1. We're looking forward to our trip to Europe.
2. Do you enjoy looking after children?
3. What are you looking for?
4. We'd better hurry up or we'll miss our flight.
5. Bill gave up trying to solve those algebra exercises by himself.

III. Circle the right answer.

1. b   2. c   3. a   4. b   5. a

IV. Write questions/ phrases for the following answers.

1. Does Nancy like to look after children?
2. How long has Alice been married?
3. Have you seen that movie? / Have you seen that movie before?
4. How long has Josh lived there?
5. What are you looking for?

V. Fill in the blanks with a phrasal verb from the box. Make sure you use the appropriate verb tense.

1. "I'm looking for my car keys. Do you know where they are?", Magda asked Tim.
2. "Hurry up! We're late for school", Bob told Josh.
3. You can trust James. He's a reliable guy. He won't let you down.
4. "I was born in Boston, but I grew up in Miami", Gary told Sean.
5. Amanda could be a baby-sitter. She loves to look after kids.

LESSON 29
DIALOGUE 29 – COMPREHENSION QUESTIONS

1. He's been doing regular physical exercise, he's been going out with friends at least once a week and he has also been doing some new tasks at work.
2. No, he doesn't, but he's been thinking of joining a gym.
3. No, he hasn't. He lost touch with Ted since he started dating Dana.
4. He's excited about the possibility of getting a promotion at work.

PRACTICE SET 29

I. Listen to the questions and circle the right answer.

1. How long has she been working there? a) Since July.
2. Why don't we eat something different for a change? c) Good, maybe we can go to that new restaurant downtown.

3. Has Paul made up his mind? b) No, he hasn't made up his mind yet.
4. Why is Samantha in a hurry? a) She's late for work.
5. How long have you been studying English? c) For about four years.
6. Have you been working a lot recently? b) Yes, I have.
7. What has Patricia been doing lately? c) I don't know. I haven't seen her in the past few weeks.
8. Why don't you get rid of that old computer? c) I know I should. I'll probably buy a new one next month.
9. Have you ever been abroad? c) Yes, I've been to the U.S. and Canada.
10. How long has Rita been living in Italy? b) She's been there since October.

II. Dictation: listen to the sentences and write them.
1. I'm sick of fast food. Can we have a real meal for a change?
2. Brian thought he would never learn how to play golf, but he soon got the hang of it.
3. I wish you would quit smoking once and for all.
4. Alice is working as a waitress now, but she doesn't plan to do that for good.
5. Rachel rarely changes her mind once she makes up her mind about something.

III. Circle the right answer.
1. b   2. a   3. b   4. b   5. b

IV. Write questions/ phrases for the following answers.
1. How long has he been living there?
2. Has Fred made up his mind yet?
3. Why is Carla in a hurry?
4. How long has Jeff been a teacher?
5. Does Sarah have brothers or sisters?

V. Fill in the blanks with an idiomatic expression from the box.
1. "We always go to the movies on Saturday. Why don't we do

something different for a change?

2. "I'm telling you the truth. I had nothing to do with what happened", Rick told Tony.
3. "I can't talk to you right now. I'm in a hurry. I'll call you later", said Nick to a friend.
4. Steve rarely changes his mind once he makes up his mind about something.
5. "Don't worry, you'll soon get the hang of that new computer program", Ron told Jack.

LESSON 30
DIALOGUE 30 – COMPREHENSION QUESTIONS

1. Because Steve had already left home when Frank stopped by his place.
2. He's worried about their school assignment.
3. He might go downtown to watch an action movie.
4. Because he needs to catch up on his sleep.

PRACTICE SET 30

I. Listen to the questions and circle the right answer.
1. Had you already taken a shower when Rita arrived? b) No, I hadn't.
2. How long had you been living in Berlin when you moved to Amsterdam? b) For about eight years.
3. Does Monica look like her mother? c) No, she looks like her father.
4. Can you pick us up at school? b) Sure, what time?
5. Have you seen Ted lately? a) Yes, I talked to him yesterday.
6. Has Rachel been on a diet? c) No, she hasn't.
7. Can I try on a smaller size please? a) Sure, I'll get a smaller one for you.
8. Did you throw away yesterday's newspaper? c) No, I didn't. Do you want to read it?
9. What time did the plane take off? b) It took off at half past eleven.
10. Can you turn on the TV please? a) Sure!

II. Dictation: listen to the sentences and write them.
1. Can you turn off the radio please? I'm trying to study!
2. Tony looks like he's in shape. Has he been working out at the gym lately?
3. Can you pick me up at school earlier today?
4. Do you know why Bill turned down such a good job offer?
5. Why didn't Steve show up for class yesterday?

III. Circle the right answer.
1. c   2. a   3. b   4. c   5. b

IV. Write questions/ phrases for the following answers.
1. Does Carol look like her father?
2. Can I try on a larger size?
3. How old is she?
4. How long had Brian been working there when he was promoted?
5. Did Dave show up for class today?

V. Fill in the blanks with a phrasal verb from the box. Make sure you use the appropriate verb tense.
1. Don't forget to turn off the lights before you leave.
2. Does Cynthia look like her mother or her father?
3. Japanese people usually take off their shoes before entering their houses.
4. "Can you pick me up at school tonight?", Sandra asked her father.
5. David showed up late for work today because his car broke down.

GUIA DO ÁUDIO

Track 1: Dialogue 1 – What do you do for a living? p. **15**
Track 2: Dialogue 1 – comprehension questions p. **16**
Track 3: The alphabet p. **17**
Track 4: Practice set 1: I. Listen to the questions and circle the right answer. p. **21**
Track 5: Practice set 1: II. Dictation: listen to the sentences and write them. p. **22**
Track 6: Dialogue 2 – Why don't we go camping for a change? p. **25**
Track 7: Dialogue 2 – comprehension questions p. **26**
Track 8: Practice set 2: I. Listen to the questions and circle the right answer. p. **31**
Track 9: Practice set 2: II. Dictation: listen to the sentences and write them. p. **32**
Track 10: Dialogue 3 – What does your dad do? p. **35**
Track 11: Dialogue 3 – comprehension questions p. **36**
Track 12: Practice set 3: I. Listen to the questions and circle the right answer. p. **40**
Track 13: Practice set 3: II. Dictation: listen to the sentences and write them. p. **41**
Track 14: Dialogue 4 – You have a great memory! p. **43**
Track 15: Dialogue 4 – comprehension questions p. **44**
Track 16: Practice set 4: I. Listen to the questions and circle the right answer. p. **48**
Track 17: Practice set 4: II. Dictation: listen to the sentences and write them. p. **49**
Track 18: Dialogue 5 – You missed out on a great party! p. **51**
Track 19: Dialogue 5 – comprehension questions p. **52**
Track 20: Practice set 5: I. Listen to the questions and circle the right answer. p. **57**
Track 21: Practice set 5: II. Dictation: listen to the sentences and write them. p. **58**
Track 22: Dialogue 6 – It's great to be back home! p. **61**

COMO ACESSAR O ÁUDIO

Todo o conteúdo em áudio referente a este livro, você poderá encontrar em qualquer uma das seguintes plataformas de streaming:

Ao acessar qualquer uma dessas plataformas de streaming, será necessária a criação de uma conta de acesso (poderá ser a versão gratuita). Após acessar a plataforma de streaming, pesquise pela **Disal Editora**, localize a playlist deste livro e você terá todas as faixas de áudio mencionadas no livro.

Para qualquer dúvida, entre em contato com **marketing@disal editora.com.br**

Este livro foi composto nas fontes National e Newzald e impresso
em **julho** de 2024 pela Paym Gráfica e Editora Ltda.,
sobre papel offset 75g/m^2.